IN THE WAY OF IT

John McGreal

Copyright © 2013 John McGreal

The moral right of the author has been asserted.

Apart from any fair dealing for the purposes of research or private study, or criticism or review, as permitted under the Copyright, Designs and Patents Act 1988, this publication may only be reproduced, stored or transmitted, in any form or by any means, with the prior permission in writing of the publishers, or in the case of reprographic reproduction in accordance with the terms of licences issued by the Copyright Licensing Agency. Enquiries concerning reproduction outside those terms should be sent to the publishers.

Matador
9 Priory Business Park
Kibworth Beauchamp
Leicestershire LE8 0RX, UK
Tel: (+44) 116 279 2299
Fax: (+44) 116 279 2277
Email: books@troubador.co.uk
Web: www.troubador.co.uk/matador

ISBN 978 1783062 256

British Library Cataloguing in Publication Data.
A catalogue record for this book is available from the British Library.

Printed and bound in the UK by Berforts Information Press

Matador is an imprint of Troubador Publishing Ltd

MIX
Paper from
responsible sources
FSC
www.fsc.org FSC® C021018

Dedicated to Dylan

Also in this Series:

The Book of It (2010)
my it to you (2013)
The Poetry of It (2013)

With special thanks to VW.

'Those who read twice can see twice as well'.
Menander
(Attic Poet 4BC)

CONTENTS

Preface	xi
Chapter 1	3
Chapter 2	15
Chapter 3	31
Chapter 4	53
Chapter 5	71
Chapter 6	97
Chapter 7	117
Chapter 8	143
Chapter 9	159
Chapter 10	173
Chapter 11	185
Chapter 12	199
Chapter 13	213
Chapter 14	231

Preface

I am pleased now finally to publish here my book *In The Way of It* simultaneously with *my it to you* and *The Poetry of It*.

The singular visual form of the work is characterised by use of monosyllables, the No 7, double columns in a two page format, abbrvns and anagrams.

The use of monosyllables In this volume is a further investigation of their literary possibilities first explored in *my i to you* in 2005. At the time I had become aware of their role Samuel Beckett's works like *Lessness*. With the exception of proper names, single syllables are used throughout *In The Way of It* to write Mac's story. Paradoxically, in their simplicity they are deployed to spell it out as clearly as possible how *The Book of It*, with its new, open, literary form of rich polysyllabicity, emerged from his art practice and was embarked on in 2006 in all its spacial and temporal complexity. Like those in nursery rhymes, many short words with one syllable make for a certain close ness and involvement, not to say intimacy with accompanying feelings which resonates from child hood. Though not consciously intended, one effect in the text perhaps is partly to offset the distance attempted in writing Mac's story in a detached, third person, adult narrative.

As with other works, the No 7 is deployed in a simple way mathematically to space the text. There are 7 spaces between the words on each line, 28 lines per column and 14 Chapters in the whole work.

The double column on these pages has been used since the earliest days of printing in the mid 15th Century, notably *The Gutenberg Bible*. In more recennt writing it has been used in Literary Criticism by Jacques Derrida in *Glas* (University of Nebraska Press, 1974). In Literature itself it has been employed more obliquely by BS Johnson in *Christy Malry's Own Double-Entry* (Collins,1973).

In conjunction with the two-page landscape format derived from Mallarmé's *Un Coup de Dés,* the double column is used here in part on some pages to shape the echo of Eugene Gomringer's *Silencio*. At times monosyllables may be used to achieve clarity but equally they set a limit on what can and cannot be said in their own terms. It is as though both writer and reader are presented with variations of audial and visual sound and silence imposed by interpretation and translation into an other foreign language.

The pwr of angrms and cndnsd abbrvtns is evident when the artist armed with a dream may reclaim a secular miracle and open the space of new forms of art. In this respect I am glad to publish *In The Way of it* on the Centenary of Modernist works like *Le rêve transformé* by Giorgio de Chirico and in Literature itself *Le Grand Meaulnes* by Alain-Resnais, as well as *A Man Without Qualities* by Robert Musil and *Swann's Way* by Marcel Proust which both figure in the text.

JM
June 2013

IN THE WAY OF IT

Chapter 1

When he came out of the dance at
The Irish Centre Mac saw and heard at
once that he was in a new scape.
He gleaned that he was in a new
time and place. He would have to make
his own way. His sole chance now was
to prise his mind and heart free of
the old ways of ing and ness. At
first he paused for he was quite tired.
He had caned it all night on the
dance floor for all it was worth. He
tried to get things clear in his thoughts
as one or two drops of rain fell
on his bare head. When he looked up
at the sky Mac then saw that it
might soon throw it down. The low clouds
had got so dark as they had swept
in on the wind from The West. He
hailed two kids in capes who pranced on
the back wheels of their bikes. As they
braked near a cone and sped past him
they both left skid marks on the road.
/He asked his self what he had to
lose and took his chance. He dwelt
on tews as he 'gan to wend his
own way. On the wind 'neath the tall
spire near by he heard chants as he
went to the end of Blacks Road and

crossed the top of King St. There were
no frowns or lours when with a wry
grin he passed by way of *The S*wan.
The old lair still had charm for him
so he gave its taps a wide berth.
On his right in front of *The George*
the old ings of rail still stood. They
sang in the wind of the men past
with dark eyes and fine heads of hair
in dark blue suits, white shirts ties and
blck shoes that shone. The men who 'mrgd
frm Mass at St Augustine's as they leaned
frm great heights and spat in the clouds.
The old men with weals on hands from
hafts and helves who drank on The Tans.
The young men who would sick up stew
and act the goat in fights and frays
and bray and brawl wth those frm Wales.
/It was a long march for Mac past
Aelxander's Barbers dwn The Grove. In a bit of
a trance he moved down its ness of
straight and mused on The Ides as a
few cars drove by Pat's. With out a
snag he got near the end and turned
in to the side streets and wynds where

wild men with hair of straw still roved.
He was 'mazed to find the chants had
come from the aufs who sought to greet
him at the same big old house with
The One Room in *Sycamore Gardens* in which
he had lived with his Mam and Dad
for the first five years of his life.
It was there that he first used to
dare to walk and talk; on his Mam's
knee to read and write. It was the
room where he had first heard sung with

his young elfs, love's sweet song of the
self. It was there he had first learned
to trance and dream. Out side to greet
him as he stood on his own once
more at the foot of the five worn
steps which led up to the front door
was him self aged five and his small
Bro still stood in the same door way.
On guard with a firm back and arms
down by his sides young Mac looked straight
at you while Mike with big waves in
his hair stared down at some thing held
in his hands. Years had long gone in
which Mac used to come back to stand

and brood on that same spot at one
with the dead. When he dwelt on the
shared life they lived in The One Room
where he had first learned as a tot
to dade, bleared thoughts of what his Mam
and Dad and he and his small Bro
might have said and done came and went.
The same blurred thoughts used to float up
in to his mind as they came back
to him of those near far off days.
/How Mam and Dad had both come from
The Land of Ire. How Moll was née
in Galway in 1916 in that so tense
year of *The Easter Rising*. How In 1908
Mell was born in Westport the home of
John McBride who had helped to lead it.
How Moll had hoped to stay on at
school but her dow had been to leave
when her Mam died in child birth with
her last one. How Moll's Dad drank and
the home broke up when they lost the
farm. How Mell's Da had died when he
was young and he had left school as
soon as he could. How each had gone
on the boat to The Land of Eng
to work in diff parts of The North.
How in The War they met in Leeds
in Moll's Aunt's pub *The Prince of Wales*.

How Moll had dropped her course in ing
of Nurse to work in The Bar when
her Aunt's spouse had died. How the lass
loved to hear Mell sing and play the
spoons. How when the dew was still fresh
they walked down the aisle to wed in
Leeds Cathedral. How they moved to Lon as
Bing sang *Too Ra Loo Ra Loo Ral.*
How he found The One Room just
off The Goldhawk Rd quite near The Bush
then quite full of teagues with brogues
as The Ink Spots had a hit with
In To Each Life Some Rain Must Fall.
How the costs of food and rent were high
but the Dad did War Work and soon
got a start on a new site where
he could earn more. How The Ma took
a part time job as a char and
did ings of clean and and wash for
well heeled folk who owned a large lux
flat near Marble Arch. How in cold months
they lived in Rome. How for the wage
Moll used to droil and drudge as they
went to *The Proms* to hear Bach and
Brahms as well as Bruch Liszt and Rach.
/How the house in Sycamore was full of
life. Up stairs was a young Welsh man
who taught in a good school and was

said to have wracked his own brains. Two
Land girls from The Corps had worked on
on a large farm in Herts. When they
brought in the crops they used to thresh
the husks from bolls of grain. They had
baled hay and knew how to sort the
wheat from the chaff. On top of them
was a big clan of loud Scots from The
Lands of High. Its Chief had a blade
in his belt and a rood round his
neck. He bawled as his cots of bauld
bairns howled. At the top on his own
lived a swart Moor who read and wrote.
How Mac was born when 'peace' broke out
and *'Small Boy'* and *'Fat Man'* dropped on
The Land of Jap. How it was from Sycamore
that his Mam took him up The Grove
to the Nursery in Brook Green where Spock
shot to fame while she made light bulbs
and valves for *Osrams* and then served Cops
as a Bar Maid in a nice Lounge
in Hamm. How he was scared to go
down in to the dark coal hole with
all its smut. How it had been so
cold and had such a damp stench
it must have smelled like the cave which
hid *The Dead Sea Scrolls*. How he
and his young friends with warts and all

played hide and seek in the wreck age of the bomb sites and combed them for what they could find. How boys used to strip glost lead from pipes and roof ducts to melt ells of it on a fire in a pot with a sharp pong to sell it. How on trips they sneaked on board trams that went near the Marts in in The Bush and Hamm where the old dear with the gift of the gab sold 'alf crown shop in bags'. How Moll had kept the veil to which The Da had set fire on their first night and Mell said he was in the wrong. He had not meant it but had a drop too much. How such pleas were not yet rife so she quelled her vile doubts and took him at his word. How Mam's womb had grown so big that she had to rest. How he got fed up when the lamb child born in the same year as The Prince of Wales. How the bub used to blea in his crib. How King babe sucked on Mam's teat and Mac could not. How he used to bleat when she picked him up and still would not husht but used to meaw and miaul and yow and yowl. How cooped up they were for two more long years years in which the cub used to crawl on his toys. How The Da used to snort at tins of stuff and woke them up when he snored at night. How Mam used to comb his hair for nits. How he had loved it as a child had when his Dad was at work and his Mam made up her mind to for get her angst and took them out for a walk. How Mac had helped to push The Pram in which Mike lay or held the side of it. How he was proud of her when slim and svelte she got decked out in her blue frock or the nice print dress with dots. How she put her hair up in a coif or got it done in a perm. How at times she wore her cloche hat that trailed a coil of dink trim or a small toque. How some days she put on a shawl with frills of lace and some tight gloves. How she used to wear round her thin neck a small loose string of cheap pearls. How he was in an odd land of er and wond as they went right up The Grove thru The Broad Way and then down Hamm Mall to Ravenscourt Park. How he dirled and thrilled at The Lake with its

ducks and frogs. How arms or legs might
get sore from the gnats and flys that
stang as much as swarms of wasps and
bees from hives. How he still loved the
same old place out of sight where they
sat midst the diff sorts of Rose each
with their own soft tangs. How Moll hummed
a song that still warms the heart by
Nat King Cole. How in his smooth voice
on The Wire Less he sang that he
would not get her for un or some
thing like that. How she sang Old Ones
like *The Harp That Once Thru Tara's Halls*.
How Mac had loved all the thrills and
spills of The Play Ground. How he could
not wait to rush in and out of
each bricked Rail Way arch with its own
vault and curved space for a Slide or
Swings or See Saw or Round A Bout.
How the trains passed on top of them.
How in The Sand Pit he built walls of
a fort just like his Dad on site.
How he dug holes to make moats and
filled some but they used to leak. How
he made roads on which he drove a
car round in the loop of an arc
How in The Pool he splashed and then
swam the sea to The Land of Ire.

/How Dad shrugged when the bets he had
not hedged did not come off and his
Mam used to blate that they could not
spare it. How Mell said he did his
best but Moll used to prate that one
sows what one reaps. How she pawned her
Gold Ring to buy food when they were
down to shives of toast and sold her
best coat and an old fur to make
ends meet. How in those grey years large
tins of pears came in The Post from
Perth where one of Mam's Bros had gone.
/How Mac stood up like a guard with
a spear when his Aunt with big hips took
a snap of him on the steps. How
he and mates with eith and ease turned
a spare box in the street in to
a kind of ark or steam boat. How
they shived bits of cork to make ships
out of card and board and would swob
the decks and the bows with a frayed
old mop. How one took the helm as
they cruised off to The Land of Ire.
How they drew with a lump of white
chalk and played hop scotch screeved on the
paved stones out side the house. How next
day they were free as Huck Finn when
the kerb was the sharp line of the

sea shore on the beach or The Nile.
How he got rides when big boys made
push carts with frames of broad planks from
shides of wood gnarled and burled with knots
and knurs. How they used lengths of rope
nuts and bolts and flanged pram wheels with
smooth rims and greased cogs on the hubs.
How he saw Joan's pink pants when he
lay on the ground and she jumped up
in the air. How he used to slink off
and skulk when his Ma spanked him.
/How in the lit tanks of the shop
at the end of the street fish of
all hues of the rain bow swam in
the wind. How Mac and his pals got
up to all sorts of pranks. How they
shrieked and laughed be hind his back at
the small fat fub with a fob watch
in his light buff coat. How they thought
he was a fronce and a fop. How
they chased The Rag and Bone Man on
on his horse and cart that stank on
his way to the dump. How they used
to mock The Lame Man who limped with
a crutch. How they teased The Old Codge
with a cod's face when he doffed his
cap. How now and then they used to
flam a small lad with a hair lip and

a lisp. How Mac used to frump and
sulk when Mam smacked the bad boy.
/Mac thought too of how cows and old
mares and curs and pigs and fecks and
fucks flew in the One Room with Gee Gees
and Baa Baa Black Sheep in the months
when The Big Bang burst in to reams.
How Da was tanked when he came home
for his meal and threw his eggs or
spam in the air since there was no
meat. How Mac kept his head down as
real ings of feel and loud words sailed
thru the air at night. How with jonks
and jooks he just ducked out of the
way when one of them lost the plot
with a polt and a slap. How he
would flee from the whangs and bangs of
loud brawls and switch off in the midst
of bemes and blows. How he felt safe
when he hid be hind the lear couch
and lived closed off out of sight in
his own er wond world of 'mics and
books with his gang of close friends like
Brer, Nod, Big Ears, Mole and Toad. How
he peeked and peeped out to keek and
sken the room to see if it was
safe to come out. How he had soon
learned so to keep his young eyes ope

and ears tuned to their moods as he
knew it would make it worse if he
had the sauce in some way to cause
a noise to 'noy them. How his small
Bro had a fine head of fair curls
which his Mam washed and brushed. How Da
swore Mike looked like a girl and Mam
cried at such a smear. How The Brute cut
them off and she cried but Mac could
not bear it and numbed out. How he
learned to fade out and not make a
sound with no thing to say. How when
they clashed he learned to play mum chance
like one who shuts down and acts the
mute in a weird deaf and dumb show.
/How the chit waifed and wailed and balled
his eyes out when his Mam said his
bad Dad would not take Mac with him
to the Land of Ire at Yule. How
once his Dad took him out for a
walk when his hand got a sharp sting
that was worse than a flea bite.
How his Da was feal and rubbed a dock
leaf on his skin to stop the itch.
How the inf ant had the wis and
dom not to show them or his self
what he felt in the depths in side.
/As Mac stood in front of the house

the storm which had brewed for some time
now broke. He was awed when in a
mist it was as if the loops of
an old spool of rime were played back.
As the cold rain teemed down so hard
it came back to him how his Mam
said they had once gone to meet his
Dad at *The Sheperd's Bush Hotel* on the
Green. How they had to wait by the

sea food stall with its heaps of prawns
shrimps and whelks as it was still quite
a long time for the last ing and
up of drink. How Mac had glimpsed his
Da's shape wreathed in the thick blue smoke
as he sat perched on his stool at the
bar with the men of woad. How Mac thought
his sharp eyes, hooked nose and large, flat
ears made him look like a Hawk. How the
loud din from the talk, the laughs and
shouts from in side the dark place with
all the noise of its screaks and shrieks
and yells and youps had held the child
in awe as he whiffed the fumes from
the hot fug. How out side it had
been a cold, clear day and he was

tranced by the glims and glints of the
tall Pints of light ale with their froth
tops as they gleamed in the light on
the ledge next to black Pints of stout
by the slat on the sill. How at
last The Da drained his Pint and came
forth with the gift of a dead fowl
in a bag from his pal and a
pack of salt crisps for each of them.

/How they were in a rush as it
was late and had to crunch and scrunch
them in their jaws and munch them to
wolf them down as quick as they could.
How he and Mike both ate them much
too fast and they stuck in their craws.
How the sun went in as they reached
The Play Ground on The Green and the
sky turned black. How the clouds burst.
How the rain poured down and clad in his
thin coat Mac was drenched. How Mike was
doused too but put in The Push Chair.
How Mac was soaked to the skin and
scared as the rain coursed through him. How
it whooshed down on his head and ran
down his hair; it sped down his cheeks

and chin; it slid down each inch of
his neck and chest; it rushed down his
thighs and knees; it gushed down his calves
and shins and flowed down both his feet.
How he was steeped in the rain as
it washed in to his eyes and dripped
in to his ears; it swashed in to
his mouth and nose and seeped down his
throat. How the lad got a huge fright
and his heart froze. How he felt a
tight pain in his chest and gasped with
the gliff in fear he would drown when
he could not catch his breath. How at
sight of this Mell had got ten for
his own cares and slung his coat on
Mac's head but too late. How by then
in shock the boy could not breathe to
get air in to his lungs and Moll
grasped that they had to get him to
The Doc. How they tried to keep out
of harm's way on the path but lost
it when the old drains got clogged up
and deep pools formed as it streamed down.
/How by then the hard rain had sluiced
thru the scraw of thin grass on parts
of The Green where small shoots had shown.
How the turf was scoured on most of
it and turned in to a real bog.

How they slopped and sparged in it. How
they sloshed and plashed it. How they were
pressed down in to the dank depths of
the mire as they splashed and splurged
in it. How they sank down in to
the slub and sludge of the marsh as
they quelched and squelched in it and they
squished and swoshed in it. How with the
scare Moll was rilled and keen to blame
Mel for the fact that Mac had got
a chill and said he should be in
gaol. How Mam claimed her hopes were sunk
and that it could not be worse. How
he swore as they reached their goal and
snapped back that she was too harsh; that
he had no choice but to get up in the cold
and dark first thing each morn to tew
and toil on the site for a wage
and that he had earned his Pint; that
when she mouthed off she had more of
a gob on her than Queen Mab; that
none of them had been spared as they
had all got wet; that she should not
foist the blame on him as The flood
was not the fault and less his ness.
/How the next day Mac woke up and
found him self in a dry warm bed
with clean, stiff white sheets and a Nurse
who smiled. How he still found it hard
to breathe and could not take deep breaths.
How he had a chill and sneezed. How
he felt cold and was till bunged up
so she kept the drapes closed. How his
Mam's lips were moist when she came to
see him on the Ward and kissed him.
How she took him a few sweet grapes.
How she brought him a book to whet
his wit in which he could fill things
in. How she spread some toys on the
flat bed pane for him to play with.
How he cried and cloyed to her as
he had a real fear that she would
not come back. How The Nurse laughed since
his Mam came to see him at the
same time each day like clock work and
was not late once. How she squeezed the
mite and scruzed him tight. How she told

him a tale of a young deer or
a short yarn from The Wild West or
a dere of yore parsed from one of
his big books in which she had to

make cuts. How his young chest wheezed like
a reed for some weeks. How The Nurse
used to hoist him up if it rasped
and wap him on his back in a
firm but kind way that worked and in
time eased his choice of soft iced buns.
/How Mac got well and his Mam came
and took him home to The One Room.
How once there he found a new toy
from his Da. How it was a Bear
whom the child called Ted. How he had
a wide girth but on the whole he
stood up right on his own two feet.
How he had a well stuffed coat of
thick brown fur but with quite a few

lumps and bumps. How the tears in it
had been sown up tight but the slight
one on his left calf had not been
yet. How he wore a short scut tail.
How Ted had a small snub nose with
a turned up snout that tweaked the air.
How his conk sniffed it like one who
takes snuff. How his ears were both a
tad flat and some what slack. How his
bead eye was a bit loose but had
a kind of glint in it like that
of one from a brae who lacks fear
that bade one not to breach his grith.
How with the wide stare from his good
eye his furred friend had a kind of
fixed girn on his face. How with a
sort of wink now and then he had
a broad grin that stole up on him.
How he held a large mug in his
left paw and a jug in his right
one. How Mac put the key on a
wire ring in his back and wound him
up tight. How Ted filled his mug full
to the brim. How he then tipped his
head right back and quaffed it straight down
his throat in a deep long draught. How
he had a look in his eye that
said: 'You don't know the half of it'.

Chapter 2

In his mind Mac was five and a
half when they were re housed on
The White City Estate. They moved to a
new block of flats named Baird House full
of hope to make a fresh start. With
a spring in his step he stretched his
short legs and leapt up the stairs two
at a time. He held on to the
rail to turn and spin up each of
the flights to their new home on the
third floor. The Land of Ing was up
in the sky. From it for the titch
the versts of squitch grass on Wrmwd Scrbs
spread past the gaol like Steppes of Russia.
/The paint work smelt fresh and clean. The
braid of Mam's hair and the pleat of
her skirt shone in the bright light of
the rooms which poured in from the winds.
At the front these looked out on to
the big play ground of Canberra Prmry Schl
where kids leaped and played in their breaks.
At the back they gazed right down on
Hamm Park flanked by the huge new site
of The BBC Television Centre with its en
trance in Wood Lane. In the court yard
at Baird The Man in Muff rang his
bell on Mon. A Lean Man with a
grind stone on his bike who ground knives
dinged his on Wed. A Fat Man in
a van sold Fish and Chips wrapped in
The News of The World so they did
not need a plate on Fri. Huge men
streaked in coal dust humped sacks of fuel
up for the new coal fire on Thur.
In doors they had a new pan and
brush set with tongs. When he came to
clear the flue of soot with his brush
on the end of long poles The Sweep
put sheets out in vain to keep things
clean. A wide side board, soft couch and
arm chairs were new too like the bath.
Mac blabbed and blubbed if it was cold
or he got soap suds in his eyes
when Mam washed his hair. He longed for
a bike and felt let down with a trike.
/When Mell was out at work or in
the pub peace reigned they would all sit
round the hearth at night and list en
on the smart new 'gram to favs like
'Take It From Here', 'Have A Go',
'The Al Read Show' or 'Ray's A Laugh'.
But the old war on the home front
soon broke out there and raw fear set
in to mar the move. It gealed and
Mac 'gan to dread it when Mell got
drunk and some nights he would start to

do things like turn off the gas to spoil Ma's fare of half baked tarts still in the stove. Moll fumed and 'gan to lock Mac and Mike in the front bed room with her. They dared to push the big bed up 'gainst the door and jam it to keep Mell out. They feigned sleep but great was the noise when he tried to burst in and barked threats to break it down with his axe to wreak and wreck the place. Now and then The Law were called in their cars to such brawls and they stayed with friends in the block. When babe Mike rolled off a small camp bed and fell on to a glass one night Moll still in her night robe rushed him to The A & E at Du Cane Rd in a cab. The stitch left a scar on his cheek as if he had been in a duel which he bore all his life. When she turfed him out Mell did not come home but at times Mam then took them to meet him on The Green. /They oft used to wait but like *Godot* he still did not come. Once a week they had to queue at The Magistrates Court in Southcombe St off North End Rd to find out if Dad had paid in what was now due to them. If he had and there was a leam of light in the ness of dark they went to the Cafe for a meal and shared a Braised Steak or Mixed Grill with Chips. If not they had to face it and queue with the lame and the lost in the smoke and the maw of shame to make dole at The Nationl Assistance Board in Hamm. One day it was still a huge shock to Mac when The Law told them that his Dad had fled. In a spin Moll cried and raged that her man had gone off with a whoor named Nell. She yelled that if she found her for two pins she would give her a good ing of slap. / Mac had to ask his young male friends what a whoor was but none was sure. By now the scamp was in a group of small pals who swopped lots of 'mics with tales of Bosch, Huns, Japs, Nips and Wops on the door step. There was a new Yale lock on the front door that was left on the latch for folk to come and go. Moll made a plea to some so that on their small black and white TV Mac could watch *Muffin The Mule* *Bill and Ben* and *Tex Ritter*. Out side

he and his friends played *O' Grady Says*
'tween The Pram Sheds in The Yard and
ball games in The Cage and The Park.
With scabs on his knees he climbed trees
and joined in Leap Frog on the grass
at The Back. He feigned to joust on
horse back in the lists and played at
knights and knaves and base rogues. A few
of the big boys called Mac a shrimp
and and a squirt but some did not
shun him. These new mates taught him how
to make fires and camps on waste ground.
They made low huts like crude yourts with
small walls of old bricks and roofs of
bits of wood turf and tin. They showed
him how to fight and swear in a
world of Cops, Teds, Spivs, Coons and Queers.
He heard how to arm him self with
the wares of war like sticks and steel bars and
how to throw stones when they fought with
kids in the next block. With the rest
of the scamps he picked up how to
play Kiss Chase and touch up the girls.
How to take a slash up the wall
at a slant to give them a laugh.
He joined The ABC Minors and found out

how to get in free through the fire
door to Sat Morn Pics at *The Savoy*
in Acton. He soon came to know how
to raid shops and nick sweets. In some
way which was not clear he learned to
shout for The Light Blues when it was
time to took sides in *The Boat Race*.
With pals in the same week he joined
and got thrown out of The Sea Scouts.
/The big boys showed Mac too how to
bunk in to the ground at Loftus Road
to watch QPR in The Third Div South.
He learned too how to get in to
The White City Stadium each year to see
things like *The Royal Searchlight Tatoo*.
At *The Royal International Horse Show* he and
Mike went to see the well groomed show
how to do Ing of Jump and Hunt
to Hounds as their Grays and Roans used
to jaunce and prance on well heeled steeds
with well shod hooves. They cheered when som
some one like Pat Smythe or Harvey Smith
or The D'Inzeo Bros got a clear round
in the Heats to get thru to the
Jump Off 'gainst the clock as well as
the times a twerp one hates in haste

fell off their horse to the ground. In the world of Tics and Ath Mac loved to let go when he watched Ings and Meet of both The AAA and Int. /In a few years Mac would then see Chris Chataway beat Vlad Kuts to gain the 5000m World Record. He sipped a lime juice as he saw Derek Ibbotson break it in The Mile. To train them selves Mac and his pals ran round the out side of the 'Stade. They jinked and jogged for a few slow laps and then all went and did the High jump and Long jump on the grass at The Back near Baird House. As they lived next to The Track for a few pence Mac and his mates used to 'mind' cars parked by the kerb in front of the flats for those who bet on The Tote and went to The Dogs twice a week. In all these ways Mac was drawn in to life on the 'State. /But in imp or tant ways Mac was not part of that ure cult. At the time his Dad left he was still at *The Sacred Heart* Schl in Hamm. Mst kids frm White City went to schools on the 'State but Moll had made sure to get Mac a place at The RC Infant School where he would learn to read and write well so that he could then move on to St Mary's RC Junior Boys School in Brook Grn. At *The Sacred Heart* the mite learned not to be scared to scribe: how to print and then to write in long hand. In his school book he wrote, *'It is a lovely day We like to go out to the paro for a wark' (sic).* As George VI was laid to rest he said that, *'on our school wireless we can hear the bands playing sad music'*. His new class made trips once a week to get books out from Hamm Library. As he was fledged Mac's life was thus split in diff worlds from a young age. He was brought up on the hard edge of the White City 'state and its ure cult of pov. At the same time Baird House it self was built on one side of it, a short walk in The Smog out to Wood Lane for a bus to Brook Green. First of all as a babe when Moll used to steer him in the pram to

The Nursery and then as a child when he went to St Mary's' midst the grass and trees with their green leafs Mac got used to the sight of well kept homes.

Though he still felt like a waif in some ways as he grew Mac was drawn to the clean smart folk who lived in them and wished to be part of that mid class life. On the way to and from St Mary's he used to ride the bus for which he had a Pass and did not need to pay the fare. Once or twice a week he used to walk down Shep Bush Rd with his friends. Each day for years they passed a tramp with dank hair and a long grey beard who sat on a low brick wall. In his old grey coat with frayed cuffs and worn boots he itched to scratch and scritch his yuke. Now and then he said a few terse words to him self but of the time he just sat and stared in to space or dozed. He scared them so they ran past him with tense laughs and loud shouts.

/All the kids on The White City were poor. At school Mac's scalp was combed for bugs like fleas and lice. He knew it was false but folk of their ilk were looked down on as trash by some of those who owned shops on the edge of the 'State and The Law. Moll was ired when Mell left them all deep in debt. They were rid of some of their fear but it still felt like a blow. They were in dire straits as they owed back rent and had fear they might be thrown out. The list of new stuff for the flat was bought on 'HP' at *The Provident* and at *Edward Evans Store* in King St. Moll did what she could to make ends meet but it was hard on the dole. She darned slits in gloves and patched holes in socks and pants. She sowed up the hems of her dress. A loud Suit from The Town Hall gave them chits to get new clothes and shoes from a ware house. They were shamed but just had to make the best of it. At night Mike 'gan to grint and grind his teeth. When he 'gan to wet the bed the spate of rank sheets in the morn got Mam in to a real tew. With no funds she woed the least bill owed or things on the slate to Mr Jones who called in on the rotes of his milk round. Strapped for cash she eked out mashed spuds and puds

with lots of stodge, bread and lard or
marge with corned beef, fish or meat paste.
When the crusts ran out Mac was shamed
with cheeks flushed and sent to ask one
of the folks next door for sliced bread
a drop of milk, a twist of tea,
a tin of beans or a few eggs.
/Men from *The St Vincent de Paul Society*
for those in need of alms came once
a week and gave them hope. When Mam
cried and bared their soul with tales of
woe both were kind and helped them ride
out the storm. The one with a beard
brought Brach and Farl Cakes, Swiss Rolls and
Jam Tarts which could be stale and drie.
He got them cut price at work in
Cadby Hall at Brook Green parts of which
Mac would see from the play ground high
up on the fenced roof of St Mary's.
/It had been a shock to Mac when
he heard that his Dad had gone. In
a ness of numb he found it hard
to take in the words. He was stunned
and did not know what to think or
say. His friends had Dads who took their
belts off to strap them but they stayed.
He was glad that at least he did
not have to dread it when Mell came

In from the pub. The fact that he
felt hurt and spurned he tried to hide
from but now and then it used to
steal up on him as his chest heaved.
In plain ways Mac could not ex he
felt crushed deep in side but put a
brave face on it and braced his self.
In a state of siege with the world 'gainst
the three of them, he and Moll fused
and forged strong bonds. In ways they merged
as they took it in turn to calm
the fears of each and those of the
lamb. If her darl could not sleep the
soft lilt in Moll's voice soothed Mac with
waves of ing and love. When she fret
and said that all her hopes were slain
he held that all would be well. Told
he was now The Man of the House
Mac had to grow up fast through a
mute pact. Moll would make it up to
them for the fact that his Dad had
gone if he pledged not to leave her.
In turn with vows and vums the man
child swore he would not be like his
Dad. He would be good as gold and
save them in their plight. He would graft
and work hard at school and get a
Good Job. She said he would be Great.

/At the same time Mac had learned at
Home and School and in Church that he
had been born a Bad boy with the
dark stain of Sin on his Soul. His
fear was that Moll would leave too. He
that doth sin shall go to Hell. He
knew he was no saint and at times
fear of it would not let him sleep.
He made his First Conf and First Comm
at St Aug's in Hamm at the same time
as Anne Troy his sweet heart in plaits
from the pre fabs on the 'state. Mac's
Guilt eased if he helped his Mam so
in the years to come he was there
for her to bring up and mind his
small Bro. He went to the shops. He
learned how to do the house hold
chares and chores. He tried to keep the
flat neat as he could not bear it
if she cried and said the place looked
like a pig sty. At times he cheeked her.
His life in a daze with Mell on
the run from The Law, when his Ma
was out Mac used to stand on a
stool and get down the bag of tools
his Dad had left that was lief to
him: an Adze, an Awl, a rough File,
a Fret Saw and Hack Saw, a hinged
wood Rule, a Plane with a haft of
dark red wood, a big Wrench and a
sharp toothed Saw. In it too were stacks
of nails, thin flat brads with a lip
on one edge, round brods and of lots
of small tin tacks. Mell's own Sparth
with its light helve still hung from a
bit of string on the cup board wall.
/Mac was shocked on the first morn at
St Mary's when his Mam kissed him left
him on his own at the front gate
of the school. He was more or less
pushed in by a crowd of big boys
who tore in to the play ground which
was small but full of noise. At first
he was scared and shy as a snail
but he soon made friends. He liked to
play out but his thighs and heels got

chapped in the cold. He was good at sports and learned to swim at The Baths in Lime Grove. where his class went each week. They played foot ball on the ash pitch in Rav Ct Park, near where he had first learned to walk. Mac was good but used to hog the ball so that he would stand out and be seen. In time he was proud to wear the blue and white shirt of the school team tho a few times they got trounced. /As it turned out Mac liked St Mary's. He was keen at school and did his home work. It was strict in class but he loved the ness and norm of lin or der. He learned to write with pen and ink: to use a steel nib in the right way so as not to blot or smudge the page with blobs. He tried but could not blame his neb when he could not keep his work books clean and neat free of blotch or splotch. He worked hard. In his first term asked to stay in the class room at Play Time to write out with care *The Pied Piper*. He loved to work in the peace and calm ness of the still space. Now and then tho' he slept in class and mis spelt odd words. The bell rang and woke him and he wrote 'gran' in stead of 'grain'. He used to feel that his head weighed him down and leaned to one side. He would fret that he was bad at Maths and tensed up. At times it felt too much like a race in which he had to get a head to please those who taught him as well as his Mam and Mike. At home he had time off with Jet, Doc, Mitch and Lem to list en to *Journey Into Space*. He basked in praise when he did well and got a good mark or a prize. When Mr D took Play Time Mac used to go quite near him and hope that he would be seen. Mr D had black, greased back hair and a big fore head which creased in lines

when he was irked with the gruff and
the grump. When he frowned and loured his
dark brows pinched up just like a swan's.
Mac longed for a nod or smile but
in vain. It was in this phase of
his life that *Oh Mein Pa Pa* topped
The Charts and the trum of Eddie Calvert
hummed the pet for nine weeks. It took
one more year of hard work for Mac
to feel that his time had come. Just
as *Rock A Round The Clock* was a
hit he was put in the top class
for the last two years to prep for
The 11+. It was taught by Mr D
who was strict but fair. With whangs and
whms & whcks & whops he thwcked thm
all with a thick starched strap that made
their hands sting. In Mac's last year for
parts of the course he was glad to
be in a group coached by The Head.
In the mean time Moll saved for a
Conway Stuart pen for Mac to use in
the test. It was tough for him to
face up to the fact that there was
a chance that he might fail. He had
great fear and pain in the guts but
tried to do his best. Of course there
was an ode of great joy at home
and at school when Mac learned he had
passed. Holes in his shoes were filled with
card board when Moll took him in a
storm to be seen by the Head at

The Crdinal Vaughan Schl in Knsngtn. Thn as
he got a grand place at The Grammar
for next year more great gusts of joy.
In just a few months Johnnie Ray topped
The Charts with *Just Walking In The Rain*.
/In these years Moll tried as well to
keep her side of the pact with Mac.
She did her best to swage the hard
fact that their Dad had gone and to
make up for what he had not done.
She laid bare big new worlds. When The
Aunt came with her niece she took them
all out for a great treat to the
new well lit Tree Walk and Fun Fair
at *The Festival of Britain* in Battersea Park.
In those days Moll oft en used to
take Mac and Mike to The Pics. They

loved Burt Lancaster in *The Crimson Pirate* and
Bing Crosby in *White Christmas* at *The Broadway*
in Hammersmith; they gazed at the bust of
Mrn O'Hara who co starred with Jn Wayne in

The Quiet Man at *The Gaumont* in The Bush.
They all downed tubs of ice cream as they
watched lots of films with big male stars
ke Jack Palance, Kirk Douglas and Robert Mitchum.
They laughed at Laurel and Hardy and sat
in The Gods with Zeus at Xmas Pantomimes in
he Chiswick Empire and *The Sheperd's Bush Empire*.
In Sum Moll brought them to feed the
ducks in The Round Pond. They got the
Bus to Rich mond Park to look for
The Deer. They took trips up town to
The Bank, St Pauls and The West End.
/When Moll sent Mac out of the nest
with Mike to stay with her Aunt in
Scarboro for the Sum Hols, she gave them
the chance to exp quite a diff way
of life. He was eight when they went

by Steam Train thru the North York Moors.
With tags tied round their necks they both
rode with dogs on leads and The Guard
in The Freight Van. The Aunt had her
own posh flat with large high rooms in
Prince of Wales Drive on The South Cliff.
She took them to The Spa and to see
Shows like *The Mikado* by Gilbert & Sullivan
at The Lake in Peasholm park, as well
as The Tree Walk. She took them Out
to Tea with her friends The Sitwells who
lived in a huge Pile out in the
Dales where Mac and Mike had to sing
Don't Let The Stars Get In Your Eyes.
In the RC Church the old Aunt had
her own pew with her name on. It
stood at the front next to the font.
When they sat next to her at Mass
Mac and his Bro had to stretch with
straight backs. In the lounge of her flat
she had a small black and white TV
and a book case with glass doors plus
a large couch round which she chased
them in a rage if they told her
a tale when they stayed out late; spilt
great deals of stuff and made a mess
on their nap kins or asked to sing
with Form a long watch by George.

Mac liked it best when The Aunt told
them to take care but let them go
out on their own to range free. They
would race to the cliff and zig zag
down the paths all the way to the
front. Mac loved the smell of the sea
air and when he felt the wind on
his face. He and Mike played on the
sand with their bucks and spades. They built
forts with walls, dug round moats and fought
the tide as it came in. They wore
their rings and sprang in to the sea.
They sparged in the waves. In the rock
pools on the strand of The South Bay
they looked for crabs and star fish. They
searched and hid in the caves and vugs.
On the quay they watched the men in
sea boots land their catch in cawls and
creels from the loads of boats in the
the fleet of ing and fish that made
its way down the East coast each year.
Sat in warm coats, Mac and his Bro
gazed at them as they used to mend
their worn oars and ropes or the
tens of holes which gaped in their nets.
/One year they met a kind old salt
named Len Tonks who used to fish off
the beach and pier. He had fyke and
corf box as well as rod and reel.
He gave them an I Spy Book to
lere the rich names of all kinds of
fish like Bass, Birt, Bream, Brill, Burt, Carp,
Cod, Chub, Cusk, Dab, Dace, Dorse, Frog, Fluke,
Gade, Ged, Hake, Huss, Kelt, Lant, Launce, Ling,

Loach, Parr, Perch, Pike, Plaice, Roach, Rock, Rudd
Ruff, Saithe, Scad, Scrod, Scup, Shad, Skate, Smolt
Snook, Sole, Spod, Squid, Tench, Trout & Wrasse.
Len taught them both as well lots of
knots like loop knots, reef knots and slip
knots. He told them that Bitts were posts
on deck for ropes made from stuff like
hemp; that Brails were small ropes on sails
used to truss them be fore they were
bunt and furled; and Vangs used on the
gaff of a fore and aft sail. He
went on to tell them that a *Barque*
was a *Bark* or a B*arge* which might
be rowed or pulled or sailed; that a
Brig was square rigged with two masts and

a low for and aft sail with a
gaff and boom; that a *Buss* had sails
on two or three masts and was used
by the Dutch to fish; that a *Caique*
was *a* light skiff rowed by Turks; that
a *Dhow* with one mast sailed in the

Gulf; that a *Hoy* was rigged as a
sloop fore and aft with a jib stay
and a bow sprit that stood, used to
take folk and goods for a short way
on the coast; that a *Ketch* was a
well built boat with two masts used on
the coast too; that a *Koff* was a
slow boat used by the Danes; that a
Punt or *Scow* was a flat craft with
broad and square ends shoved by Toffs on
The Cam and The Thames with thrusts of
a long pole who liked to boast they just
yawed and messed a bout. Len told them
a *Schuit* was a flat Dutch boat; that
Sculls were rowed in pairs fours and eights

like those they had seen lots of times
from the clubs on The Thames Mall; that
a *Smack* had one mast with a sail
rigged fore and aft like a sloop that
fished on the coast and had a well
in which these might be kept; that a
Trow was a boat or barge used in
the South of the Lands of Cot and
the North of the Land of Eng to
spear fish by torch light; that a *Yawl*
was a ship's boat with six oars some
times used to fish; that a *Yacht* was
a craft in which the smart class sailed.
/Once The Aunt gave them their six pence
a day to spend they were free. They
might scale the cliffs to the heights of
Scarb Castle. They might shout and scream at
The Fun Fair on The Pier or row
boats in The Mere on Oliver's Mount.
The swam in the brine and slid down
the chute in The Op en Air Pool.
Mac's trunks of blue wool weighed a
ton wet and when he took them off
he liked to wring them out and put
them thru the old mang. He and Mike
both loved cones of soft *Jaconelli* Ice cream.
Best of all they both liked to putt
on the smooth green at the top of the

South Cliff. A Hole in One made Mac's heart soar. A nice man worked there who took their six pence and gave them the white Score Cards, clubs and balls. If Mac and his Bro got there 'fore time they watched him cut the grass and put out the red flag pins. He had a sharp round piece of tin which he sank in the earth to make new holes and to fill in the old ones once a week in the erd. The man used to rem them with a smile when they turned up each year. One Sum their Mam came for a few days. For two she stayed in Lon and worked long hours in Lyons tea shop. One year she could not come as she was ill in Du Cane Rd Hospital. /In his last year at St Mary's when Mac had passed the 11+ Moll wished to treat him. She scrimped and saved so that he could go on The School Trip to The Isle of Wight. The boys went by coach and boat to stay for 10 days in a Guest House in Ryde. It had a Gong which was rung for most meals morn and night. Mac shared a room with three young males. They bounced and jounced on on their well sprung beds and pissed in the sink. They sang *Blue Suede Shoes* and had a great time. They swam in the cold sea and played foot ball on the flat beach. From Ryde they went out for walks thru stiles down old path ways on which they kept up the sort of good pace that in the end lames keen small boys. On each long slog they took packed lunch in a beige knap sack and a cape for when it rained. They got down the deep gorge at Blckgng Chne. In the gulch each found a niche to fill in their Logs. They put sands of diff hues in test tubes at Alum Bay. On a bg air field they sw a Brabazon plne tht ws wdgd with chocks & wrppd in moth balls it flew no more. They climbed the steep steps of a tall white Light hse which warned ships a way from the rocks on the coast. When things were

dropped from the top The Keep said that
they were pests. On one trip they scaled
the walls of Carisbrooke Castle. Thru the
court in the bawn a don key turned
his life on a wheel. Mac sent his
Mam and Bro post cards on which he
wrote that he thought of them and prayed
for them. He spent his last pence on
a cheap brooch with a hasp for her
and a big stick of Rock for him.
/Mac had done well at St Mary's so
that in his last year he had been
made a Prefect and the House Captain of
More House, one of four in to which
the school was split with Mayne, Fisher and
Campion. As such he wore both a blue
Shield and a wide Badge. He was praised
by all when he did re search and
then wrote up a short *Life of More*
to read it out loud in each Class.

He was all the more shamed one morn
ing when The Head sent him out to
The Front of The School Assembly. He
had picked him out of the line as
his shoes were not clean and both were
scuffed. In The Break Mac raged as his
his pride was hurt. He felt let down
and thought that he might run a way.
Lunch Time he crept in to The Head's
room and left Shield and Badge on his
desk pad. At the end of The Break
The Head stormed in to Mac's class. In
a speech he made it clear to all
boys like him could not just re sign.
In shame Mac had to go right out
to the front of the class to pick
up his Badge and Shield and take them
back to his desk. As he gripped them
in the palm of his hand, he had
thought to throw them at The Head. The
poss that he might spoil it for his
young Bro who was then in Class 4
flashed in to his mind. In the same
year *Look Back in Anger* by John Osborne
burst on to the scene at The Court,
Mac had a fear as well that it
might put at risk his own place at
The Vaughan and so did not do it.

Chapter 3

When Mac got a place at *The Vaughan* his Mam took him to a posh shop in High St Ken called *Hope Bros* to fit him out for the new school. He had got a Grant for a grey serge suit to be worn in the first two terms and a black blaze for the Spring term, as well as a tie, new shoes, socks and the rest. He had to wear a new black cap with a large brim which he used to hate. The peak made him stand out on his way to school and back. Some of the hard kids at White City said he looked like a cunt he felt like one. He was duffed up in front of his Bro by one of the slobs from a gang of boys on the 'State. He knew that if the yobs sought him out, such toughs could bash him up much worse and so he swore to keep the cap in his bag 'till he was near school. He got Lines to write if seen with out it on his head but felt it was well worth the risk. /So each morn Mac took The Tube from White City to The Land of Hol and Park and thus crossed the tracks in to a diff world. The avs were broad and lined with tall trees. The shops were full of nice things. The lux flats opp the school had high rooms with warm lamps in the winds. The new boy was awed and proud to be there but was shamed too. In his first term at *The Vaughan* Mac felt shown up on Mon morns each week when he had to queue in a mean line with the waifs and strays out side The Sec's room for Free School Meal chits . It brought him down to a low state that he could not think of much or talk of it at all. He was glad to get lunch but it did not seem right that they had to be marked out from the rest of the boys with mon. He kept his doubts to him self and thought he was fine when he tried to do more work to make up for it. At times if tired in his mind's eye he saw The Head from St Mary's look at him through the wind and he would try more hard and get on with it. The new Head ruled with fear and used a cane to thrash boys sent to wait out side his door by the strict Staff who wore black gowns. At the start it was all quite strange to Mac. He found

out fast that they did not like the
way he and some of his new mates
spoke. The dolt was taught by Miss Sim
twice a week he had to change and
to be blunt how he ought to speak.
Mac was told how not to slouch but
to sit up straight when he formed words
and to shape them with poise; how to
ope his mouth and not talk with it
closed; how to purse his lips; how to
use his teeth and tongue; how to take
a deep breath and at times to pause
as he spoke and how not to race
and rush; how to hear his own voice
how to take care with each phrase and
thus chant in a way that was clear,
'She sells sea shells on the sea shore'.
In all Langs Miss Sim frowned on slang
with a glout and lour and *'is not'*
right had to take the place of *'ain't'* when
it came to use of *'nuts'* for glans. One
did not say *'Ay'* or *'Aye'* or *'Yea'*
or *'Yeh'* or *'Yep'* but *'Yes'*. One did
not use terms like *'Ah!'* or *'Bah!'*
or *'Cor!'* or *'Dang!'* or *'Eh!'* or *'Eh?'*
or *'Fie!'* or *'Pah!'* or *'Poh!'* or *'Pooh!'*
or *'Ha!'* or *'Hah!'* or *'Ha Ha!'* or
'Ha Ha Hah!' or *'Heh!'* or *'Hey!'* or

'Hist!' or *'Ho!'* or *'Oh!'* or *'Oi!'* or
'Phew!' or *'Pish!'* or *'Ugh!'* or *'Yo!'*. Nor
did one use *'Strewth!'* or *'Whew!'* or *'Wisht!'*
or use terms like *'Gee'* or *'Shucks!'* which
The Yanks did, though one could say *'Hup!'*
or *'Whoa!'* or *'Woa!'* to one's horse. One
did not sing Ella Fitzgerald's *It Don't Mean
A Thing If You Ain't Got That Swing*.
As a kind of re ward in the
Third Year she took the boys to the
Show, *'Fings Ain't Wot They Used To Be'*.
/From his first day at *The Vaughan* Mac
had sensed that he would have to change.
He made new friends with whom he learned
to play Chess and the big diffs 'tween mites
like pawns and the rest of The Knights,
Rooks, Kings and Queens. He tried to read
The Times. The Daily Mirror was banned. If
a boy was caught with it The Staff
might smite him and set some hard Lines.
At home he still liked Desperate Dan in
The Dandy, Dan Dare in *The Eagle* and
too The Bash St Kid in *The Beano,*
as well as Roy of The Rovers and
the rest in *The Hotspur* and *The Wizard*.
At the same on The Wire Less he
could not wait for *The Barlowes of Beddington*
and lived in *The Mill on the Floss*.

/Mac looked on when lads flipped and swopped small coins such as Batz, Cents, Dimes, Frncs, Janes, Mrks, Old Pnce, Placks, Pyx, Rnds, Reis, Sens, Sols, Taels and Yen. The Vaughan was a new and at times quite strange world in which he had to learn fresh words and names for things. On a school trip to The Zoo he found winged Zimbs; Apes and Sais; snakes like small Asps, long Boms and Kraits; Bears like Ted big and small; both wild Boar and tame Swine; Brocks and Das; old and young Bulls, Yaks and Zhos with long manes; a rare Fox and a Lynx; Gaurs; wild Thars and Tehrs that weaned & yeaned young goats; Hogs; Kobs and Mhorrs; a fine Moose in the rear; a huge Ox and young Stirks; a group of Pards in their own cage; Skinks like sneaks that used to scoot here and there; Skunks that smelled; lots of Ais and Sloths; Sharks with sharp fins; Shoats & Yelts tht squealed; Stoats; Toads; horned Yales & tons of Zoons that snoozed a while to pass the time. /In The Bird House small loud Choughs chirmed and churred while bald Coots plunged; Crakes like Daws chirked & chirled; big black Crows & Rooks cawed for corn; large Cranes ducked with long legs and bills; a Finch chirred with the tone of The Spink; black blue and Brant Geese canked while Claiks screaked and a true grey Lag Goose clacked; Grebes mde steep dives; Gulls with long wings and webbed feet skirled wth high shrill screams Mac took note that The Hawks and Perns with short round wings had a jess, a short strip of silk on each leg with a ring on the end for a leash the old name of which was a loyn or lune. He was glad there were Jays here and there and Kites with long wings and forked tails most of which were Gledes. Larks rose in the trees with Lings that looked like them as well as Black Merles. Barn, Brown and Beech Owls perchd while Chu and Grey Owls, Hoot and Screech Owls with Long Horned Scops and White Owls all 'merge in dribs and drabs. Strnge Rocs swooped roun Ruffs with ear tufts. Shrikes screamed & skirle A few Sprews glossed in their coats as Storks billed their lng lgs. Shrikes hooked thei toothed beaks while a rare Thrush kissed its mate. Tits and Twites winged it as did small Wrens and Yites with the low yells that hark back in their own closed world. /As Little Richard sang *The Girl Can't Help It* and had a hit with *She's Got It*

Mac would write up such trips with zeal. If he did not know what things meant at once he looked them up at night. His small desk in the front bed room at Baird House faced out on to the park. There he would dare to read new things and took some care with his home work. He liked to read and write of those like The Celts, The Danes, The Finns, The Franks, The Gaels, The Gauls, The Goths, The Greeks, The Jutes and The Lapps. He did not loll and laze much in class but was slow at Maths. At the end of his first year there were tests to split the boys in to two Streams for the rest of their time at the school up to the Fifth year when they took their O Levels. Mac did his best but tensed up. He had to leave one test with pains in his guts and rest on a camp bed in The Staff Room. He felt low and shame when put in The B Stream. What made up for it was that a few dear friends were in the same Form and they all liked Sports. Mac had been keen and took part in all he could from the start of the First Year. He had wished to join in at once when kids from all years played Foot ball in the small play ground. For the first few terms they used a ball made of card squashed up and tied with string. Mac got in to strops if the big boys did not choose him to play in a team and he was left out. From these he made a friend named Szem who came from The Land of Po and lived in The North of Lon. He was two years in front of Mac and good at sports. He had no Sis or Bro and so he liked to go home with Mac and spend time with his Mam and Mike at Baird House. He showed Mac how to win at Subbuteo and took him to see *The Spurs* play *The Busby Babes* in the same year Man Utd had crashed in Munich. Mac liked to play but got a prob with his left knee when twelve. His main sport was then Cricket. He was quite good with bat and ball. He could bowl. He liked the fast catch in the slips and throws to hit the bails from a good way off. Out in Chingford he trained at The MCC School once a week. In the Fourth Year at school he was picked for The 2nd Eleven and then for two more years he played in The 1st Eleven. From the first day Mac had loved The P E Class with Mr Cross in The School Hall but he found it hard to keep up in The Run round the block each week. Mac was lithe but his thighs were thin and his legs were not strong.

He could not hold to a fast time as he got out of breath. Not once did he come near the front but at his own slow pace used to go all the way. In the school Gym he liked to vault The Box and The Horse, to climb The Ropes and The Wall Bars but one day he got a shock on The Beam. As Mao made his *Great Leap Forward* in China, the boys in the class were asked by Mr Cross to climb up on to The Beam and to do a back flip in to his arms. He would catch them all as they fell back and in that way break their fall down on to the mat. Mac lined up with the rest of the boys and climbed up The Wall Bars on to The Beam with ease but once there he froze with fear. He would not move. He just could not trust Mr Cross to catch him. It took tears and shame 'fore Mac was coaxed and he forced him self to let go and to do it.

/At the time of this scene Mac's Mam was not well and he had to hold on to him self a lot at home. As he had grown in to his Teens and The Monotones had sung *Book of Love* in the Doo Wop style, both Moll and her son got more and more in tense. The Aunt in Scarb got Mac his first pair of long jeans when he was still in short pants at twelve. Moll wished The Man of The House to do well at school but he had to steen his heart and fight to grow up as a male. It had been hard for Moll since Mac had been at *The Vaughan*. She had stuffed her bra and worked on tills in shops and good pubs like *The Chef and Brewer* in Edgware Rd when she could but the hours were long and the wage not high. high. In lots of ways she loved to work with folk and things would go well for a while but none seemed to last long. She toiled for not much and came home tired and out of sorts. She went for a short lie down on the bed a lot and spent hours there. As Buddy

Holly sang *It Doesn't Matter Anymore* she used to chide Mac at times while in his own mute ways he would cheek her back. Moll used to gorge on bread and jam to stuff down what she felt. It was too much to sift thru it. When she ailed she had to go on The Sick. If she fell out with some one, she had to go and make dole. She still got in to a to do and had fits if Mac or his Bro were ill. She used to fuss and fret if one got a bad cough or cold as it meant more time off work. In the weeks that led up to the scene on The Beam in the gym, Mike had got the Mumps. With ringed eyes thru lack of sleep Moll had to take time off to dab him him with some thing day and night when his throat glands swelled up. She girned in rage when Mike had just got well but he fell off his skates in a race and broke his nose. The mite had been in Mac's care so Moll used to scold him as she lost more time off. As Conway Twitty had a big hit with *It's Only Make Believe* Mac still had a shock and the seals of love were stretched in the hall at home when drugged Moll fell in to his arms. It was a bomb shell when she blur ted out that that a big tab and dose she lets sleep of ing and pills had ta ken. He got a fright but led her to her room and layed her down on the bed. He ran out to the Phone Box in the street where a man he knew who lived down stairs on the ground floor was in the booth. It took a few hard hits with his fist on the door and shouts from Mac to get him to break off his own call and then to ring for an Amb. One came soon and took Moll to Du Cane Rd Hospital. Mac and his Bro slept at their friend Den's whose Mam took care of them for a few weeks. She had a stab at it but said that she just could not get the funds from The Town Hall and could not keep them so they were sent in great fear by car with a man in a grey suit to *St Vincent's Orphanage* in Mill Hill. It was a sad, harsh place then run in their own stern way by *The Daughters of Charity*. Mac and Mike feared these swans of wrath each of whom wore a large starched white head dress. Kids were forced out to play forts in the play ground bared to the cold when hoar frost still lay on the play ground. They shived and sneezed as The Swings froze. The chaste Nuns kept tabs on them and used Ping Pong bats to whack and whop the cheats if they did not eat up the stodge of bread pud. In four weeks Mac and his Bro were moved on to a place near Chelsea Bridge in Oakley St, off the Kings Rd. Both liked it there as it was small and warm. It was near their schools so they could pick up their less ons. By then Mike was at *The London Oratory*. A man told them that their Mam had been pumped out at Du Cane Rd and sent to *Springfield Hospital* in Tooting. A course of drugs and ECT had made her well and they would all be home in a few weeks. Mac leapt up the steps two at a time when the day came and Moll ran down to meet them. As she put her arms a round them both Mac was glad that she smiled and laughed a lot but he could feel she felt tense. She was brown and looked well in one way but at the same time her face was aged and lined. She had lost a great deal of of weight and seemed small and thin. They were in fear and mute shame. It did not take long for the time to come when Moll could not bring her self to say the name *'Springfield'* with out tears and rage when she spoke of what they had done to her. Mac put a brave face on it but in side he was scared. At school he had a calm mien but that was a mask. When she could not get a job Moll cussed and cried that they were cursed and there was a hex on them. If she went on in such a curt mood and would have no truck with him Mac tried to snap her out of it. He made to cheer her up but his own hope waxed and waned. He would vex her and not know why. Now and then Moll would be a ghast when some one claimed to have caught sight of his Dad in one of the drab pubs with lots of Brass in The Bush. He had turned in to a kind of ghost who could spook them and rouse their deep fears. It used to daunt him but Moll would count on Her Son to go with her to look for the ghoul in his old haunts where Drabs were bruised and Bards still sang in the blue smoke to hard men of woad. On a sur prise treat for her 50th Birth Day his Mam and Bro had a great time, as Mac did when he took them both out to see *South Pacific* at *The Dominion*. /To help out Mac got a Paper Round in the shop a cross the road. He used to get up at 6 o' clock in the morn to run round all the flats. The old Blocks did not have lifts so he had to flit up and down lots of stairs but at least the climb kept him quite fit. He did not like it when it was cold and dark but he had a lot of get up and go. He had verve and once he was out and felt the fresh air on his face he was glad to do it. He loved the thick strong smell of the news print that met him in the shop. An opp came to work there on Suns from 8am to 2pm. He stopped The Round and sold lots of pop, scoops of ice cream and sweets like Chaws and Chews in stead. When he had done that for a few months he 'gan to steal. The cash was kept in a card board box which The Boss checked once an hour or so. Mac found he could slip coins in to his jeans and not be seen. In one way he felt guilt but he was fed up of his Mam's sobs when she was short and they were left with just stale dry bread. It meant that he could help her out to get grub so she did not need to get stuff on the slate from Mr Jones. Mac him self did not have to tell tales to ask Moll for mon. He could buy a cup of tea or a Coke with his mates. The cold fear that he might be caught if he filched did not go. His Mam took pride in the fact that she did not steal and had raised him to think of it as wrong. Mac knew that it would have been a slap in the face and she would have died of shame if he had been found out but went on and risked it. In side he could not help it when his spite grew as some of his pals took skis to the piste in The Alps. /Mac had not worked in the shop for long when he fell for a small dark girl called Mill who came in each week. She lived near in Batman Close. Like his own Mam and Dad her's both came from The Land of Ire. While he cleaned the winds of the flat at home which looked a cross to those where she lived he used to moon on dates with her. As Cliff had a hit with *Livin Doll* Mac blushed with ease when his Mam saw this and teased him. The sad fact was that he felt quite meek and shy when it came to girls. His cheeks went bright red at the word Sex. Since he had been at *The Vaughan* Mac had tried hard to be a Good Boy, not to say a Saint. When he 'fessed to The Priest each week Sex and Sin had come to mean the same thing. The boys had been told that at night they should all sleep with both of their hands out side the bed sheets. Mac did so but in his mind he was not sure what it all meant. As his pubes had grown in some ways his frame had shut down on sex. With guilt he read *The News of The World* to find out a bout it. He picked things up from boys at school. When it hit the shops they marked with a stripe the most blue parts of *Lady Chatterley's Lover*. Moll had sent Mac to The Doc with a note but he said that Mac prob knew more than him. From his shelf the Doc would have loaned Mac a book like *The Way of All Flesh* by Samuel Butler. He looked but just could not find it. In the Sum Hols The School Journey from *The Vaughan* was to Rome but it was dear and Mac could not go. The Church then fixed it up with the St John's Youth Club in the East End for him to go once more to their own Sum Camp at Gosfield Lake nr Halstead. Mac had been Nine the first time he went. He rued the white socks his Mam had made him wear when he met the coach and found them hard to live down. He had to hold his own with some tough kids with whom he shared a Bell Tent. Mac had got used to the camp and 'joyed its ways a part from one thing. At night he had got up set at the rude sex jokes in the tent. He told The Doc who let him sleep in The Sick Tent for a few nights. When he went back the gests had stopped but in ence of sile the kids stared and gawed him.

Months had passed in the shop till Mac
braved it out and got up the pluck
to ask Mill to go out. She did
not know it was his first Date. He
felt grown up when he got good seats
at *The Metropole* in Victoria to see *Spartacus*.
The film rolled and Mac got Mill in
a clinch in The Back Stalls. As the
slaves fought to get free in the film
he snogged his way thru it with her
and told his friends how great it was.
/But his inf with her was cut short
when he glimpsed a small card one gets
in the wind ow of *Black's Newsagents*. it
was an Ad with a Phone No. to
ring for *'Personal Service'*. Mac was drawn
to the nymph and the vamp but he
was scared too and 'shamed of his lust.
He loathed him self as the thought of
a slut 'ticed him and a sense of
sin lurked in his soul to tempt him
In his head Mac dwelt on vice but
letched for weeks and told no one. He went
back lots of times to stare at the
card but fear and shame that he might
be seen won out and he would walk
a way some times close to tears. He
played a round so with the Phone No
in his head. In a kind of mind
he mixed up it game he so could
not quite rem it. Time passed and he
got the nerve to ring. A girl with
a sort of French voice told him that
if he had the mon he was old
en ough. He asked if he could stay
the night and was told she would have
to see when he got there. Thoughts of
ess and obs of bawds and whores went
on to poss him and grew like tares
in his soul. They stayed in his head
and weighed on him for a while but
he did no thing. In the end he
put them out of his mind and did
not ring a gain for a long time.
/Mac had all the while kept up with
his school work as best he could. He
now tried to make up for the time
lost when he had been a way in
Mill Hill. The Staff knew it was hard
for him at home and backed him. He
bunked off with his mates on odd days
out but on the whole he turned up.
He got sent home a few times by
The Head the first time to have his hair cut
when it was too long. Like his mates
he used a caul of his Mam's to

wave his hair. Then once he had to
change his shoes as the points on the
toes of his Chelsea Boots were too sharp.
/By The Fourth Year Mac had made some
head way and he was in the top
half of the class for most things. He
did not like Maths at which he was
poor but by now the bulk of his work
meant a lot to him. In Geog he took
care as he drew maps in his book.
When Cook the class 'hard man' threw an
app core from the back and spoiled one,
it sent more amps through him than a
volt sends through an ohm. Mac's great wrath
at the mess made of his hard work
was such that he lost his fear of
the hulk and chucked it straight back in
his face. The fight meant the youths were
both thrown out of the class room and
had to do lines but in side Mac
was chuffed when they came to be friends.
/The Wind of Change tore in and swept
Mac in to The Fifth Year when some
Staff told him that they thought he was
bright. They said that he could do well
in The O Level Exams and that he
should aim for The Sixth Form. Mr Bull
who took History was six and a half
feet tall and kind; Mr Mo who taught
Geography slept through Mass and had a dry
sense of fun. Mac felt that both of
them were on his side and as Elvis
sang *'It's Now or Never'* he gan to
swot and to fill his mind with facts.
The boys learned much by rote so he
had to stow a way a great deal
in his head. 'Twas the same for the
next few years when Mac would stay in
and swat as the sun shone at Wimbledon.
As Rod Laver made his way thru each
round to beat Chuck McKinley, Mac made his
to cram all the facts that he could.
While the kids on the 'State crowed and
showed off taws in The Open Air Baths,
in to his head Mac rammed in more.
His great need to do well was such
that Mac prayed hard and made a deal
with God. He would be such a good
boy from then on if God just helped
him to get through that once. Great was
the joy at home when a small form
came in the morn Post to tell them
that Mac had passed all five of the
O Levels he had sat for in French,
Eng Lang, Eng Lit, Hist and Geog. He
thanked God for a good week or so.

/Mac was then quite torn. As Sam Cooke sang *That's It, I Quit, I'm Moving On* most friends that had been near to him left the school to get a job and earn mon. In a way he felt that he ought to do the same thing and not try to cheat fate but in his heart he wished to stay on. He sensed that it would be a real feat to and go in to The Sixth Form as he was urged to do by The Staff. It was a tough choice for at home they were still poor. They could not go to hear Mike sing in the school choir with The Boys of The Schola Polyphonica and The BBC Symphony Orchestra at The RFH, led by Igor Stravinsky him self when he did *Persephone* that year. They had to list en to it at home. As the piece came to a close and the 'gram shook with all the claps n' loud cheers they were so proud to join in as well. Though she was quite low, Moll still backed Mac up in his wish to stay on. She and he took pride in the fact that they both aimed high for him. They were not just hung up on the hooks for him to bring in a wage as soon poss. They wished to do the right thing which was for him to go on and get his A-Levels. They were of the same mind that he could then aim to teach and help kids in a school.

/At the same time Moll was stressed and fell ill once more. A hot rash of Shingles burned her skin. A patch of red spots spread and scorched her side and scalp too which had to be shaved. She wore a wig which did not fit and was sort of held in place with a clasp. She could not work and so they were pressed down by the lack of means. When Moll tried there were lots of stops and starts. She used to weep and youp when she could not hold jobs down. She would cry out that she was just sick to death of it all and that she was no good to her self or them. At times with puffed eyes she blamed Mac and his heart quailed when she called him names that hurt. In years to come it left him with a tache on his soul. He got quite scared of her when she raged that Mell would not be dead as long as he lived and was cowed by her loud ang in some ways. His Dad

was like a wraith who still used to
haunt them all at times. One day
Mac got a shock when he went home
to find Moll had gone. She had run
a way to her Sis named Norah who
lived in Leeds. Mac broke down in tears
and cried in front of his friend Ton
who seemed hap with his Dad and Mam
and two Bros and a Sis in a
nice house in Acton. Moll came back full
of shame and re morse at the end
of the week and she said Mac had
made the right choice to stay at school.
/Thus in the same year the first man
out in space went round the earth Mac
found his own way and went in to
The Sixth Form at *The Vaughan*. For the
first time he was on a plane with
boys from the A Stream. He chose to
do History, Geography and French and mixed on
a par with those who did the same.
In the new space his mind grew when
for the French Course he read *Athalie* by
Racine, *Dr Knock* by Jules Romains and too
The Knot of Vipers By Francois Mauriac. The
Geog Course was Economic and Physical Aspcts of
N America and W Europe. His main Course
was Englsh and European History 1485 to 1815.

He loved to search the past. From the
start his work was good and he was
told to 'keep it up'. In the next
two years he learned to read, to use
source mat and to think for him self.
/One way in which Mac did so was
to let go of his Catholicism. He had
ceased to go to Mass when he 'gan
to work in the shop on Sun morns.
His deal clinchd with God that he would be
'good' if he got his O Levels had
failed. He felt a hyp when he tried
to do the same for his A Levels.
In The Sixth Form he had to do
Apologetics, a branch of Theology that 'proves' the
truth of Christianity. By then his doubts in
in The Church and its weal had grown
and freed his thought so that he felt
what it preached was a lot of cant
and quite wrong. In his child hood Mac
had learned The Creed but his faith in
God and The Trine had lapsed. He had
prayed hard and spent his life on his
knees but he now felt that there was
no one to hear. He had no more
faith in God than he had in Baal
or The Boodh. He had no more trust
in priests than he had in sprites or

sylphs or will o' the wisps or guys
who held to The Four Yugs or went
on The Hadj. Hymns and psalms tht moved
him as a child lost their ring. Things
came to a head for him one eve
when he felt shame to be seen near
Our Lady of Fatima. It was a mom
of truth and a point of ing and
turn for him when the runt felt that
he had earned his stripes and as Dylan
sang *'A Hard Rains A-Gonna Fall'* in streaks
of tears he had to walk a way.
/In The Sixth Form at *The Cardinal Vaughan*
all the boys were seen by The Staff
as Young Men and were keen to be
thought of as such. For the first time
The Man of The House at home had
to find his own place as A Man
of The World out side it and school.
In the guise of a grown up Mac's
way was to drink with male friends in
The Pub. To be big in those days
was to have a quick out of bounds
drink at lunch time in *The Norland Arms*.
To do so and thus to be served
at the bar when in Law one had
to be 18 was part of a shared
rite de passage to be come a man.

At the Wine and Cheese Party for 'Young
Gentlemen' at *The Vaughan* they all got drunk
and some one smeared a soft cheese that
stank in side all the desks for quite
a few weeks. Mac looked young for his
age. As The Chieftans came on the scene
and played *Comb Your Hair and Curl It*,
like his mates Mac brushed his dark hair
with a fixed quiff that curved up and
back as smooth as Tony Curtis'. He shaved
but his side burns just would not grow
and the hairs on his chin were sparse
as were the few on his chest. He
was lean and could be vain a bout
his looks but felt shame that he lacked
brawn. He had grown up with the big
men of woad who stood right at the
back of *Our Lady of Fatima* when they
went to Mass so they could get straight
out to the pub. Now on a Sun
Mac too and a group of his mates
found their own way to swig a few
pints at *The General Smuts*. On just two
they used to belch and bolk and it
was all just a bit of a laugh.
In the morn his head might belk and
throb but they all looked down on
Half Pints who did not drink like men.

Mac him self had been fledged by his Mam not to drink too much. As kids he and Mike had sips of Ginger Wine at Xmas while Moll just went bright red if she had a *Baybycham* or a drop of Port. When he joined The Sixth it was seen as the norm by folk like her from The Land of Ire for youth of Mac's age to drink. It was viewed as strange if they did not. She was pleased for him so when he used to meet his best friend Ton too each week for a drink at *The Goldsmith's Arms* in East Acton Lane. Mac soon found that a Brown or Light Ale helped him to talk. In some ways Mac had low self worth and was still quite shy but a drink or two did let him come right out of him self on stuff like sex and what was ing on go in the world. Ton had boils and blains but did well with the girls while Mac dreamed but drink let his wroth show when it came to The Wealth Gap or The Cold War. With his head still high in the clouds Mac was piqued when his Oxfam tin was not filled at once when they did the rounds of all the pubs in The Bush.

/In The Sixth Mac was a School Prefect two years and had charge of a class in School Assembly. In a way it gave his self worth a boost but it caused him to stand out. Some times he would give Lines to those who cheeked or jeered him or sauced him on school lore but on the whole Mac had to brace and mask him self in the role of ness and strict. When he had to take charge in front of a class or read a text out loud in one of his own he felt one could see through him which he did not feel in the pub with Ton. His head might belk and throb in the morn but that was part of the game to moan of or vaunt next time.

/At the end of his first year in The Sixth Mac and Ton had an ing of work in days of Hol. They went to pick fruit and beans in the fields mong the dikes in the skied land scape of the Norfolk Broads at a Concordia Student Sum camp. In The Charts at the time Cliff sang *'It'll Be Me'* and on the way Mac could not get the song out of his head. He and Ton kipped mid big stooks of straw and small mice 'neath

the joints and joists of an old barn
with a score of boys their age from
round the world. The girls slept in one
next door. The beds made up from spare
hard boards were the banes of their life.
They had bran and pears for break fast
and skied their cores to files of ducks
tht quacked & frogs tht croaked in the
pond as cows in a field chewed the
cud. In the day Mac and Ton filled
sacks with the large kind of broad beans
that one reaps from the good earth
of those parts. At night they drank pints
of strong ale in the pub and smoked
tipped cigs like *Gold Leaf*. On the eve
of their dept there was a loud dance
at which they all stayed a wake to.
Twst The Nght Awy wth Sam Cooke. Mac
slept with a girl for the first time
on her camp bed. He tried to grope
her but she would thwart him if he
got brave and tried to touch her tits.
She laughed he was so con trite and
asked for ness of give in the morn.
/When he went back to *The Vaughan* for
his last year in The Sixth Form some
of The Staff helped Mac to raise his
sights. Mr Bull and Mr Park who now

took Hist urged him to try for a
place at University. At first he was stunned
as he was not sure what one was.
It took him some time to see that
they meant it and what such a step
would mean for him. His heart leapt at
the poss that he could on go with
his ing of learn and at the thought
too that it would give him a way
to leave home. It had been hard
at Baird House since he had been in
The Sixth. He sat to do his home work in
one world in which he was asked to
judge *'The Break with Rome'*; to weigh up
'The Reigns of James 1 and Charles 1';
speak his mind on *'The Whigs and The
Glorious Rev'*; to think thru *'The Roles of
Burke, Fox and Pitt'*; to take stock of
'The Poor Laws'; to rule on *'Clive and
The East India Company'*; and to write up
'The Life of Albrecht Von Wallenstein'.
Yet at the same time as Gerry and
The Pacemakers asked *'How Do You Do It?'*
from his desk by the wind in his
bed room Mac looked out and saw the
boys from the 'State in their world play
on the foot ball pitch in the park
while thru the wall he could hear the

low thrum of The TV all the time.
For spells the Mam was pressed right down
in to the ness. She wished for Mac
to learn and make use of his mind
but for her self she would just read
Mills and Boon and stuck to *Tit Bits*.
When she was tired and high strung Moll
just glared loud at him and raged. At
times she might tell him to get right
out of her sight. At such points when
he took the brunt of her worst rage
he locked him self in the loo or
just left the flat and sat in the
park for a while. He felt that she
talked at him and could not hear him
if he did try to speak as she
strafed him with words. In the end he
just read as she droned on while he
made grunts here and there. Moll vowed to
call him in the morns but when pressed
and scared to be on her own left
him to sleep late. He could not bridge
the gap that had oped and felt the
deep need to get a way from home.
/Mac dropped sports to have more time to
work for his A Levels. Oft he sat
and tried to read in the sun midst
the cheeps of birds in Hamm Prk where

they played Bowls on the ing of green.
He asked him self if would dare to
aim for grades that would get him a
place at University and be a route out
of the White City. As Martin Luther King's
'I have a Dream' speech rang in his
ears, Mac filled in an App Form to
read History at Leicester & Nottinghm which did
not req 0 Level Maths or Latin. He
had been told by school Staff that he
should do well and was put in for
S Level History and Geography as well as
A Level French. Mac felt him self stressed
that he had to make it. The strain
did not show 'til it was time for
his Mocks at Easter. On the morn of
the first one in History, a fear that
he would fail gripped him and he lost
his nerve. By the time that he got
to The Tube at White City Station the
dread took hold of him and he knew
in side that he could not face it.
He did not get off at Holland Park
but stayed on the train to Queensway. He
get out and went in to Kensigton Gardens.
He walked in tears round *The Round Pond*.
He rang a friend but clammed up and
in shame he mooched here and tehre all

day on his own in *Hyde Park* and
tried to weigh it up in his mind.
He had dared to get that far but
his hope had gone and Mac felt he
had lost his chance to get a way.
Yet when he went back to school next
day he found that Mr Park took it
all in his stride and calmed Mac down.
When the real test came in the Spring
Mac did well. He was tense and could
not sit still. He used to fike and
fidge but turned up and kept his nerve.
Tho Mac had been on a Sixth Form
Trip to The Sorbonne, it turned out he
failed in French as did his whole class
which had spent too much time at Whist.
But a Grade C in Geography and more
Distinction in Scholarship Level History was just
fab news as Gerry and The Pacemakers sang
'I Like It'. Mac's faith in his self
grew with the thought that his Mam had
been right and he might in deed do
some thing great. The mixed grades meant
that he had to wait for a poss
University place the next year and as Leslie
Gore cried *'It's My Party'* he had to
get a job at once to make ends meet.
At the same time he sent an App
both to Leicester and Nottingham for the next
year to read Social Science (which took in
a course in Economic History) as well as
History in its own right. He left school
on a Fri and on Mon was a
full time clerk at The Head Office of
The Metal Box Co Ltd in West Acton.
As Cliff crooned *'It's All In The Game'*
Mac filled in forms for this or that
batch of tin cans to be filled with
fish or meat, beer or soft drinks. He
was sent on a course round The UK
to see where the tin plate was made
at the big steel plant at Neath in
South Wales and works in some towns where
cans were made like the one at Rochester.
In Chatham he dared take a girl with
green eyes and tints in her dark hair
to *The Rolling Stones* at The Corn Exchange.
It was a great time for new sounds.
He did not hear much that night thru
the screams but he did not care as
it was a thrill just to be there
with a girl who made his heart race.
He was hap to scan the whole crowd
and to take in the vibes of the
wild band on stage. While he did a
stint at The Works in Leicester Mac was

seen in The History and Sociall Science Depts. In the last one Dr Birmingham at once put him at ease while they talked and then at the end of it gave him a place to start in October. When Mac wrote to let his Mam and Mike know great was the joy. On his way home Mac was so hap that in The Bar at Leics Rail Station he had his first drink on his own, a clear Pint of Bass on draught in a clean thick glass jug.

/Mac re turned to work as a clerk at the Head Office in West Acton but then had to have his Appendix re moved in Du Cane Road Hospital. When he went back in a week the Nurse who took out the stitch asked him what was wrong. He said no thing but then found him self in front of a tall Psychiatrist in a suit who asked him the same. Mac held that he was not hap as his Mam had not been well and it had now got to him too. She had been low since she had a Hysterectomy at the same Du Cane Rd Hospital. She got some care and a free lunch three days a week at a Psychiatric Day Centre in Hamm but she was still pressed down and had need of more help. Mac had done his best but was due to take up a place at University and would leave in The Fall. His Mam wished him to go but some times clasped him to her so hard that he could not breathe. The Doc said that in the circs Mac should hang on as he would soon be gone and that

he would write and ask Moll to come see him. She would not and said that Mac had tried to get her locked up. For a few more months Mac filled in forms at Metal Box but could not wait to leave. He felt that such a job was quite well paid but not what he had worked hard at school for and he yearned to feel free. As Roy Orbison sng *'Its Over'* Mac knew as Moll did that he would have to go. The hard fact was that in some ways their old pact made in his child hood must now come to an end. As if to bear it out The Stones had a big hit with *'It's All Over Now'*. At the time Ton passed his Driving Test and got the gift

of an old *Ford* car from his Dad.
It was sound a side from a loose
front seat and odd leaks of oil that
he tried to caulk with a rag but
left a strong smell of an old crock
that will not start and dies too soon.
/In The Sum they drove up the east
coast of Eng to The Land of Cots.

They stopped to see *Love's Labour Lost* at
The Edinburgh Festival where they had a rare
treat of cream teas with jam and scones.
The Swain stuck in his mind as they
went on as far North as Loch Ness.
It was hot in The Lands of High
so they camped and swam in cold tarns.
Egon Ronay was the guide to slake their
thirst in the best pubs on the way.
With more large pints to sate it they
jobed at the Jocks in kilts of plaid.
This helped Mac to for get the rants
at home. They roved down The West Coast
thru The Lakes to Liverpool where they had
to go to The Cavern. *The Beatles* were
not there that night to sing their hits
but Mac and Ton had a good time

with *The Rockin Vicars*. Some shite broke in
to their car and took off with their
suits and a lot of stuff. The heist
did not spoil a great trip but Mac
was glad for them to get back to
Lon don. He and Ton were still good
friends but they had fought all the way.
As Cilla Black had sung *'It's For You'*
Mac had lookd at T Bottomore's *Sociology* and
read of 'Social Class' for the first time.
RH Tawney's *'Acquisitive Society'* and *'Equality'* too
were both proof to him of the deep
ness of wrong wth the 'Selfish Indvidualism' and
'The Wealth Gap' of Capitalist Society. They spoke
to him in a fresh way and his
watch wrd nw was *'Production for Man not
Man for Production'*. Tracts like these new to
him were the ripe seeds of a keen Socialism
that saw class strife in black and
white terms and was irked by Ton's grey
Liberalism. With this mix of ang and fear
and hope Mac said his sad fare wells
to Moll and Mike at St Pancras. As
Marvin Gaye sang *How Sweet It Is* Mac
felt some guilt as he left them both
but he had real grounds to go too
as he made his own way to Leicester
then to set out to change the world.

Chapter 4

Mac went up to Leics on the train thru The Lands of Mid. The low clouds meant the light was dim as he got a bus out to Oadby. He had a place in Beaumont Hall, a Hall of Res three miles from town. His room was in one of the new low blocks built in the rear of Beaumont House, an Edwardian Mansion built in 1904. With a wry smile Mac saw once more that he was in quite a new world as he strolled in The Bot Grdns midst the clumps of shrubs with ferns and fronds and rare plants with long bines and stems. It did not seem quite real as he sat and read on on the stumps of old Elms and Limes. /He soon made friends with three young men like him self from the class of ing and work. Like him they had come from Grammar Schools in Lon on a Grant. When they sat down to eat in The Refectory they were served by girls each dressed in a smart black skirt & white blouse. At times Mac felt awk as he thought of their low wage and asked him self if their homes were like his own. In one way he was in a new place but his Mam wrote three or four times a week to say how much they missed him at Baird. How it was not the same since he had gone. How things had not changed and how Rent was owed or there was no mon to pay The Gas Bill. With his main Grant and help from *The Thomas Wall Trust* Mac felt flush for the first time in his life and at first was hap to help out more than once. In grand style he wrote to them and friends on a pad in which 'Beaumont Hall' stood out in black print at the top of each page. /Mac and his three new pals formed a small group and stuck close in 'Fresher's Week' All the Socs had their stalls spread out in The Queens Hall on the ground floor of The Percy Gee Building in which too were The Students Union and The Dining Hall. Mac did not join one but at the end of the week went with his friends on Sat night to The Fresher's Hop in The Union. Like them he stood round the edge of the dance floor glass in hand and drank pints as he looked at the girls bop to The Stones' *Little Red Rooster* and *Alwys Smethin Thre to Remind Me* by Sandie Shaw. It was hot in the hall and he had to take off his don key jack lined in bright red silk. He tried to look cool in his round necked shirt, flared Levi jeans & Chelsea boots. His long dark hair hung straight down his neck.

He had a fear of ing to lose it. If he had gone bald it would have been a blad but when Mac went to The Doc's he had said no prob. In side Mac felt scared but a few quick pints made the diff to sort out the nice girls from the slags. It got got him on his feet to speak to the birds and dance with a few chicks. When they got home Mac and his pals said they had a good time but the Hop was a bit of a meat mart. They laughed it off in a shame faced kind of way but most Sat nights were the same for the rest of the year.

/A drink at the week end and a dance at The Hop helped Mac to have a break from his work. He was quite in tense from the start of his new BA Course in Social Science. He was on a great high from his first trip to The Unvrsty Bookshop. It was so light and clean. The books smelled as if they were fresh off the press. It was as if in their pure state they were in wait for him to be read. Most of the time his mind was on his work and he was shocked at how calm and laid back most of those on his Course were. In their first year they read Economics and Economic History, Geography, Sociology & Politics. These were all imp to help him to grasp ways in which things in the world could be changed. He had just used his vote for the first time and helped Harold Wilson to form a new Labour Government in The 'White Heat' of a New Tech Revolution. In side him self Mac was pent up and stunned by all those who had an air they did not care much how things were in the world. As they traipsed each day to and from The Union to The Gordon Rattray Lecture Theatre most of them looked to take it in their stride. They took screeds of notes twelve times a week but on the face of it their main aim for the rest of the whole time was just to try to have fun. It shook Mac how few hours most took on their own work while he spent most of his fixed on more stuff in The Library.

/At the same time as he walked to

and from The Rattray with piles of books
on The Guilds and Trades in his arms,
Mac him self could not but a ware
be of the ground work on a new
site laid out for a tall ing of
build where a lot of men of woad
worked on the spade in sun and rain.
Men with grafts dug a deep trench as
straight as a rule. By ties of er
he could not und or stand he felt
drawn to them when he passed and a
strange lure to be with them. Most times
it went in a trice since his mind
turned back to work in his own world.
/Thru out the year Mac switched off from
work too when he went with his best
pals for a few pints and games of
darts to pubs in Oad or Leicester. On
such trips out he did not wear his
his University Scarf as he was not at
ease with the split 'tween Town and Gown.
He could be quite vain and proud to
wear it in Lon don but he felt
it made him stand out and was too
much in the face of the folk in
Leics with whom he wished to blend in.
He left it in his room when pals
took him on a spree to *The Hind*

for his 20th Birth Day. In the pub
he got quite drunk with a large group.
Out of the blue he left it with
a girl whom smashed he thought mongst all
her peers with out her broad rimmed specs
lookd like Louis Lane. At Salisbury Hall where
she lived he tried to take his clothes
off but just kecked and retched and threw
up in the bath. The Head of Hall

put him in a cab and he woke
up the next morn on the floor in
his room next to his desk with a
sore head and much shame. He took a
Rose with a Card round to the girl.
She gave him for and The Head of
Hall put it down to youth and high
jinks. It was all laughed off by them
and in a while he took her to
see *The Knack... and How To Get It*.
/In fact since the start of the year
Mac's heart had been set on a girl

back at home. In Lon be fore he
left for Leics he had got quite close
to Ton's girl friend Di. When Di wrote
to say that she had missed him Mac
re joined that he felt the same way.

He felt a bit of guilt but in
the first term he got a spare seat
on a fast coach that went down from
Leics to Lon for an Anti-Apartheid Rally in

Trafalgar Sq so that he could meet her
for a few hours. She was not sure
what she felt a bout Ton. It was
awk for Mac but he could not help
his inf and was drawn to her so
they went on with it. Di sent him
cards with hearts on and pink notes that
had whiffs of scent and said Luv Yu.
She went up to Leics for a Hop
and stayed for the week end at a
Women's Hall of Res. They had a good
time with kiss and ing of dance. She

ticked him off for ing of drink but
said that he was fab and so were
all his friends. Near the Xmas Vac he
for got him self and sent her a card
which *said 'God gave us memories so that*
we might have roses in December'. A note
came to say that while she much liked
him Di was not in love with him.
As Dylan sang *It Ain't Me Babe* she
said that she was now back with Ton.
/On the coach back to Lon don at
the end of his First Term Mac 'gan
to lose his sense of Self. As the
miles went by he got more and more
tense. He was gripped with fear and felt
he would die. He took deep breaths and
it passed so that by the time Mac
reached home he was glad to be there.
His Mam and Mike were hap to see
him and things were fine 'til he used
the word *'individual'*. Whn he said that he
was glad to be one Moll mocked him
and scorned his new use of such long
words. She wished him to change but to
stay the same too. In an ence of
sile they hung mute in the air and
the scene passed. Mac had got a Temp
Job at The Post Office in The Bush

and got up at five o' clock in
the cold each morn to take his sack
full of cards out to clear his Round.
The inv to bed from a warm young
house wife did not come to pass but
he still liked the work. For him self and
Moll and Mike at The Odeon in Hammersmith
he got seats for *The Beatles Christmas Show*.
/When he got back to his own room
in Beaumont Hall at the end of the
Vac Mac breathed a sigh of re lief.
He was glad to spend some time with
his Mam and Bro but he could not
bear the thought that he might have to
live at home once more for good. The
cold fear grew in him that he would
then have to do so if he failed
at the end of the year. His work
had thrived in the first term and he
longed to go on with the whole Course.
/In The Spring Term he worked hard too
and in The Easter Vac he shared a
a flat in Lorne Rd with a friend
so he could stay up and do more.
He loved space to think in the peace
that reigned in the Vac but was still
tense. He went out with a girl who
served in The University Library. She was irked
by him when they lay on his bed
and he failed to touch her proud breasts.
She flounced out in a huff and left
him high and dry when her boy friend
came back from the sea as Tom Jones
sang a hit song called *It's Not Unusual*.
/At the same time on his Course the
'Science of Sociology' was for Mac a real
find and he fell in love with it.
Key terms like 'Social Stratification', 'Social Mobility'
'Class Diffs in Distribution of Income and Wealth'

helped him for the first time to make
sense in depth of class rage and the
ness of rich and poor he had lived
thru him self. By the Spring term as
he took brief notes in The Rattray on
The Classical Sociological Works of Comte & Marx
Durkheim & Weber Mac knew tht he could
not wait to read more. When he got
a 'Grade B' Pass at the end of
the year great was his re lief. In

a dream it meant that he could opt
for Sociology as his main choice and stay
in Leics for at least two more years.
/In the Sum break Mac got a paid
emp Job in The Sociology Dept on Norbert Elias'
'Young Worker Project' which had looked in to
The Adjustment of Young Workers to Work Place
and Adult Roles'. As a 'Coder' Mac weighed
up what scores of boys and girls who
had left school came back with when they
d in 'Opn Ended Questionnaires'. For two months

he shared a house in Lancaster Rd with
Keith and Nina who did the same work.
He went out for a drink on his
own a few times when he felt lone
but then saved mon to go down to
Lands End with Ton in his old Ford.
They cooked on a stove that used turps.
They used Ronay as a guide to the
best pubs in The W Country where they
supped the sort of stire that tires the

guts and rots the mind. To off set
it they climbed tiers in spurts to tops
of knolls and tors where they piled stones
on tops of cairns. They scraped their way
up the hard clint and flint of scarped
cloughs and crags as well as screes of
loose shards on the slopes. They camped in
The Land of Doone midst turds of cow dung.
In St Ives they bought blue smocks and went
to the Folk Club in *The Sloop Inn*.
In the way that one vies with a
drink in side they did their best to
keep up with its rites when they had
a few tries to see who could not
sing with a cupped ear. They had a
good trip but then went their own ways.
Mac just did not care at all for
the fact that Ton had joined The OTC
at Aberdeen Unvrsty where he had gone to
read Medicine or that Di had been to
see Churchill as he lay in State. At
The Dove in Hamm Mac fell out with
Ton's Dad. They had been pals but on
top of a drink Mac's rage had blazed
up at Mr Bird. It was like a
slap in the face when he said that
men who had gone on strike at Plessey
where he worked as a Manager should

be shot. Mac stayed at Baird for a
week but then as The Walker Bros sang
Make It Easy on Yourself went back to
Leicester to seek a house for that year.
/Mac soon found the right place to rent
and gan to feel at home in it.
He shared *Alonza* in Knighton Fields Rd East
with his old pals Al, Geoff and Pip.
On Suns friends named Pat, Mave and Jean
cooked lunch while they bought the wine. Mac
had a small room at the top. It
had its own fire place but ice still
formed on the winds when it got cold.
He was in one of the new small
groups The Prof in The Sociology Dept askd
round for drinks and made them feel at
ease in his house. In it Mac made
friends with Paul and his wife Elaine who
had two small tots named Rufus and Jan.
/Through more pals Mac met and fell in
love with a girl called Jilly. She had
brown eyes and high cheek bones. He had
seen her in the First Year when she
did a Combined Studies Deg in French and
English Lit but he did not then go
the vole. They had looked but as she
then had a boy friend named Mike not
said a word. As The Small Faces still
in The Charts at start of term asked
Whatcha Gonna Do About It? Mac asked
Jilly out the first time to have a
drink in The Lounge at *The Clarendon*. The
seeds of love were sown in smoke as
they rolled their own fags and in her
voice with a touch of scouse she gushed
out Ionesco while he raved of Marx. They
braved the cold breeze and deep snow in
Vicky Park and went for a Chinese meal
in town. Ice formed on each pane of
glass in his wind when they got back
to Mac's place and went to bed. As
he kissed her lips and the smooth nape
of her neck it just seemed too good
to be true that she would give her
self to him. It was the first time
that he swived so and was awed in
a new world. She was his first love
and touched his heart in a way that
no one else had done or would do.
She reached in to him and made him
feel whole. He cared for her so much.
In the next weeks and months he was
dirled and thrilled just to be with her
and proud to be seen out with her.
The love in his young heart was leal
and it raced when she came near him

at her place in West Avenue. He glowed
when she looked up at him. She hanced
his sense of self a fresh and deep
in side his soul felt full. In their
young frieze of life wide eyes were gazed
and glued as they both sat and stared
while their drinks went cold in The Union.
In the dark Film Club at The University
they held warm hands all the way thru
Splendour in The Grass. As Xmas neared at
the end of term Mac had to go
home to work on The Post. It was
such a pain not to be with her.
He could not wait till he heard from
her as he hared fast round the tops
of the flats to clear his sack of
cards and sang The Beatles' *Please Mr Postman*.
With long hours he earned the funds to go
up and to stay with her at *Byeways*
in Waverton for The New Year. The coach
trip took ten hours but was worth it.
Mac got on with her Mam and Dad.
When they were at work he and Jilly
went out for walks or just smouched and
schmoozed whle her grand dad slept next door.
When it came to sex Mac tried to
be cool but was a bit of a prig
and a prude. As The Supremes had a

hit with *Baby Love* Mac's pride would not
let him tell her that he was still
not at all sure how cubs were born.
He and Jilly feared that she would get
preg which made for probs. When he was
tense and came too soon he blamed her.
Mac did not like sheaths and she was
not sure of The Pill. In the next
years they had quite a few frights. They
were still young too and in a way
wished to be free to branch out. At
times they had all sorts of moods based
on they knew not what and it was
not hard for them to feel cooped up.
From the start Mac stressed how imp
it was to be 'free' but a lot
of it was show and in side he
was scared to lose her. He winced with
pain at a dance when she kissed some
one else on the cheek. They split up
at times when too shut in but then
both tried hard to patch things up as
The Beatles sang *We Can Work It Out*.
/As the year went on in Leicester Mac
and Jilly as a pair thus tried to
get hip. They longed to be with it
and in the groove. They felt like squares
not sure what clothes they ought to wear.

On a trip to Lon they went to
Biba's in Ken Church St and 'Boutiques' in
Kings Rd to look for the right Gear.
She bought some beads tights and short skirts
while he got a pair of dun cords
but it was so dark and loud in
most that he just got in a rage.
They had some fab times like when they
groovd to new bands like *Manfred Mann* at
Granby Halls and *The Who* at The Poly.
They both dressd up for *Georgie Fame* and
danced all night at The University Rag Ball.
/In Lon Mac was wont to meet Mike
for a drink and a game of darts.
They would each take turns at the side
to chalk up the score on the board.
Mac's Bro was no more the short podge
he had been in the days when Mac
felt that he used to cramp his style.
At The London Oratory he had shot up
and now looked down on his big Bro.
There was nowt to stop them and they
met up quite a lot for the crack
with pals in town at *The Duke of Clarence*
in The Bush, *The Hoop & Toy* in
S Ken and *The Queens Head* right on
Brook Green. They loved to go and hear
Connolly Folk play at *The Hop Poles* in

Hamm and some times took a long Moll
when they would ask for *The Galway Shawl*.
/Mac had worked hard from the start of
the year. His Prof had liked a crit
of Talcott Parsons in a text on Functionalism
and as the time had gone on it
was thought so that Mac would do well.
His Deg was framed such that he had
to do a Finals Paper in Econ History
at the end of that year and the
rest of his six Finals Papers in Sociology
in the last term of the third year.
Tho he had spent such a lot of
time on The Econ Dev of Japan since
The Meiji Restoration Mac got stressd as it
loomed up. On the eve the fear raged
in side and Mac got in to a
funk that he might let folk down. He
felt that he would not make the grade
and went to tell The Prof that he
could not face it. When he was not

in Mac went to *The Clarendon* for a
drink. He meant to calm down but went
from pub to pub gripped with the dark
fear in side that he would flunk it.
As The Stones sang *Paint It Black* he

got in to more and more of a
tense state. He thought that it was his
fate to fail. In due course he found
him self on the side of the main
Welford Road. With wet feet he stood for
some time in the rain and thought to
throw him self in front of the fast
cars the tyres of which hissed as they
came down the hill. He stayed on the
verge for a while but then broke down
and went home. His friends could see that
he was down. There were more tears but
not much was said and they put him
to bed. In the morn they got him
to The Queens Hall where The Finals were
held and so helped him to get the

First for which he had had worked.
Mac put what had passed out of his
mind and that is where it stayed for
a long time. He did not speak of
it to Jilly and they marked his feat
of a First with a meal in town.
/It helped to take Mac's mind off him
self as he had to make preps for
his 21st Birth Day. He got a tun of
beer and hired lots of steins from a
pub. He made cards and sent out invs
to all his friends most of whom came
and drank gawns of ale. The Bro rolled
up with his pals from Lon and crashed
in the front room on floor and couch.
The whole joint swang for the week end.
Mac's friends gave him a tank' with his
name and their own graved on it which
he kept safe for quite a long time.
/The Sum Hols were full too that year.
At the end of term Mac got a
Temp Job at White City Stadium which took
on more Staff as it was one of
the sites of The World Cup. In the
role of Bar Porter he filled shelves and
stocked casks of real ale and kegs of
beer. It meant he could watch live the
whole match as France drew with Uruguay 0-0.

Whn The Land of Eng thn bt Germany 4-2
to win The Cup Final he saw it
on the TV at home with Moll and
Mike. Jilly came to stay at Baird for
a few days as Mac was soon due
to go to Israel. They went to see
A Man and a Woman by C Lelouch
with a Film Score by Francis Lai. Still
in The Land of Er and Wond Mac
could not get it out of his head.
He was thrown by the Kitchen Sink Realism
of *Alfie* with Michael Caine which in a
lot of ways was more close to home.
/Mac was glad to get a way for
the rest of the Sum Vac in which
he did an External Research Project in Sociology
for his Degr Course and was marked as
a Finals Paper. It was a source of
great joy to Mac that he had the
chance to do his in Israel. With a
Grant from the Lon County Council Mac flew
for the first time on a Student Flight
frm Heathrow to Tel Aviv. The Sociology Dept
had close lnks with The Hebrew University in
Jerusalem. It set up a rare opp for
him and a friend named Lin to do
'Participant Observation' in a well knwn Kibbutz at
F'ar Hanasi quite nr Galilee and a smll
Moshav at Beit Herut. While they did so
Mac and Lin had to work most weeks
to earn their keep. They got up at
dawn to work in the fruit groves or
to pick veg in the fields. They helped
to clean out the fowl in long sheds
and to feed fish in ponds. Mac had
been drawn to strains of Soclalism in Zionist
Ideology of which he had read and wished
to see how they had worked in the
real world. The folk at Beit Herut were
keen to talk so he went with the
flow and his full notes grew in to
a Dissertation, *'Elites in a Moshav in Israel'*.
/It was not all work and once Mac
had brief sex with a girl. At the
end of most days he and Lin went
to the beach at Netanya for a swim.
They had time to make a bus trip
thru The Negev Desert down to Eilat. They
took a dip in the pool at Ein Gedi

and learned to float in The Dead Sea.
They got up at dawn and climbed to
the heights of Masada. Mac sent Moll lots
of cards from each such place as well
as Acre, Bethlehem and Galilee. He was glad
to be there but felt more than a
twinge of guilt that it was him and
not her that had such an opp to
see 'The Holy Land'. He was not free

to en joy it for its own sake.
/On the way back Lin and Mac got
a boat and crossed The Med deck class
through the Greek Isles to Bari in the
South of Italy. The dolphs leapt in as
it cleaved through the blue waves for three
days. He lay on deck next to a
girl called Liz neath the black stars for
three nights. When he laughed her tears off
as they docked Lin said he was hard.
The truth was that he could not wait
to see Jilly. He and Lin hitched up

to Salzburg and met up with Mike and
friends in Heidelberg. He was proud to hang
out and drink with his young Bro when
they camped by The Neckar. They got on
well as they drank with a few boat
crews and it meant a lot to him.
/At the end of the Hols Mac went
to Jilly's new flat in Leics on the
top floor of a house in Severn St.
He took her a bag of soft black
yuft. He was not sure how she would
be since she had spent two long months
on her Course in France. (As they had
gone their own ways for the Vac she
had said that the test of their love
would be not if they were sad but
how they felt when they saw each oth
once more). She told him that she still
loved him thru and thru but she had
been out and danced with a French boy.
She hoped he did not mind as they
they had planned to be ind. It had
been hard but she had need of it
and thanked him as he had helped to
make her see how she was free. His
heart gan to race and from then on
found it hard to trust her. In side
he raged but he told him self that

he did not care. He knew that at times he gt wll browned off and just wished to screw a round. He got bord with her and when he saw a fab girl robed in a cool dress and orbed in long loose ear rings he yearned to take her to bed. As Dave Dee, Dozy, Beaky, Mick and Tich had a hit with *Bend It* Mac tried to laugh it off with a few quick jibes and *bon mots*. /For Mac the way out of what he felt was to get down to work with great zest. In the first term of the Third year he had to do his Course work and to write up his Dissn. Al and Geoff had found a new flat at 321 Clarendon Pk Rd in which each hd their own room and his had space for both a large bed and desk. A small fire left the room quite cold but kept him a wake to work. In the late eve he and his friends used to go for a pint or two and a game of darts to *The New Road Inn* or *The Stork's Head* just up The Welford Rd. At the time Mac could take it or leave it and judged all thse who drnk at lunch time or got drunk in the week. It was a stroke of luck for him that Jilly's Mam was then Sec to The Duke of Westminster and skilled at her work. Gwen ws gald to type Mac's prized Dissertation for him and took a lot of care with it when she was not pressed down. At Xmas Mac once more worked on The Post in The Bush. When Jilly wrote that she loved him so much and missed him he went to Byeways for New Year. /In the Spring Term Mac got the nod from his Prof that he had done well in his Dissertation. He was more or less told that he was on course for a First Degree. He was still full of self doubt but by then a part of him thought that he could do it. In side he had 'spired to be a Don for a while and now he let his hopes soar. In the last two terms he did three shifts a day each of four hours.

He formed a small close group to read
texts and to probe trends in their work.
/At times it was a test for Mac
and Jilly. His ings of feel were up
and down when he drove him self. She
asked if the strain was worth it if
it did not make him hap. She had
moods but did not push her self so
hard. A friend had just got stressed out
in her job and had a break down.
So it was not all toil and in
March Mac went with Mike and half of
those from White City and The Bush to
see QPR win The League Cup Final whn
they beat West Brom well 3 – 2 at Wembley.
They were thrilled to be there
and all the more so when The R's
turned out to be the first team from
The Third Div South to win The Cup.
At the end of the month he went
up to *Byeways* for a few days. As

M Gaye and K Weston sang *'It Takes Two'*
he took time out with Jilly but then
it was straight back to his shift work.
/Mac chose the 'Theory' option so he had
to take two Finals Papers in 'Theoretical' as
well as those in 'Applied' and 'Empirical' Sociology;
'Social Psychology' and 'Sociological Methds'. It was a
tense time for him in the last months
of prep but he stayed quite calm. The
deep fear that he would fail was still
there but he knew well that The Staff
had faith in him and the love of
those close to him was a great strength.
The fact that prev he had done well
helped him to keep his nerve. He braced
him self to face the test and kept
a clear head. All the prep Mac had
done showed in the first Finals Paper and
the words just flowed out of him. He
was in his own world and he could
not wait to do the next one. He
was then in his bliss and at the
end of the day he rued the fact
that they had to come to a close.
In one way it was no shock so
to see his own name at the top
of the list with a First when the
marks were put up out side the Prof's

Room. At the same time it had all
the ness of strange in a real dream.
Great was the joy when his Mam and
Mike went up to stay the week end.
They were all so proud and the good
news ws soon spread when they went home
to White City. A Social Worker who used
to help Moll drove them all back up
to Leics for The Deg Congregation at The
De Montfort Hall. Mac got his Dip and
The Free Press Book Prize from Collier Macmillan.
They took pics of Mac and Jilly in
their caps and gowns hired for the day.
She had done well too with a good 2:1.
Moll was thrilled to go for tea with
her Mam and Dad at The Prof's house.
/When his Prof told him that for the
first time his Gree gave him some choice
and sway in his life Mac thought that
he had made it. His plan was to go
on with the work he had done in
Israel but bsd at Manchester Unv. At a
lunch he went to Mac got on with
Max Gluckmann in The Anthropology Dept. The Prof
gave him the gift of a Studentship to
do a PhD for which he thanked him
at the out set but in days Mac
changed his mind. The fear came back when

he found that in a year's time he
would first have to face more ex ams
for an MA in Anthropology. He was tired
of them and had a wish to go
his own way. He sought in stead to
do a PhD at The LSE in Lon.
He was drawn there by its rep as
the site of Student Protest. At the start
of the year there had been opp to
the App of Dr Walter Adams as the
next Director due to his close links with
Ian Smith who had dec UDI in Rhodesia.

There had been a Sit In that had
stirred Mac and the poss that he might
take part in more such acts lured him
back to Lon. He went to talk to
Dr Percy Cohen who gave him a place
to do an M Phil in The Sociology Dept.
If the work went well in two years
its grade would be changed to a PhD.
/Mac had worked at his old job as

a temp Bar Porter at White City Stad

for a few weeks so that he and

Jilly could go a way for a while.

She went to stay with her Sis who

gave birh to a boy but they rang

and wrote all the while to hatch plans.

It was 'The Summer of Love' and they

set out with joy. She cut her hair

so that he was shocked when they first

met. He had to look twice to rec

her but then laughed. They flew on an

eap NUS flight to Amsterdam and then camped

Grmny, Yugoslavia and Bulgaria to Turkey. They

hitched all the way and had good luck

to reach Istanbul in a week. They stayed

a few days to see the sites and

wam down the coast of Greece. They climbed

thru the clouds to Mount Olympus. While The

Beatles sang *'All You Need is Love'* they

had a scare at The Parthenon for as

they looked down at Athens Jilly was late.

A friend had helped to fit her with

a Cap but they were not sure of

it. They breathed a sigh when she came

and got a boat deck class from Piraeus to

Brindisi in The South of Italy. They hitched

up to Rome where they were barred from

The Vatican. The Swiss Guards would not let

them in as Jilly's skirt was too short.

They thumbed up the coast to Florence where

they looked at a lot of art but

they drank too much red wine and had

their first row since they had left. When

she laughed and said he looked so stern

Mac blanched and could not bear it.

He palled and slapped her in the face.

They wre bth shckd as she blenched and

in the ing of morn he tried hard

at once to make it up to her.

They thumbed to Milan and then to the

S of France. They went up to Paris

whre they stayed with some of her friends

for a few days. With their young limbs

bleached & browned they bth flt tht it

had just ben a fab trip. Mac was

a bit tense but could not wait to

start a new phase of his life at

The LSE so with Jilly he crossed the

The Channel on the crest of a wave.

Chapter 5

When Mac went back to Lon it did
not take long for the wave to break.
He had not thought of where or with
whom he might live or just how much
such a move so close to home might
weigh on him. In a few weeks spent
back at Baird House he was in quite
a state. A flat share fell through and
at the start of term he was still
at White City. With Moll keen for him
to stay he was fraught as his dread
grew he'd get trapped in her lair. In
desp he took a small dark room on
the low ground floor at the back of
a house in Warwick Way. He daubed it
with black and thin licks of ornge paint.
The vile stair well that had grime on
the rail had a dank smell of mould
and must. Near his room it stank of
filth and old trash. He did not know
Pimlico. The back of Vic Stn seemed full
of B & B's with VAC signs in
the winds and folk on the move. Mac
felt lone and cut off from friends.
In Leics he had got used to the
fact tht they had been there for him
but now most had gone their own ways.
He had grown up in Lon but he
felt lost and un sure of him self.
Once a week up in The West End
of town he met Stu who had come
from Leics too in *Ward's Irish House* in
Piccadilly. In flight from the ness of lin
and lone in his room, in bouts Mac
'gan to bouse and bourse too much on
his own in old near by pubs like
The Marquis and *The Warwick*. In them he
was wont to stand at The Bar and
stare in to space or to sit and
read *The Guardian*. As a Grad he was
blind to it but his ing of drink
gan to drag him down and to blight
his young life. He lived more and more
in his head with sure plans of what
he would dare to do or say next
day but which in the cold light of
morn were not said or done. At Xmas
he took flight back home to White City.
/At the start of term the wave had
soon crashed on Mac's work at LSE. He
was met on his first day there by
The Dean. R McKenzie's face ws knwn to
Mac from the TV on which he used
to move his 'Swingometer' to show trends at
General Elections. The Prof gave Mac a job
in The Sociology Dept as a Grad Tutor

which meant he had to teach four hours a week on the 2nd Year BSc Degree. He got the opp too to take a Sociology Class once a week at St Mary's TTC in Twickenham. In some ways Mac loved the work but he found it a strain. He used to fret that he was not good en ough and when he was tense wld for get things. It was hard too on the morns when his mind was not clear and his head ached a lot if he hd drunk much the night be fore.

/At first the plan for his PhD had been that in his first year at LSE Mac would learn Hebrew at SOAS for a year to help him with his field work in Israel. He soon grasped that it just did not feel like the right way for him so he made an imp change. He switched to a new Phil prob which asked 'Can Sociology be value free?' Some staff then put it to him that he should do an MPhil more based on 'Facts'. Tho he was less sure of him self Mac was stll quite self willed and would not hear of it. He thought that with a 'First' he ought to know it all. He had to shed tears in The Library to learn he was out of his depth when he just could not grasp Sartre's *Problem of Method*. Mac was stunned but not to fess up to it and to keep it to him self he sank a few pints in *The George*. It had not helped when his Mam gan to haunt Mac at LSE and he got a shock one day when she turned up in the cafe. He knew well that she was pressed down at home. Mike was there yet but she still felt lone. Her ness of sad weighed on Mac and he went to Baird once a week to see her. He had felt en raged and scared when she had marched in to his own space. From then he did not just use The Library to read but to hide in and he hid as well in *The George*.

/As Vicki Carr sang *It Must Be Him* it was in the pub at the start of term that Mac read how proud Jilly was that he had got to LSE but the wave soon crashd too on their love. She had stayed in Leics to do an MA in English Lit. She wrote to say that she missed him so he spent a long week end at her new place in Tichborne St. He tried to tell her how

things were but he was not sure him
self. The rifts oped up first when Mac said
he did not like it at LSE and
was at a loss back in Lon. She
said that she wished to be there for
him but longed for him to be strong.
They went to see The Alan Price Set
sing *'Simon Smith And The Amazing Dancing Bear'*
and it was like old times but back
in Pim Mac sensed tht some thing had
changed. She liked him when he was hap
but she found him diff when he was
down and he felt the same with her.
/It was still a huge shock when Jilly
came down to Lon and told him out
of the blue that she had slept with
some one. She said that she was weak
and full of self hate for what she
had done but that she wished for more
from him; that thru his pure obs with
work Mac cut him self off from life
and she felt caged in; that she was
not sure of them as she had been
and felt mixed up with guilt that she
had let him down. From his side Mac
was in fear. He felt safe when they
were close but knew that he leaned on
her too much. The more he had grown
to need her the less she did him.
They shared a mute sense of blame that
sex had not been as good for them
as they would both have liked. Mac could
not bear more strife and tried to patch
things up. He for gave her but it
did not work and they soon split up.
/In the New Year Mac had seen an
Ad for a room in a large flat
in Fitzjames Ave in West Ken. His flat
mate turned out to be a Night Guard
who liked to throw lost souls out of
The BA Terminal at Gloucester Rd. Once more
Mac did not feel in the right place.
He drank pints of ale in pubs like
The Live and Let Live, The Famous 3 Kings
and *The Cumberland* Arms in North End Rd.
He had met a girl called Terry who
his friend Stu brght with him when they
went to watch Chelsea draw with Man Utd
1-1 at Stamford Bridge. In Green Lanes they
shared a small flat in North Lon where
she burned Joss Sticks. The Art Grad had
long straight blonde hair and wore a tight
shrt skrt. They gulped pints at *Ward's* in
Piccadilly and *The Tally Ho* in Kentsh Town
where there was great Jazz on Suns
when a friend plugged in to the nice

vibes and played a cool reed. Mac liked
her vague air and they had good sex.
He learned to roll joints but when he
puffed dope just got right out it. If
he took a spiff Mac felt that he
was wired up all wrong. He felt so
strnge that he wld dree his weird and
so he did not do that much of it.
On New Years Eve that year they all
got quite drunk in *Ward's* and Terry jmpd
in the fount at Trafalgar Sq. it was
cold but they laughed and thn wlkd all
the way back to North Lon. For the
nxt few mnths Mac would drink and sleep
with Terry on week ends and then go
and for lunch at his Mam's on Suns.
He tried to tell him self he was
OK but in side he felt lost and
strained in vain to feel like a man.
/Mac strived to get back on track at
LSE when he changed once more the theme
of his MPhil. He switched to J Westergaard
to do some thing on the role of
The Aristocracy in The British Class Structure. He
was drawn to look at it in part
by the fact that by then his Bro
had worked for one or two of them
who lived well out in the green sward.

Tho it was hard to get down to
it Mac found he could work in spirts.
The prob was that when he looked at
the Lit in The British Library and did
try to sift some of the facts to
ship er land and own wealth write he
just could not fill a whole page and
made a bodge of it. He used to
fit and foy scraps and scrips in to
strips and tape them down on sheets.
It all looked a bit of a mess
which was how he felt. If he did
not bin them he gaped at these botched
sheaves of stuff and was shamed to give
them in but did not know what else
to do. He sensed that he had lost
his thread and that some thing in side
him had died. His chest heavd with siths
and sighs but there was a dearth in
his heart that would not let him work
in the old way and some how had
led him deep down to go on strike.
/In side he missed Jilly. They had swopped
Xmas Cards. In a few months they wrote
and joined up once more. He looked for
a new flat and was charmed by a
nice light place on the ground floor in
Hazlitt Rd nr Olympia. Those in the top

flat were at The Royal Academy of Music
and he loved to hear the slight strains
that used to float down from their lutes
and flutes to drift in the air as
they played on the scales or tried out
a piece. Jilly came some week ends and
planned to move in with him when her
MA came to an end that year. Mac
shared the place with friends from Leics days
called Bill and Mave and was hap for
the first time since he'd gone back to
Lon. In March with raised arms and clenched
fists they took a keen part in the
big Anti-Vietnam War Rally in Trflgr Sq.
Since Jan The Tet Offnsve hd forced the
US back in Nam. It was just the
day aft er the My Lai Massacre and
the air was tense whn both Vanessa Redgrave and
Tariq Ali spoke. A part of the crowd
in which they were made its way to
Grov Sq and then down Park lane where
cars wre smashed up to The Hilton. When
Bill was seized by The Old Bill in
Hyde Park Mac felt that no way could
he lose face in front of the girls
and he had to try and free him.
So they wre both nicked and marched off
to a large van bound for Bow Street.

They were frisked and left in the cells
for three hours but bailed in time for
a quick pint In *The Lamb and Flag*.
Their case did not come up in Court
for months in which time the great fear
was that they might be sent to jail
as scape goats since a big march was
planned by the N*am Solidarity Campaign* for Oct.
/In the mean time Mac and Jilly were
charmed at week ends as Louis Armstrong sang
What A Wonderful World It Can Be. At
LSE Mac's own work went by the board
as he was caught up in the thrill
of The May Events in Paris. News came
in each day from The SWP to The
Soc Society that The Revolution was at hand.
Mac was in The Old Theatre to see
those who led The Student Movement in Europe
inc T Ali, R Dutscke and D Cohn-Bendit
with raised fists all sing *The Red Flag*.
In Aug they were all part of the

world as it watched in shock on TV
as The National Guard beat the youth who
faced them at The Dem Cnvntn in Chicago.
When their case came up at Bow Street
Mag Court Mac and Bill were charged with
Assault on a Police Officer. In the end
they paled and chose to plead their guilt
and were let off with a £25 Fine.
/It was good news but when jilly moved
in she and Mac soon found that it
did not work. Things with them got worse.
As The Beach Boys sang *Do It Again*
they both tried hard. They gave their
rooms a fresh coat of paint and made
the flat look nice but when it was
done things still used to jar. It was
their first chance to live as one but
they had run out of things to say
and in side Mac felt as if stuck
in a void. By then he had grown
to need her more than she did him.

In the ness of his lost Mac clung
to her but felt the shame of the
cling and cloy at the same time as
he felt tied down and wished to be
free at least for a while. In the
back of his mind he had thought for
some time that he would like to take
The Hippy Trail to India. The Raj had
charmed him since he had read of it
in The Sixth Form. He longed to get
a way and be gone and she was
keen for him to go. It struck him
it might be his last chance if he
did not have some jabs and seize it.
/So Mac made his mind up to take
a year out from LSE and to teach
the Lish of Eng. Out of the blue
he felt an urge to head for Baghdad.
Luck was with him and he thumbed thru
Europe to Istanbul in a week. Things went
well till he reached east of Ankara where
there were far less cars and trucks on
the road. His worst fears grew and he
had thoughts of ing and back turn when
a man in a Morris 1100 stopped out
of no where. He said that he had
a spare seat in his car and was
on his way to Karachi. It meant that

Mac was in Tehran in two weeks. They drove up thru The Khyber Pass and crossed in to Pakistan at Quetta. Mac was in Peshawar in 3 weeks. With his NUS Card 3rd Class fares were cheap so he went to Delhi by train. He stayed for a few days to see the Old Town and The Red Fort. He was stunned by the mass of the crowds who thronged each space and shocked by the lame and scarred folk, young and old who begged in each place. He went to The Taj Mahal at Agra and saw bowed heads ashed at Benares on The Ganges. As he hitched his way South he had to share the cab of one truck wth a loud soiled chimp. When Mac reached Madras he went to a film and with a tea tray on his lap he saw C Gable in *Gone With The Wind*. He met a lad who took him home to meet his folks. They lived in a slum but put him up for the night. Most of the time Mac lived on dal and rice and slept out with the low castes in the streets or those with in 1st Class Waiting Rooms in the Railway Stns. He asked at a few schools for work but with no luck so he moved on to Bangalore. He was struck by how young were the dead Brits in worn graves from the time of The Indian Mutiny in 1857. In days he took a train to Bombay where he stayed at The Youth Hostel in The Old Town near The Docks. He met those like him self from all parts of the world who too looked for work. /Mac's plans had to change when he got ill. His guts got bad. There were rafts of farts that came in gusts on whuffs of wind. With a crowl and growl and whoosh and gush he 'gan to cack and cuck till he shit and shat all the time. It was not Dengue but his temp soared and he fell in thru the doors of the A & E at St George's Hospl. They kept him there for three nights and gave him free drugs to deal with a 'mild' form of Amoebic Dysentry. His weight loss was such that he had pause to think. He did not feel strong and he dwelt.

much on Xmas at home. He made up his mind to go back to The Land of Eng. He palled up with a long haired bloke in a fez on his way to Lon who smkd strng kief. One morn in a packed mart Mac had to be helped to his feet with zest at a cafe when he was dazed by the ess of drow and sin brought on by bhang. /As they moved North it got much more cold so they went back a lot of the way by bus. En route Mac took Speed for the first time and talked his way thru Pakistan, Afghanistan and Iran to Turkey. The young man from Oz had no skills and aimed to look for a job in a pub in Lon. Mac was glad that he had a place at LSE to go back to. He got a train from Erzerum to Istanbul which took 3 days. He then hitchd in the cold to Munich where he ran out of mon. He was rep

to Lon by train with the *quid pro quo* he paid £16 back to The Diplomatic Service. /Thus at the start of Xmas week Mac found him self back at Baird House. It was just less than three mnths since he had set out from Lon. He cashed his last £20 at The Midland Bank in The Bush and was at once hoaxed in a fraud when a gang of crooks lured him in to a game of *Find the Lady*. In a small crowd which had formed on The Green a man seemed to have been duped by a quick sleight of hand. It had been clear to Mac that they were out to rob him so he rushed in to help and had at once lost five Pounds him self. Self willed he had to be coaxed and pulled back by his young Bro who ruled it out but too late. /When his Prof at The University in Leics heard that Mac was back at home he gave him a job for two terms as a Tutorial Assstnt in The Sociology Dept. Mac took Tutorials and Seminars on the 2nd Year BA and went to The Staff Seminar once a week. Though it was good to be back he was not too well. His weight was down to 45kg and he still had a mild form of Dysentry. He felt quite tense and fraught whn he had to teach. He smoked his own roll ups to try and calm him self but he found it hard to breath and his voice would go. He had deep qualms that he was not good en ough and was wracked with self doubt. He felt that groups he taught could see straight thru him. Mac was not at ease in his role on The Staff. He still had some friends in The Socialist Society who then led a loud Sit In for more Student Power at The University in Leics. [At LSE the steel gates put up by Walter Adams at the start of the year had been torn down. The whole place was closed in a Lock out for three and a half weeks. As the strife went on a 'Free LSE' had been set up at ULU.] Whn asked to speak at The Student Union in Leics Mac had too much fear. What he could do at that stage was to face down the Right Wing in the SCR and raise a Petition of Support for two staff who had been sacked at LSE. /When he had gone back to Leics Mac had got rooms in a large gaff in Princess Rd. He shared them with his close friend Bill who was then in the last year of his Sociology Degree. For a while Jilly used to come up for week ends or he would go down to Lon. When Mac had got back from India she had said that in some ways she found it hard to talk of 'them' but she still loved him. He said the same. They both longed to be hap and at first they got on well as in the old days but it did not last. Mac found his work diff and his Mam a strain. At Baird Moll was pressed down. She found it hard to go out and get to the shops on her own. Her debts and probs with the rent would not go a way. She made veiled threats that she would kill her self and in Leics Mac used to dread it when the phone rang. He used to think that it might be news that in the end she had done it. With a mix of fear and guilt he went down to stay more week ends at Baird. He got tired and drained of strength. He was worn out and let Jilly take more of the stress. He leaned on her too much and asked her to help Moll get out to the shops. While Mac had been

a way Jilly's own Mam had died when
she took a dose of pills and she
still grieved. Moll had been kind to her
when Gwen had died and she was hap
in one way to give some thing back.
/It came out of the blue at Baird
when Jilly told Mac that things for them
were at an end. When she said that
she had slept with some one else and
had to go he slapped her in the
face. She cried that she did not want
to end up pressed down and poor like
his own Mam. Dazed he begged her to
stay till the morn to spare Moll's ings
of feel. In the wait for dawn he
tried to get Jilly to change her mind
but she would not. She left as the
birds cheeped and chirped in a sad song
which he heard in the small hours for
lots of years to come. It was a
real blow to him which left him in
bits. Mac was choked as he had thought
for quite a few years that he would
spend the rest of his life with her.
At the time Marvin Gaye had a big
hit with *I Heard It On The Grapevine*
the seeds were sown of a deep hate
for Moll whom Mac blamed for Jilly's

ing of leave. The tares of a dark grudge
in his heart grew as he told her
in wrath when she had gone that he
did not want to hear Jilly's name from
her lips once more. He could not know
the depth of it or vent it but
as the bale and the bile turned his
chyme to chyle at great cost in mute
rage he was set to get his 'venge.
/At all rates back on Mac's bed in
Leics the tears flowd as he gowled and
howled in grief & grieve. Waves of sad
ness ebbed and flowed. In the pub
on his own he used just to sit
and stare in to space. He with drew
in to his self and sank in to
a slough as he dwined and pined a
way. He had to tell The Prof that
he could not go on with his work
of ing and teach. He broke down
but could not face it and did not
see it as such. He looked out side
him self in terms of what was wrong
with Jilly and Moll and how they had
let him down. His flat be came a mess.
It was owned by Bob Gow who taught
in the Phil Dept and was from Hampstead.
He wore a purse on his hip and

Mac and Bill did not get on with him at the best of times. Mac now let Bill's mates drunk and on dope crash out there. One night when Mac was drunk a small group of his own friends sat and talked tho he wished for them to dance so he hurled a glass of beer at them. He was saved from his ness of wild for a while by a nice young girl from Yorks who read Lish of Eng in her first year. She was kind and took care of him. She cleaned up his room and in a sweet voice sang to him *Scarborough Fair*. It was her first exp of sex which for a while was good for both of them. At the same time he got bored and at the end of the Sum Term he did not treat her well and said good bye. In side he was tense and quite mixed up. In one way Mac felt that he ought to go back to Lon to fin his MPhil but he did not want to. To try and cheer her up in May Mac had got seats for Moll and him to see *The Black & White Minstrel Show* at the Victoria Palace Theatre in Lon. It had all come back to him how he had not been hap there in the first year of his time at LSE and he feared more of the same. He asked his Prof if he could stay on in Leics but it was too late. As Junior Walker and The All Stars had a great big hit with *What Does It Take (To Win Your Love)?* Mac and Bill both had no choice but to find some where else to live as Bob Gow changed the locks on his flat. /Thru friends Mac got a small temp room for the Sum in a shared house in North Lon. He did not know the folk who lived there and as Neil Armstrong was the first man to step on the sure face of The Moon he felt small and lone in Finsbury Park. Once he bumped in to Jilly who chanced to live quite near. They went to Alexandra Plce and looked down

on Lon as they drank. Mac slept with
her to prove he'd grown and dealt with
life but it was too late for them.
Mac was obs with The Class Strug once
more by then. He rushed off to a
Speech on Nam and when they both
went their own ways things just taled off.
/Mac was glad when got an opp to
move in to a large ground floor room
in a house in Lavender Gardens down in
South Lon. Once more it seemed a strange
place as he had not lived South of
The Thames but he was with those some
of whom he knew from Leics. One in

of Post Grads from Leics who all knew
Marxist Phil well. Some of thm had been
brought up in The CP. Mac was keen
to learn but he did feel out of
his depth as they all talked a bout
Louis Althusser's *For Marx*. Mac's own faith in
the creeds of The Class Strug had grown
with the fight for Civil Rights both in
The North of The Land of Ire and
in The US. He wished to move on from
the bounds of The Red Base, the rise
of which he hd seen in The Student Movement.
Mac was glad to have the opp to
read Marx in more depth but it did
cause him some probs in his own work
in Sociology. In his year off Mac had
read up on The Black Power Movement in
The US esp since Watts and the growth
of The Black Panther Party. In his Critique
of The Sociology of Racism he now used
Althusser's Theory of Ideology in his new MPhil
on *Ideology & Race Relations* with G Newfield.
/Mac had to halt his work when he

the room next door irked him as all
the time he played *Crosby, Stills & Nash*
so when Mac drank he put on as
loud as he could The Stones' *Beggars Banquet*.
/At LSE there was then a new group

learned out of the blue that his Dad
had died. A note had come from a
an Aunt's friend in The Land of Ire
to Moll at Baird House to say that
his heart had just stopped on top of

a bus in Strood. Mac felt numb and
a bit strange at the news but he
could not und why his Mam was in
tears and upset. She did not want to
go with him when he went down to
Kent. He was not sure what to make
of it when he found out that since
he had left them in his child hood
Mell had worked on The Isle of Grain.
His dad had wed once more but not
told his new wife a thing of his
past life with Moll, Mike and him self.
In a few weeks a screed came from
her Solicitors, *Winch and Winch*. The gist of
it seemed to be that Mac's Dad had
left no Will as he had spent most
of his time in The Medway Irish Club.
/In the New Year Mac got a small
part time job wth the new Open University.
He was a Correspondence and Course Tutor based
at a school in Richmond. Most of those
he taught wished to read just for their
Course Work to get a well paid job and
that was all. They were not keen to
learn Marxist Theory and Mac was not asked
back to teach the next year. In April
at The BSA Conf in Durham he launched
in to a brash Maoist style crit of
Colour and Citizenship by Rose & Deakin and
Bourgeois Sociology of Racism inc that of J Rex.
He was warned that to take such a
line was rash and might harm him but
laughed at such ness of less spine. The
next year young Mac felt let down when
he sent an App to Prof Rex for
a job but he did not get one.
/Mac's last year at LSE was not a
hap one. At Lavender Gdns his old friends
Bill and Mave with whom he had kept
up links moved in to the room opp
but in side he still felt a lone.
He used to go out with them and
meet Stu too once a week in *Ward's*.
It was at this time that Mac's obs
wth bawds and drabs came back. Lewd thoughts
of them would dwell in his head when
the pub closed and he would slink through
Soho. Asked once or twice if he would
like a good time he just rushed past.
His big fear was that some one he knew
might see him there. It was a comp
and Mac had a deep shame that he
could not trust him self. At the same
time in the course of the year he
had quite a few brief flings with real
girls. He went out with his Sis in Law's

friend Kat who was then at Sussex U.
He liked her but when she sent him
a card with a red heart it was
too much for him. At LSE he slept with
a thin nymph with red hair and green
eyes but she tripped out on too much
dope and as time went on he ditched
her as he was shamed to be seen
with her by his straight Left Wing pals.
He screwed a few times with a girl
Grad who had just split up with her
boy frnd but forced hr out. Her Feminism
was too stern. She found him too crit
of her. He had a few months with
Mar from LSE who lived in North Lon
and whose Dad cme from Rumania. With her
long hair and large breasts he liked to
sleep with her but as with the rest
he did not let him self feel much.
Most of Mac's Self went in to his
work. As the year went on he fell
out love with Sociology and gave up on
it for pure Marxism. He put his MPhil
to one side and read Socialist texts. In
May while The Beatles sang *Let It Be*
four youth were shot in a clash with
The Ohio Nat Guard. As The US went
In to Cambodia Mac raged and he was ired

too when Ted Heath beat Wilson to form
a new Gov in The General Election. He
asked to take part in a small group
set up to read L Althusser's *Readng Capital*.
In Marxism he still felt out of his
depth but was keen to grow. He read
more in Phil like Hume and Locke as
well as those in diff fields like Bernard,
Galileo, Lacan, Pavlov & Saussure. For his
own use he trans parts of *Du Trotskysme*
by Kostas Mavrakis. In Aug he had a
break and went with his friend John Auld
and his girl to The IOW Festival. They
camped on a hill and had a great
time with Bob Dylan, The Who, Jimmy Hendrix
and the rest. While a lot of folk
stripped off and let it all hang out
Mac found him self with a prim nurse
and had to sit on his mute lust.
/When Mac left The LSE at the end
of Sept his Grant came to an end
and he had to make his own way.
As Cat Stevens sang *It's a Wild World*
he signed on the dole. He sent in
Apps for jobs of ing and teach in
diff Unvs but got no where. He was
asked by a friend called Cut to join
The Ed Brd of *Theoretical Practice* which was

a new Marxist Mag of Althusserian Phil. A
quote from Lenin on the front of its
first Number in Jan 1971 set out its
role: *'Without revolutionary theory there can be no
revolutionary practice'*. As they both drank in a
pub in Maida Vale Mac was asked too
if he would like a job to trans
all of *Du Trotskysme*. The TP Board had
fixed with RKP to trans a no. of
such books from French to Lish of Eng.
With a few pints in side him Mac
tripped up. He did not give it a
thought and grabbed at the chance. It was
a job in which he could earn some mon
and his pride liked it that when asked
what he did Mac could put on airs
and brag he worked as a Free Lance.
He got a Reader's Ticket so he could
use The Readng Room at The British Museum.
It went clean out of his head that
he had failed his A Level in French.
/At a do in Croydon Mac bumped in
to a girl called Jill whom he had
taught a bit in Leics. In her long
fur coat and high black boots she had
turned up once or twice to his room
in two Terms so that he had not
seen much of her. Now in South Lon

they went out and soon shared his bed.
Things went well and Mac was more hap
than he had been for a long time
when the bad news came out of the
blue that Moll had tried once more to
kill her self. A large dose of pills
had put her back in Springfield Hospital. Mac
had known that she was not well.
For a while when pressed she had used
to blirt and blub at the least thing.
He had done his best to cheer her.
In May for a treat he had got
seats for them to see Tom Jones at
The Odeon in Hamm. The night be fore
he heard the news Mac had just gone
with her to see David Lean's *Ryan's Daughter*
set in The West of The Land of Ire
in 1916. In fear of what more drugs
and ECT would do to her Mac asked
diff friends and his old Prof in Leics
for help to pay her bills and to
get her out. In The New Year she
went home but still pressed in the ness
of down as P Como sang *It's Impossible*.
Mac liked Jill and asked her to move
in with him. He told her of his
probs with his work at LSE and with
Mam and Jilly whose pics he tore up.

Mac felt that he had failed and saw it as a chance to make a new start. Jill had not done as well at Leics as she could have and felt that she had let her self down there. She was on a TTC at Goldmsiths which she did not like so she too wished for a change. They took it in turns to seem poised and sure of their path but in side both were full of self doubt. Their faith in them selves came and went and so they were both keen to prove their own worth thru work. They set a new rule they would not smoke and put the brakes on on trips to the pub. Mac made Jill give up a few of her old friends who still did dope and give a way her Hard Rock LP's. They both read Marx and built up a file for lots of sites of class strife round the world so fast that in the end they were lief to give it up. Mac went on with his work on a Marxist Leninist Theory of Racism. He stayed on The Board of *Theoretical Prctce* tll its April Number but was not at ease and left. He still felt out of his depth in Phil and the fact that Jill had gone out with one of them in Leics did not help. Mac and Jill had felt cut off from the mass of folk for some time so they made a change and joined *The Communist Fedn of Brtn (Marxist Leninist)*. They aimed to keep their feet on the ground. In The Rush Hour at Clapham Cmmn Tube they tried to sell *Struggle* but soon found that the mass in the street did not wish to read it. The cold wind was sharp and they went back to their books. /Mac still looked for opps in Sociology but he could not get a job. One time he was flown to Aberdeen and put up in a plush Inn near the University. He was tense and drank so that when he spent the next day with Staff in The Sociology Dept he was not in the best shape. He wore his gold rimmd specs but still did not get the Post. To make both ends meet that year Mac got a few temp jobs. He heaved crates in Youngs Brewery in Wandsworth. In the yards he used to load the carts hauled by the drays. In lunch breaks he read *The Workers Press*. He stocked goods in Derry and Toms for a few weeks. He worked on a GLC Road Traffic Survey in South Lon for months.

Jill had dropped her Course at Goldsmths and
with Mac's help she had got en ough
faith in her self to app to read
French and Phil at University College. In the
mean time she taught kids wth Learning Difficulties.
/At that time few of Mac's friends wed
but he and Jill thought they would be
diff as T Rex sang *Get It On*.
The Banns were read in a few days
so Paul and Elaine came from Leics to
ness their wit at The Reg Off in
Wandsworth in Aug 1971. Mac had got an
unf flat with two large rooms on the
first floor of a near by house in
Lavender Gdns. He got stuff to furn it
cheap from The Auction Rooms in Falcon Rd,
Clapham Junction. They went to hone and eye
the moon in Dorset. Mac was mazed that
a babe was soon on the way. He
was pleased but as Jill changed shape and
turned in to a Mam he found it
hard. He ran a way to some friends
a few times in Dalston and Finsbury Prk.
His lust grew when he drank and his
eye roved. On a long pub crawl down
the Kings Rd where he did not know
a soul Mac roamed from pub to pub
on his own and lost his self in
the ness of lin and lone some where
tween *The Chlsea Potter* and *The World's End*.
/Mac was thrilled whn Fran was born at
St Thomas's in May 1972. In the cab
home tho, next to Jill with the babe
on his lap, he felt deep down that
he too was the one in need of
the care. In one way he was so
pleased to have a child. As Rod Stewart
sang *You Wear It Well* he was proud
to take her to Clapham Common where she
learned to walk but he fnd it strange
in his new role as a Dad and
the word had an odd ring for him.
He felt bad that in a way he
was shamed as a man to be seen
out with the push and ing of the
pram. One night when they went to friends
Mac got drunk and planned to run off
with a young French au pair but felt
wrong and changed his mind in the morn.

He used to fret a bout his Mam
who was still pressed in the ness of
down. At one point Mac thought it might
be best if she left her flat at
White City and moved to a room near
them in Lavender Gdns but it was no
use as she was scared to give up.
When he and Jill took the babe up
to Hull to show his Bro and Sue
there was a scene when Mac got drunk.
In wrath Jill waved a knife at him
and with Fran took a train to Lon.
On his own Mac went on a jag and
drank him self to Robin Hood's Bay where
he did not know a soul but booked
in to a small Bed & Breakfast and
binged in a Club out of his head.
They both took the babe to Jill's home

for Xmas where Mac tried hard to get
on with her Dad. He was a top
Civil Servant who worked for Sir Keith Joseph.

As Cat Stevens sang *Can't Keep It In*
Mac rang Jilly late when drunk at the
New Year. She too had a child with
some one else by then and so asked
him not to ring more which hurt him.
/Mac was pleased in lots of ways to
be a Dad but had not planned to
be one. When he and Jill had wed
their joint gift to thm selves had bn
Lenin's *Collected Works*. They still both went to
a Lenin Seminar run by Ben Brewster at
LSE each week. For her last four months
Jill had gone with the babe in side
her. Mac wished for a home life with
wife and child but was not at ease
with the resp or calls on his time.
His aim ws to be a Marxist Intllectual
and as such he longed most of all
to be free to think and read or
write when he liked. In those days he
loved both to stay up and get up
late. He was shocked when Jill laid out
the knives and forks for break fast as
they went to bed. He chafed & champed
at the bit and felt odd in side
if Jill called him Dad in front of
the child or a chum. When born his
friend Cut on the *TP* Board had called

Fran a 'Little Irrationality'. Mac thought it was too much but at the same time he just could not stand the dull chores each day and the set way of life that went with them. He had a fear that he would get like the cat that got slow and fat when Jill had him spayed. /As the last US troops left Nam in March 1973 Mac half moved to Cut's flat in Kilburn. He signed on the dole in Neasden. He worked at Malvern Mews in the week and spent week ends with Jill and France. His deep obs wth Marxism had grown to the point where when Mike came for tea to his new flat Mac felt shamed in front of his friend that his own Bro did not know much more Marxist Theory. /Once at Malvern Mews Mac worked there and in The Reading Room at The BM. Each night on TV he and Cut were keen to watch The Senate Com Hrngs on Watergate. As R Daltrey sang *Giving It All Away* Mac might have a few pints with Cut in *The Chippenham* near by but then roved on his own too. Pressed in the ness of down as well as lin and lone he went on dark pub crawls and scrawls in rough low bars round The Harrow Rd in which he knew no one at all and spoke to no one. He chanced to get out in one piece when he got so drunk in a Shebeen in Maida Vale that he rowed with some one when he came out with a lot of tosh re M Garvey & The Back to Africa Movement.

He bought a small Honda as he liked its ness of blue. He did drive it round the block once but fell off it in The Mews. He left the bike parked for months till he gave it to Mike. /Ben Brewster was not hap with Mac's draft of Mavrakis. Mac met The *TP* Board which wished to pay some one out of his Fee to made good the text. Mac felt shamed and lost it. He told them he would throw it in The Thames first. He raged at the whole room and at each

one of The Board in turn. He felt
Cut had let him down and 'trayed him
so in throes of wrath Mac left Malvern Mews.
He found a room in a mixed house
in Camberwell with 3 Grads. Olney St was
a poor rough part of South Lon. On
first night he moved in lumps of brick

had to cut right down on the use
of his stove. He still made dole and
lived on bread and cheese but their price
shot up too and he found it hard
to cope. Few friends came round for him
to play the host. He took a job
three nights a week in *The Temple Bar*,
Walworth Rd. It pulled in the crowds with
Topless Danecrs who lured Mac as well but
shamed him too and he felt he should
not be there. In a few weeks the
the hots cooled and he soon gave it
up. At week ends he went home to
France and Jill who was ing and do
her new BA in French and Philosophy at
University College. When she talked on of a

flew through the wind. He mixed a bit
and went to a pub with the Grads
but was pressed down. One pint would trance
him in to a dark place. He drank
more on his own in near by pubs
like *The Red Cow* in Walworth Rd and
The Mother Red Cap on Camberwell Grn. By
then the cost of ing and liv in
The Land of Eng had soared. Things had
gone from boom to bust and there was
a deep slump. The price of oil had
just shot through the roof and so Mac

Don who taught well Mac raged in side
as Marvin Gaye sang *Let's Get It On*.
/In his work on Althusser Mac came to
see that in the end he too was
trapped in the closed Subject Object Circle of
Classical Philosophy from which he claimed to be
free. Mac put his ire to one side
and shared his Crit with Cut who left
The Board of *Theoretical Practice*. In the way of
It, Issue No 6 in May 72 had
turned out to be the last as the
rest of The Board chose not to go

on. It had been the same month Mac's
'Little Irrationality' had been born. By mid '73
he was firm that he had forged a
fresh path of Discursive Materialism. He was sure
by then that he had made a break
thru to a new Science of Discursive Reproduction
which dis placed the old 'Philosophy of Knowledge'.
He wrote to his Mam at Baird in
thanks for her gift on his Birth Day
and sent her mon for the gas bill.
He planned a first new book by Nov
which should make it poss for him to
help her go to The Land of Ire.
/Mac still strove to live the life of
a Marxist Intellectual but inc found it hard
to think as he tried to get by
each day. The book came to be a
faint hope as Wizzard had a huge hit
with *I Wish It Could be Xmas Everyday.*
While the men in the mines fought for
a big wage rise Mac in his head
tried to dev The Science of Discursive Formations
but found it diff to make ends meet.
He was glad when Heath was brought to
his kneees in the Three Day Week and
Wilson formed a new Gov which raisd their
wage but he felt all the more poor
him self. He still lived on bread and
cheese. He read out his own new work
to a small group at Birkbeck and a
few backed him. He still yearned to be
an 'Intellectual' and not just an 'Academic' but
he made up his mind to try and
get back to a safe place at University.
Mac plannd to use his work on Althusser
to do a PhD in Marxist Philosophy at
Sussex University. It was a choice based in
large part on fear of pov but at
the sme time he hoped tht he would
then have the strength to stay 'True To
Him Self'. He got a good Ref and
a small loan from his blithe Prof in
Leics which helped him to get out to
Falmer and talk to John Mepham on the
Staff in The Phil Dept who turned out
to be keen for him to go there.

/To earn the mon to pay back the
loan and to save for the next year
at Sussex Mac got a start in March
on a site of ing and build just
off the Kings Rd near the *Paris Pullman*.
Most of the wild men there had come
from The Land of Cots. On The Lump
they earned lots of dosh cash in hand.
On the week end they drank their wad
and asked for a Sub Mon morn. At
first Mac saved. The work it self was
hard and full hods of bricks were too
much for him but he was lithe and
fit to do a score of tasks well.
For a spell he used to go and
stay at the end of a day's work
with Jill and Frances. He felt tired but
more like a man shod in his boots.

For a short while it was fine till
Jill told him that she had shagged
some one at Birkbeck. 'Free Love' was meant
to rule and Mac bluffed his way. As
he had done twice since she had first
moved in with him he tried to mask
and put a brave face on his hurt.
As The Electric Light Orchestra had a
hit with *Can't Get It Out Of My Head*
he tried not to care but had to
curb a strong urge not to clump him.
With a wodge of notes in his back
pock he joined the men to drink more
at week ends. When drunk he rang a
whore's card in Gloucester Rd Tube and felt
shamed and a mess when he lied that
he had been there. He picked up quite
a fat girl in a pub who did
Domestic Science and they slept at his place
or her Hall of Res in South Ken
when it seemed like a game as he
sneaked down the stairs and out the back.
/Mac then gan to take one of his
house mates to bed in Olney St. Sue
was a Biology Grad at St Mary's Hosp
in Pad. Her PhD was in Immunology. At
the same time he went on ing of
work at the same site for some months

but then fell and sprained his foot. He took a job as the Night Watch Man. Mac thought that it would give him lots of time to read but he was too tired and scared him self in dark of night. His great fear grew that he did not know en ough. He took fright once more and felt such a lack that he tried to force him self to read all nine Vols of F Copleston's *History of Philosophy* in a few weeks. The job meant that he spent a lot of time on his own in which he used not to think but to brood and hoard his thoughts in an obs way. He got it in to his head that from then on he had to be on his own and that he had to make a new start. He met Jill in *The George* and when he had drunk en ough he told her that things were at an end for them. The next day he asked him self what he had done but hid his guilt and pressed on. /As The Rolling Stones had a hit with *It's Only Rock N'Roll (But I Like It)* by the time Mac was due to go to Sussex he knew in his own mind that he was close to the edge. Nixon had re signed in Aug when there was a move to imp each him. Mac's guilt was such that he felt as if he had done some crime too. It had been made worse whn Sue had told him that she was ill and did not have long to live. Tho he did not know her he felt in a way as if he ought to stay with her. When he set out for Brighton in fear he knew that

he verged on a real break down. The truth was that at some point he had read that Pyschotherapy was to be had in a 'Progressive Health Service' at Sussex and that fact had stayed lodged in the back of his head since he had a mind to go there to do Phil. He was scared to speak to a soul when he got to Brighton Station. The NUS had stalls to greet those like him who were new but he went round them. He had fixed up

a place for a year in Park Village
at Falmer but could not stand it. His
clean room looked out on to broad fields
of green grass in which slow herds of
of cows grazed and scrazed on the lea.
The lack of noise and dirt in which
he lived and worked in Lon was too
much for him. He could not sleep but
dozed and drowsed for a few hours in
his dark room in the day. Each eve he

had a few pints of ale in the
Bar but did have the funds to drink .
To get some air he dared to walk
on his own in the shads at night.
He had got to hate light. As his
deep dread of it grew he hid him
self and sighed with re lief in the
black heat of the shared TV room.
In side with closed eyes he felt safe.
He had two brief meets of ing with
Staff but then dodged them. For a few

night mare weeks he filed in to Prof
Lakatos' large class on The Philophy of Science.
He was whelmed by waves of shame and
could not face small groups. He did not
have a shred of steem for him self
so low he did not meet a soul.
/Dire weeks passed till Mac gan to break
and in the end he lined up to
see The Doc in The Health Centre. At
first Mac said that he had two probs.
He had saved some but did not have
funds for a whole year as he had
planned. Mac told him that his mind raced
too with probs in his work on a
new Science of Discursive Formations. The Doc said
he could not help with those but if
he cared to when he wished Mac might
come back and see him to talk more
of what he thought and felt in side.
A few weeks went by till his ness
of stub and born gave way and he
went back. In the end he broke down
in tears and was forced to yield. He
had to cede that he was in need
of help as he just did not know
how to live and how to go on.
He was not sure what it was but
he knew some thing was wrong with him.

Chapter 6

As he walked through the gate for the
first time Mac saw that etched in the
wall was 'The Cassel Hosp for Nervous Diseases'.
It scared him but he pressed on for
his meet with a Therapist which The Doc
at Sussex had made for him there. It
was a rare Therapeutic Community in The NHS
that had been set up by Tom Main
at the end of World War II. It
was to be found in the grand C18
house on Ham Commn used by E Cassel
in 1919 to treat men with 'Shell Shock'
from World War I. Once with Dr Lan
Mac told him how he had spoiled his
opps and failed at life. Mac was shocked
when it was left to The Doc to
point out that he had gone in to
his probs with his Mum at length but
had not at all talked of his Dad.
Mac was firm at first that Mell had
gone and left him in his child hood
and so there was no thing to say.
It took a long ence of sile for
Mac to start to find some words and
then him self in a flood of tears.
/At the Bus Stop on the way home
Mac both cried and laughed to him self
with a kind of wild re lief as
he thought of what Dr Lan had gone
on to say when Mac had told him
of his lone trips from pub to pub.
He had put it to Mac that he
had made them not just to drink but
to search too for his Dad. His grief
was tinged with a kind of joy and
a spirt of hope since it was the
first time that one had helped him to
make some sense of a part of his
life that had caused him so much pain.
/As Mac had to wait a small while
for a place to start at *The Cassel*
in the New Year he moved in with
Sue back at Olney St in South Lon.
She had a small house near Mold in
North Wales to which they went for a
few days. He found it a bleak place
on its own strip of poor land but
when she came back to Lon he chose
to stay for a break in which he
meant to go thru Hegel's *Phenomenology of Mind*
The wind howled and scared him on his
own which made it hard to read and
in the end forced him back to Lon.
Mac felt guilt that he ought not to
leave Sue for *The Cassel* as she still
held that she had not long to live.

He had to go to her work place
to find out that for months she had
lied to him. The fact that it was
not true set him free to look to
him self. Mac's guilt that he had left
Jill and Frances led him to meet with
his wife in Gordon Sq. He was not
in a good state. In the same breath
Mac fessed that the obs in his head
were all ing of fuck him up but
said he would for get *The Cassel* and
re turn home with her and France to
make a fresh start. They both knew tho'
that he had need of help at least
in the short term and had to go.
/Mac had mixed ings of feel when he
found him self in side *The Cassel*. It
was a strange space for him where he
shared a large room with two more of
The Lost. At the same time he felt
safe and glad to be there. When he
sat in the deep and long ence of
sile in The Firm Meet ing on his
first morn Mac knew that he was in
in the right place. He felt glad too
for his Ind and Group Therapy that would
be held two morns each week. For days
he clutched to him self all the time

M Foucault's *The Archeology of Knowledge*. A curt
Nurse soon put it to him that he
had sat with his head in a book
and done no thing all morn. As he
cleeked the cleach and cleech, he mocked
her out loud for ing of think that
to read was to do no thing. In
great fear Mac asked him self how he
had slipped right thru the net to fall
in to such a spot with such boors.
His fear was that they would not keep
him and that he should be thrown out.
For some days when Lunch was at an
end and his time was free he used
to go all the way in to town
on the Tube to The British Museum so
that if he was turned out he would
still have links with The Reading Room. The
trips made sense to Mac till he had
faith that Dr Lan meant it when he
said that he would not be cast out.
/In a way Mac had just got used
to *The Cassel* when the bad news came
from The Land of Ire that Mike had
crashed his Honda and was 'in a coma'
in St Joseph's Hosp, Dublin. Moll had flown
at once to his bed side thanks to
help from Desmond Guinness for whom Mike worked

at a time when he drank hard with
the rich Jet Set round Leixlip Castle. Since
he left school his Bro had done a
Foundation Year at Ealing College of Art where
he fell in love with his Susan and her
with him. They wed quite young and Mac
was their Best Man at Acton Town Hall.
Next day they went up to Hull School
of Art. Mike had learned how to paint
in the Hard Edge Style as well as
to print and sculpt. In the Vacs he
and his wife had worked for her best
friend's Mam, Karen Finch, who had set up
The Textile Conservation Centre at Hampton Court.

At the time she was one of few
in The Land of Eng with skills to
to re store tapes tries, rugs and chairs.

/Mac felt a lot of guilt as he
had passed on the Honda to Mike. He
had seen Dr Lan just a few times
and still did not feel safe or well
en ough to leave *The Cassel* for Dublin.
His Mam was ang with Mac when he
did not go and when she found out
that he had hid from her the break
down in his own life and the fact
that he was ill in hosp him self.
/So Mac stayed in *The Cassel* and felt

some new hope. It took a while but
he gan to let go of his dark
obs and to feel like his old self
when he was well. He saw Dr Lan
twice a week and was in a Group
run by The Chief Nurse. Mac formed a
small self help group with Thor and Mat.
Like quite a few who were ill there
they came from well off homes. Mac saw
for the first time that such pain of
their sort could not just be read off
from their class posn but had to be
grasped in terms of their own psyche too.
/At the same time there were down to

earth tasks to be done each day when
Mac had to get out of his head.
He had to join in first thing each
morn and help hands on to clean the
place and used an old wire brush to
scour out the loo. He took his turn to
prep food and cook the meal for the

ing of eve. He helped to org a
Fête to raise funds for a new fridge.
/At first there was free time when lunch
was at an end till the eve meal.
With friends he walked down The Thames Path
from Ham Hse past the Ings of Petersham
'neath The Hill to Richmond or up past
the wide weir to Kingston. He and Thor
played a lot on the Tennis Courts in
the grounds. In ings of eve they had
time to play Chess and Scrabble. Mac still
read lots of books like *Siddartha* by Hesse
and Mann's *The Magic Mountain*. A few months
passed and aft er lunch he gan to work
on his own up stairs in the Library.
Un well at Sussex Mac had been loathe
to do it but he let John Mepham
coax him to sign up with John Spiers
of The Harvester Press Ltd to trans late
:ien Seve's *Marxism and The Theory of Personality*.
Mac had now bought him self a good

Harrap in 2 Vols and worked at peace
for some hours on the text each day.
/In a few months when Jill went to
see Mac, he made out that she was
hap and had changed in some way. It
still seemed strange when his wife said that
she was In Love with Mik, a friend
of theirs whom she had crit for years.
In weeks Mac met Mik in Richmond at
The Old Ship in King St. When he
was asked how he felt, pint glass in
hand Mac gave him a green light by
say ing that things with him and Jill
were at an end and it was OK.
With in a few months he was galled
in side and felt 'trayed by them when
he found out not just that Mik had
moved in with Jill but that she had
swopped their own old flat in Lavender Gdns
for a house in Carthew Rd, Sheperds Bush.
/While he was at *The Cassel* Mac did
not drink on his own and when he
drank with friends who liked one or two
now and then he did not think of
it as a prob. Most ings of eve
he stayed in but now and then he
would join a small crowd that had a
drink near by in *The Hand and Flower*.

If they drank fast he lagged be hind.
It was a sign of how much less
he drank when one of The Lost was
thought by The Staff at the Hosp to
have gone on a lone binge Mac was
part of of a resp group asked to
go out and find him to get him
back safe. They looked in *The Royal Oak* and
The Ham Brewery Tap in Ham St but
found him in the end at the far
edge of Ham Common in *The New Inn*.
/Tho Mac did not think of it as
a prob, he was some times not quite
the same when he did drink. Now and
then with Thor and Mat he used to
go to Richmond to take a few pints
in quaint old pubs lke *The Waterman's Arms*
in Water Lane or *The White Cross* on
The Thames. One night on the way back
Thor jumped a red light in his van
and they were chased by the police. He
did not stop but sped on and then
turned a sharp left and hid in a
cul de sac. The police who found them
were armed as The IRA were a threat
in Lon at the time and freed them
with a sigh and eyes to the stars
when Mac said they came from *The Cassel*.

Like Thor, when he drank Mac did not
feel that The Law was for him. One
night he got back from the pub to
The Cassel and told The Nurse in Charge
that it was OK so he was ing
and go to sleep with his new girl
friend Ann in her room. Next morn Mac
was warned by Dr Lan that if he
did it once more he would be out.
In June Mac went to Leics for the
week end as he was 30. When drunk
he tried to sleep with some one's wife.
In Southwold where he went with Thor to
spend a few days at Mat's they used
to flit from pub to pub. He caused
a row in one with the Bar man
as he would not drink up in time.
When he met Mike for a drink at
The Orange Tree in Richmond, it was clear
to Mac for the first time that drink
was a prob for his Bro. Mike was

back at work in Leixlip with a new
girl friend named Penny but he was drunk
all the time. He slurred his words as
he drank too much Scotch. While they got
some French Fries which he would not eat
Mac tried to coax him to cut down.
/When Mac left *The Cassel* his friend John
gave him a lift in his van back
down to Brighton. He had fixed up a
light room on the ground floor at the
front of a friend's house in Gladstone Place.

It had been ten months since he was
out in the world so he was quite
scared in side but thrilled too to leave.
He had worked hard to get well
and was set to face life once more.
To mark that fact the first thing that
they did in Brighton was to go for
a drink. It was Guy Fawkes Night and
they went to Lewes to find Idi Amin
in flames on one of the huge fires

piled up with pine beds and teak chairs
that burned as D Bowie sang *Space Oddity*.
/In the new house Mac went on with
his trans of Sève. Up stairs Kate and
Martin typed too and at times it was
as if they sang in the same key.
He mixed with them a bit but on
the whole he kept to him self. He
cooked Sun lunch for Jill and Mik but
he felt lame and lone as he tried
too hard to please them. They had been
to the pub on the way and it
was diff to take as they both laughed.
/Mac knew she had asked for Legal Aid
at The Mary Ward Centre to file for
a Div and when he went up to
Lon to see Frances he had to leave
when wrath flared as a row broke out.
Mac was not hap and once more gan
to live in his probs as his hopes
dipped. As a male on his own he
felt a bit of a freak and blamed
the lack of back up from *The Cassel*.
He had a small loan from The Bank
but still felt poor and the lack of
cash in his pock left him weak. He
he felt fraught as if he had failed
in the world and soon slipped back in

to the old ways. He gan to drink
on his own once more in near by
pubs like *The Bear Inn*, *The Gladstone* and
The Franklin Tavern on the Lewes Rd. For
the first time too he gan to take
home Quarts of Scotch. He spent a sad
Xmas at Thor's flat in Parsons Grn with
a group of The Lost who too had
just left *The Cassel*. It was nice to see
them all at first as Stevie Wonder from
Talking Book sang *I Believe When I Fall
In Love It Will Be Forever*. Like him
tho they were all in the ness of
lin and lone and drank a way what
they felt in the *Duke On The Green*.
Back at the flat it was more of
the same as they shut down and sat
and stared in the long ence of siles
as Stevie sang *Blame It On The Sun*.
In The New Year Mac got to know
a young Mam with two small boys who
lived nxt door in Gladstone Place. He spent
time with them but broke things off in
Spring when he met a friend of Kate's
nmd Sue. She ws a Psychologist who worked
part time in The Health Centre at Sussex
Universityty. She and Mac both seemed to hit
it off at once as they walked on

The Downs and by the sea. They got
on well and shared a lot. Mac more or
less moved to her flat in Waterloo St,
near Yates' Wine Lodge in Little Western St.
She showed him how to make strong coff
and to brew blends of tea; how to
add yeast to flour and to knead and
twist dough in to snaked lengths to bake
fresh loaves of brown bread; how to make

cray fish and bird soup like bisk; how to
use stuff like kale and kelp as
well as yams in stews; and how to
make jam not too sweet. He read Pushkin
to her in bed. That Sum he worked
thru her new Freud's *Collectedd Works*. At
a time he was not sure what to
do with him self they were a boon.
He and Sue went to see *Equus* at
The Theatre Royal in Brighton and in Lon
All The Presidents Men at The Empire in
Leic Sq. Mac got on well with Sue's
friends El and Paul. He liked Paul's show
of art works for which he had drawn
men in months of toil in the mines

on a fine scheme backed by The NUM.
Mac got seats for them and Sue and him
self in July to see The Bothy Band
at *The State* up in Kilburn High Road.
/Sue had an old grey VW car in
which Mac learned to drive. They used to
pick Frances up in Lon and take her down
to Brighton for week ends once a month
or more. They had some great times on
the front at the Fun Fair on The
West Pier. It was a big change from
Lon and she was ripe for play in
the sea and on the beach where they
found chank & conch shells shaped lke gourds.
They played Ducks and Drakes wth flat stones
as they skimmed them in the waves. They
flew her kite and both held on tight
as this way and that it made an
arc in the strong wind while huge sea
gulls let out shrill screams when each one
in turn chirled and skirled in the air.
They took Fran to The Isle of Wight
for a long week end to stay with
some friends. She loved it when Mac would
heft her up on his back. She would
sit up with her legs drooped round his
neck and looped back in his arm pits
as he grabbed both her hands and ran
so fast while his own strength held out.
/Mac did not get on with all of
Sue's Feminist friends some of whom he found
butch. If he quipped she got fits of
pique. One who taught Anthropology at Sussex U
and was much too loud for him hired
an old farm house called *The Llewyn* midst
flocks of sheep near Builth Wells in mid
Wales. Mac and Sue stayed for a week
with a crowd most of whom taught and
did well in their fields. Mac felt shame
that he had failed since he left Leics.
He found it hard to cope in the group
as his mind used to go blank and
he would find him self at a loss
for words. His fear grew as he seethed
in side. At times whn Sue's friends came
round to eat at Waterloo St Mac could
not face them. He used to make him
self scarce and bolt to near by pubs
like *The Robin Hood* in Little Western St.
It had got such that in the eve
Mac had to go out and have a
drink in a pub all the more when

Sue asked him not to do so and
on the week ends when Frances was there.
In the terms of their Joint Custody it
was fixed in July that Mac had a
right to see Fran at set times. Sue
used to plead with him not drink but
it got to a stage where he just
had to go out at least for a
few pints to The Freemasons on Western Rd
and to take back cans of Long Life.
On some Sun Morns they went to meet
friends at The King and Queen where Jazz
was played. Mac's fear of folk grew once
more in side and at such times he
held Frances on his knees like a shield.
/As Mac's dread of life spread he had
to face the fact that The Cassel had
not cured him as he hoped. It was
a jolt as he still put all his
hope in the 'Talking Cure'. In Jan Mac
had got in touch with Nina Coltart at
The Lon Clinic then in New Cavendish St.
He had sent an App in Feb and
been seen by Dr Berst at Frognal Lane
in March and Dr Bak at Highgate in
April but turnd down. When Sue got a
job at The Tavistock Clinic in Lon Mac
thus sort of latched on to her. He
had held her hand thru her Clinical Dip
Exams at Bedford College and at each stage
as she had gone for the job at
The Tavistock. He had thought on it and
made a choice to go back with her
and get a job to pay for his
own Analysis. In Sept they moved to a
flat owned by a friend of Sue's in
Canfield Gdns, W Hampstead. It was not a
part of Lon that Mac knew or liked
and he felt pressed down there. At times
he could not bear some of Sue's Feminist
friends and found it hard to talk when
she asked them home to eat. She flared
when he clowned a round and joked to
cloak his fear with a drink. She did
not share the gest when he scoffed and
made fun of their stance as too stern.
He liked Mary Kelly but tried in vain
to stand er und her Post-Partum Document
in the Fall at The ICA. At Xmas
he could not laugh it off when they
went to see her friends named Ros and
Geoff. Mac did not feel good a bout
him self but in the maw of shame
that he had been in The Cassel. Geoff
was a film buff who knew Bertolluci and
was ing and work on a trans of

amsci's *Prison Notebookss* and once more Mac felt
lost and in ways out of his depth.
/In the New Year through Sue's links in
the small world of Therapy Mac was
glad of the rare chance of a one
to one Consultation with Hannah Segal. For an
hour as she smoked he told her of
his diffs with life and in days she
put him in touch with Frank Orf, a
Kleinian Analyst who lived in Regents Park Rd.
When they met, Mr Orf said he would
take Mac on three times a week. He
had a slot at lunch times on Mons,
Weds and Fri's. To get him thru that
phase and so that he could start at
once, Sue backed a loan to Mac from
the Nat West Bank for £300. It took
some weeks but Mac soon got a job
as Dep Sup at St Andrew's Psychiatric Day
Centre in Despard Rd, Islington. At first each
day Mac had to get the C11 Bus
from W Hampstead. For the next two and
a half years the job made it poss
for him at Lunch to race and rush
three times a week on the Northern Line
down to Camden Town to see Mr Orf
and then get back to work at Archway.
/It was Mac's first full time job since

he had left University but he knew too
that in some ways it was a flight
from the world. He felt split. It was
the last place he wished to be yet
at the same time he felt safe with
the ill. Tho he was on The Staff
he sensed some strange link with the fact
that in the past his Mam had been
to such a place for help and so
it was fit for him to be there.
The job was not what he had hoped.
In the back of his mind Mac had
thought tht he too might one day train
as a Therapist and that in the mean
time there he might learn some Dynamic skills.
He led some groups but most of the
folk were on drugs and there was no
scope for change. For most of the time
he had to run a set up where
they made up belts with clips and stuffed
cheap toys in bags at low wage rates.
There was a wheel where they learned to
blunge but lost him self he just looked
on as a girl came in mould a
bake to show fire how to clay once
and to folk the kiln to week pots.
/In those days when he met Sue straight
from work at The Tavvy it was in

The North Star on Finchly Rd. She was wont
to have one or two drinks and then
go home or in to town. She was
irked when he wished to sit and drink
for hours and she soon made known to
him it was a thorn in her side.
He was down in the slough at work
and when his Bro came to stay Mac
got worse. Mike still had his base in
The Land of Ire but too had lots
of work in The Land of Cots where
he used to gad here and there. Mike
liked what he did and told Mac of
his new well paid job for The Duke
of Argyle at Inverary Castle. There had been
a big fire just two years be fore
in 1975 and the Beauvais works which had
hung in The Tapestry Drawing Rm had been
re stored at Hampton Crt in 1976. Mike
had the chance to do the rest of
the work on site. He lived in a
carvn in the bawm of Inverary Castle. In
Mac's mind he was free to roam the
loughs and glens. While he felt yolked
the broth of a boy seemed to come
and go as he pleased and Mac yearned
for such a life style. He was galled
that Mike had swanned off and left him
to take care of their Mam in Lon
and with a head to throb. Mac saw
that his Bro had debts and owed tax.
He knew The Doc had warned Mike that
his health would go in two years if
he kept ing of drink but still grudged
the fact his Bro earned so much while
he had to give more than a third
of his own low wage to his Shrink.
/In one way Mac was more than pleased
to be in Analysis and he tried not
to bilk and baulk. From the start he
liked it how Mr Orf kept strict hours
but as the time neared each day he
still had such strong ings of mixed feel.
At first Mac found it hard to trust
him as he sat in his chair at
the head of The Couch. Mac could not
lie down but had to perch on the
edge of the *chaise longue* as he rolled
his own and smoked for six months 'till
he could do so. His states changed from
day to day. One time he would creep
in full of fear and be so meek
and mild. The next he could strut in
and scorn all the rugs and chairs in
such a 'nice place'. He could just march
in full of show to mock his ming

vase and the rest of his spode ware. /His Shrink based him self on Klein and much he spoke was posed to The Babe in Mac who was not sure what to make of it. Oft times he chafed. Mac found it hard to take and said it was a ruse for dopes and dupes but as time went on he felt its charm. At least for the while he was there he was more at ease but then he had to leave and rush back to save time in the grown up world of work. /When the day of ing and work came to an end at 4pm it turned out to be the norm that Mac and his Boss would wind down with a few cans of beer from the shop next door. At times they were both joined by two of The Care Staff and some of them went on to drink in near by pubs like *The Whittington and Cat* on the hill or *The Archway Tavern*. Some nights Mac had so much that he was still drunk when he got to work the next morn. His head ache bolked and throbbed and he had to spend hours in and out of the loo. When he and Sue moved to a flat in Highgate for six months which he saw in *The Evening Standard* Mac drank more in *The Woodman* up on Hghgte Hill. The nice place in Onslow Grdns looked out the back straight on to Highgate Wds. At the time he and Fran went to see *Grease* with J Travolta and O Newton-John at The Odeon in St Martin's Lne. One week end she stayed Mac got Fran's lobes pierced for ear rings in Camden Market. Mac drank too much Cointreau which had been a gift to Sue. On his way to the woods with them he fell and was shamed when he scraped and scratched his face on a fence. Due to his grazed looks he had to lie at work. By now when he had a thick head at St Andrew's Mac was wont to stand and dream and wished he had the spunk to leave as he stared out at the huge trucks which made their way up Highgate Hill to THE NORTH. He caused a row one night with Sue's friends when he tried in *The Seven Stars* in Sheperd's Bush to coax Paul to leave Lon and to get a job with him at Sulom Voe on the oil rigs in the North Sea. The plan did not go down too well with his wife. Nor did it as Mac tried to laugh it off when the meal

which she had cooked was spoiled due to
the fact that they had stayed out too
late and gone on to *The Askew Arms*.
/Thus Mac's lips were sealed as Rod Stewart
sang *I Don't Want To talk About It*
and with Harvester Press Sue brought out her
Bibliographical Guide to Sexual Politics in Britain.
In May she and Mac leased a ground
floor flat In Rosecroft Avenue for a year.
It was on the edge of Hampstead Heath
near Golders Hill Park. Mac had mixed ings
of feel whn they moved there. He loved
the peace and the tall green trees but
did not like the fact that there were
few folk and no kids in the streets.
It was just too nice for him esp
at a time when with The Punks spat in
such rage how The UK was run down
and on strike with piles of trash and
junk in the streets. As Mac mused
on his own past at a time when
there was just no hope for those on
the wrong side of the tracks and life
for the young was at a dead end
The Sex Pistols then sang *Who Was It?*
/When he left work Mac used to drink
at old pubs in Hampstead like *The Flask*.
He dodged and ducked those he had known
but was caught out in *The Holly Bush*
one night when he had gone for a
few pints of Burtons Ale. He chanced to
meet one of the old *TP* Board who
was there when he had dressed it down
in the past. He was now a Don
who had done well as a Sociologist. Mac
Mac felt shamed when his coat bulged and
made a loud noise as they sat since
it was lined with his cache of cans.
At times Mac weaved his way home down
the curved hill from Whitestone Pond and aped
old Mr O'Brien frm The White City whm
he and Mike had laughed at in their
child hood as he would tack through the
wide court yard and yaw his way home.
/In his Analysis all the while Mr Orf
saw Mac's ing of drink as a sign
of some thing else deep in his psyche.
While he spoke Klein to the Babe and
the child in young Mac, he aimed too
to nudge old Mac to 'drink like a
Gent'. He sought to get him to 'have
just one or two beers' and to 'leave
it at that'. Mac strained and strived in
the pub to down just a few pints
but it did not work. When he was
in pain and did not feel well Mac

drank to quash what he felt while at he same time he held that if you had his child hood or his job or his Mam or you lived where he did you would need to drink too. When he thought that he was on the mend he drank as he felt good. He did his best to change his ways but by then had to have a drink most days and when he had one he had to have have one more - as on those when Sue came in frm her 'Baby Observation', a part of her Course as a Trainee Therapist at The Tavistock. Some how it galled him and he would mock it. When he went too far and found he had up set her he would try to laugh it off. It irked Mac at a meal with her Mam and Dad that he grudged Mac more than a spot of Scotch in his glass and made him feel like Oliver Twist when he had to ask for more. He was glad to share his Bro's wine when he and Sue went to spend a few day at Xmas with him and a girl friend at his flat in the grounds of Dalmeny House on The Firth of Forth. Mike's work at Inverary Castle had come to an end and while he still had his place in Leixlip and had set up a rare new job at Castletown House in The Land of Ire, he had leased a new flat and work shop from Lord and Lady Roseberry to re store their tapes tries. In a way Mac grudged his grand life style but liked to share it. Mike had a 9 Hole Golf Course out side his front door. Mac loved to have a good pint with a top of froth or a wee dram of scotch in *The Hawes Inn* and *The Forth Bridge Saloon* with him in South Queensferry. At the same time, pint in hand he caused rows when in sour gluts of glum and glunch Mac told his Bro that he did not at all like the fact that he worked for The Rich. In a way it riled him when Mike got them a cab back to his flat but he was glad too. /In the New Year Mac and Sue had a do at Rosecroft to mark it when her new book *Tearing The Veil* was brought out by RKP. He helped to clean up their flat and to get the food. At first he did not drink him self as he poured the mulled wine for the guests. He then stayed out of the way with

one or two of his own friends and
drank. In side he felt they were not
as good as Sue's who all seemed to
know how to live well and to thrive
in their fields. He was irked when she
was drawn to Ian McEwan whose first book
had been out for a few years while
In Between the Sheets was on the way.
Mac fumed too when her Sis wed but
did not ask Sue to her 'Hen Night'.
When he had a drink or two Mac
tried to bring what he felt was a
daft old feud to an end on the
dance floor at *The Orangery* in Holland Prk.
He meant well but the out come was
just one more row when the Bride stalked
off and left him and Susan walked out.
/In the late Spring their lease was up
at Rosecroft. When they came back from a
trip to stay with Mike at Dalmeny for
Easter Susan made up her mind to buy
a flat and Mac helped her to search
for one. At no time had he had
the means or the thought to buy a
place him self and as he stared at
Ads in *The Ham and Highgate Express* or
Estate Agents he felt less than and did
not feel as if it was much to
do with him as his own life sank
in a deep hole of debt. He still
paid a cheque to Jill for Fran each
month and as he drank more it got
more tough to pay all his Shrink's fees.
In a few months Sue bought a first
floor flat that she liked with one bed
room in Kempe Rd in North West Lon.
Mac did what he could to lend a
hand and put down thick rolls of felt
in the large loft to keep them warm.
He liked the fact that it was near
to Queens Park but not that it was
close to the Conservation Area in which there
were no pubs as these had been ruled
out by The Temperance Society when it was
built. He got a grudge that she had
lured him there to get at him and
drank more when he left work each day

in a job which he could not stand.
When he felt as dry and parched as
if he lived in a place of drought
he downed pints of Young's with a friend
at *The Queens Arms* in Kilburn High Rd
once a week and for much of the

rest roved up and down it in those
pubs filled with men from The Land of
Ire from *The Westbury* to *The Old Bell*
to *The Cock Tavern* to *Biddy Mulligans* to
The Black Lion and *The North Lon Tavern*.
He shared a word with some one now
and then that chimed but most times he
sat or stood with his pint on his
own and lived on in a sort of
sad trance as he stared thru the men
of woad in the thick smoke of the
bar. Some nights he lost him self in
The Irish Independant. In a kind of dream
at times he stepped on to the boat
train as it left Euston for Dublin. In
the real fumes of the pub tunes and
airs frm *The Chieftans* brought tears in to
his eyes or made his heart beat fast.
He had long grudged the fact that his

Bro had both lived and worked in The
Land of Ire and had an Irish Passport.
He made up his mind so to get
one for him self and to go and
look fr his Dad's Sis named Madeleine who
he thought stil lived some where in Westport.

/When Mr Orf took his hols Mac went
to The Land of Ire for the first
time. He and Sue spent a week with
Mike who had a flat in one of
the garnd Wings of Castletown Hse in Celbrdge
owned by the Irish Georgian Soc run by
Desmond Guinesss. Mike had been hired by him
for three months to re store some of
its old chairs and rugs. It was a
strange time for Mac who knew in a
way that he should not but on the
boat got Mike some *Southern Comfort*. In a
quaint Show at The Big House put on
that year his own Bro played the part
of The Demon Barber in *Sweeney Todd*. His
his girl friend Lucy nor Sue were too
hap when Mac drank pints of draught Stout
with Mike in the dark pubs of Celbridge.
/In the coach which they took to the
West Mac was tense. Old tunes that played
on the air in the bus touched him.
He was dazed and tears came to his
eyes as he saw names like Dartford and
Loughrea where his Mam had been born and
spent her youth and of which he had
heard so much since his own child hood.
Mac got a grudge with Sue whom he
tried to rouse but who would not wake

up as they passed through. For a few days they stayed with his Uncle Michael who had a small house in Galway. On the first night when they got back from the tour of pubs in town with his young Cousin Mihal, Sue was shown to her own room with a smile by his Aunt. It had made her laugh when she found out that Mac's girl friend was a Jewess. On the next she hemmed Mac in a chair and showed him the slides of her trip to Lourdes but on Sun it was a rel lief to him when she did not make them go to Mass with her in the Church. Mihal showed them a snap of him self as he grinned in the bent wreck of a car which he had crashed. /Mac and Sue took a coach up to Westport. It was strange for Mac to see the name MCGREAL on the large signs of two Butcher's shops. When he asked Mac soon learned that his Aunt Madeleine lived just up the steep hill in John's Row. He knocked on the door of a small house and her son Rich let them in to wait till she got back from work. His Aunt was shocked but pleased to see him and fixed to meet up that night in a snug Bar at the back of a small shop in the town. Mac was stunned when she and her friends who had grown up with and known his Dad beamed and called him to mind with such warmth. It was too much for him when they passed round his pics and spoke so well of the man and boy whom they had known. Mac got so drunk that he was at a loss for words by the time that he reeled off with Sue to the place down the street where they stayed. In a pub with Rich who still seemed as sharp as a blade the next morn, Mac pledged that he would come back soon. To keep Sue hap he had just a pint of Stout and left. They hitched back to Dublin in the cab of a truck with two wild young men who had baled hay. They claimed to have guns and cheered The IRA. /Mac was pressed down when he re turned to The Land of Eng. In some way with in him he had felt at home in The Land of Ire. He had to go back to a job he had learned to hate and to live where he felt that he had no place. He could feel that Sue was no more hap than he

was and thought that she saw some one
else. They both slept with their backs turned
but he could not see a way to
mend things. He tried to share his probs
with Mr Orf but as he leaned and
lounged in The Bars with men from the
The Land of Ire in Kilburn High Road
it was not much help. As he cashed
more cheques for cash to buy cans of
beer on the way home too his debt
with The Bank grew. That Xmas Mac was
galled when Mike would not come back to
help him with their Mam. His Bro held
that she was not his resp and had
a good time with his friends in Leixlip.
/Mac's deep dread of life grew as the
New Year stretched out in front of him.
The more he tried with Mr Orf to look
at his probs with his Mam, with Mike,
with his ex wife Jill and with Frances,
with Susan, with his job, with the Bank,
with the dark place in which he lived,
the more he drank the worse they got.
By then Mac owned that he drank too
much. He did not like the small pear
shaped paunch from the bulge in his bouk
and he had tried for some time to
check what he downed as well as the

times he went out. His fear had grown
when he found that he had to drink,
for when he tried not to he used
to shake and sweat and to get tense
in a way that he could not bear.
As his ing of drink held sway it
had got to a point where he could
not pay The Fees of Mr Orf and
things had to come to a halt due
to his lack of funds. His Shrink had
wished to 'work things thru' in the right
way. He couched what he said with care
but was non plussed and to Mac it
just felt like a farce as he still
urged him to drink like a Gent. His
Shrink put The Fees off for some months
but as Mac used to act out more,
what he owed grew. They reached the stage
where both did not want the Analysis to
stop but in the end it had to,
with Mac in a black hole of debt
and his life in a mess in which
his ing of drink held sway. His faith
in 'The Talking Cure' which had been roused
when he had set out with Mr Orf
to get down to the deep roots of
what was wrong with him was soured and
his hope lost in the ness of less.

Chapter 7

Mac's life was then a hard fight to get through the long days. With out help each one got more dark. There was a part of him that was prone to lose hope and in those bleak years for him Freud was 'The God that had failed'. In large part Mac had got the job at St Andrew's so that he could go to see Mr Orf with whom things had now come to a sad end. He had found it hard to bear by then as more and more folk who had been there for a life time had cme from Friern Barnet Hosp. Mac re signed from St Andrew's on the day that M Thatcher took hold of The Gov in May 1979. For months he had mused on the lump sum which he would get from The Pension Fund in to which he had paid for two and a half years. In his mind it loomed large as he had blown it up in to a huge pot with which he could drink. On the strength of it he sat for a few months in Queens Park and read books like *The Magus* by John Fowles as he drank. Whn it ran out and Sue grouched at him Mac got a job as a Bar Man at *The Lamb and Flag* in Rose St. He tranced the pub as it was a quaint old place near Leicester Sq and sold tuns of Real Ale like Directors Bitter. For a few weeks Mac thought that he would go nuts but bore the Boss from the Land of Cots who drank Scotch all day and touched up the Bar maid. Mac was still stunned when he was just fired out of the blue. When he rang from home to ask why, he was in tears when Mr Grouse put the phone down. /By then it was clear to Mac that he and Sue had to go their own ways. As Cliff sang *We Don't Talk Anymore* Mac was sure that he did not want to wed or for her to have a babe. He rued the sad fact but by then it was hard for him to be at ease while they had Frances or if they sepnt time with Sue's close friends Mike and Val and their two kids since both his heart and mind were in The Pub. On Sat morns the norm was for them to get their week's food in the mart at Camden Town. While Sue got the meat Mac would get the fruit and veg. To keep the cost down Mac would buy it for the least he could so he could

slip in the pub. He would think what
a shrew Sue was to whine and whinge
but shrugged it off as he had a
quick pint or two in *The Elephants Head*.
/When Sue flew to Israel for her Hols
Mac got a coach up to Edinburgh to
stay with Mike at Dalmeny. On the way
he read *Saville* by David Storey. His Bro
seemed hap with a new girl friend called
Laura. Their new flat was by a ridge
of trees that could be seen as one
nears a small lake. With great feats
of will they had cleared the weeds and
built a coop for six hens each with
a sharp beak that clucked and laid free
range eggs which they boiled or fried for
break fast on the hob. They had dug
a big veg patch with diff plots in which
they grew their own peps, spuds and toms.
With a wan smile Mac watched as Mike
helped Laura to prep to treat them all
to a huge feast. He was now hap
to awn peas; to chop and dice veg
like beet, leeks and swede; to put cloves
in the rice; to chop leaves of blite,
cress and kale and use herbs like chives
in the chow; to baste and broil grouse
and quail as well to bake spuds in

the sleek stove. As Mac craved a drink
while Bro cooked a haunch and carved a
hough of beef it was all grist to
the mill and Mike got his votes as
he put stems and strigs of fruit stalks
as well as fruit like figs and geans,
prunes and sloes in to The Punch.
Mac knew that Mike had his probs with
The Bank and Tax yet still grudged his
life style and how kind the fates had
been to him. He slept with his Bro's
Ex on the last night of his stay.
/Back in Lon Mac felt in a snare
with Sue but feared the crunch and just
did not know as it was asked by
The Sex Pistols, *'Whatcha Gonna Do About It?*
He was flat broke and so in the
short term at Xmas got a job as
a Temp on the Post at Mornington Crescent.
Mac was glad when he did not have
to take the mail out on one of
the beats but could sit and sort it
as he had sprained his foot when drunk.
He saved a bit but by the end
of March it felt a dirge as the
Bank chased him for a debt of more
than £600 and Sue for the past loan
to him of £300 which she had backed.

Through a stroke of luck and their ties
with RKP Mac got a nice opp with
Sue to trans late *Martin* by Hélène Frédéric
and Martine Malinsky. On the strength of it
he got a bit more help from The
Bank as one does some times if one
earns but it was soon gone as Odyssey
sang *Use It Up and Wear It Out*.
Mac tried in vain for a job with
the new *London Review of Books* but found
him self in stead in Queens Park. In
his mind Mac thought that work out in
the fresh air each day with plants and
shrubs would do him good and help him
to drink less. He would not have to
take bus or train but could just walk
up the road. It was not what he
had planned on when black bag in hand
and barked at by this beast or that
he had to pick up the crap and
the trash. It came as a shock and
a shame to be seen thus by Sue's
friends who lived near as they walked past
each morn on their way to work at
The Institute. When late he was warned and
saw that he had a stark choice. He
found that he drank more and in a
few months one morn he was sacked.

/Mac felt poor and at a loss but
had a hope in the back of his
mind that Moll's rich Bro would save him
when he heard that Martin was due to
come soon with his wife Tess from Perth.
He had share cropped and built up a
large sheep farm. Moll had not seen them
for more than 30 years since they had
had left The Land of Ire and stayed
at Sycamore Gdns on the way to Australia.
When Mac met them at Baird it was
soon clear that Martin did not think the
same way as him. While they drank canned
beer at Baird, Mac was shamed as Moll
told her Bro of his plight and what
his Dad had done to him as a
child but Martin just shook his head and
said he should get a job. In days
Mac's Mam and her Bro fell out when
she gan to snipe in her old way
and brought up stuff from their child hood
which he could not bear. She had laughed
too when Martin told her with some shame
that he then had a pig's heart. When
they both stormed out and moved to *The
Regent Palace Hotel* in Piccadilly Mac went to
make peace and tried to broach with them
how things were. In their room up stairs

he shed fraught tears and then blacked out.
/Mac had known that it would come but
put the thought off and it was still
a shock when Sue asked him to go.
He had come back drunk with new boots
from Kilburn High Rd one Sat morn when
she asked him to leave. He felt spine
less and dragged his feet. When Sue said
she would call her Dad to get him
out he laughed it off but he was
stressed by what he owed her, The Bank
and Mr Orf. While she was a way
in Brighton he made a swift dart and
took flight. Part of his huge fear stemmed
from the fact that when Mac had worked
in Queens Park for a few weeks he
had still signed on but not told them.
Mac felt not just on the loose but
on the run as he rushed to pack
his old ruck sack with a few clothes
and cashed his last cheque for £20. He
fucked off to The Land of Cots as Abba
hit him with *The Winner Takes It All*.
Not with ing and stand his let down
in Queens Park he still thought that if
he got a job on the ground out
in the crisp fresh air of the woods
up in the North it would cure his
drink prob. He had good luck and got
one lift all the way to South Queensferry
but things did not turn out well with
Mike who was hap at the time with
Laura and had well paid work. Mac felt
shamed in front of his young Bro who
found it hard to grasp and to take
that the Big Bro he steemed now had
no home and no job. When Mac had
got there The Wood Man he met thru
Mike turned out to be an ex SAS
man and had a hand shake like a
vice. It was warm in the smog of
The Forth Bridge Saloon but too cold to
work 'mongst the pines. Mike's Ex said
that she was in love with Mac but
drunk he said that he was no good
for her and not worth it. When Mac
did walk in the woods it was to
yell in pain to get it out of
his head. In his own weird way he
aped Alan Bates whom he had seen in
The Shout, a film based on a short
tale by Robert Graves. A note came from
Sue who was glad that he had found
a job and hoped it was fun. She
had to know if he wished to come
and get his stuff or to have it

stored with his Mam or his friend Stu. In the end Mac worked for one mad night as a Guard on the front door of a pub in The Grass Market where Jazz played for Beats at The Edinburgh Festival. When he got the chance to do it to earn some cash from a friend of Mike's who owned the place Mac felt put on the spot. The joint was packed and he was not up to such work with or with out a drink which he did not risk and stood one shift. He could tell that Mike was glad when Mac made his mind up to prise him self a way and to hitch hike down to stay with his friends Paul and Elaine in Leics. His Bro slipped him £20 as they said good bye and left him by the road. /Mac sank more in to the mire when he camped out in the front room of Paul and El's house in Leics. As he sat and drank cold cans of beer in Fleetwood Rd he dwelt on the sad thought that it was the same place where he had once been so proud to pull off his great feat to get a First Degree. Now In a hope less state in which he had to trudge to the Job Centre to look for low paid work Mac felt it was his poor fate to be like Jude on the out side as he gazed at the spire of the famed Engineering Block from the far side of Victoria Park. He felt pressed down and could not see how to move on. To bear out the hard fact that there was no way back he got a note from Sue to say he could not just pick up the old life with her where he had left off. She had changed the locks on the front door. /At a stage in his life where once more Mac did not know what to do, he went with his friends and two kids on their Hols to The Land of Cots. He fixed up for them to stay with his Bro for a night at Dalmeny. When they got there he rowed with Mike who was set to leave for Lon with his pal of ing and drink and whom Mac wished to fight till they calmed him down. For Mac the days on Hol were a spell of great pain as he him self could think of nought but a can in his lap which he craved and he felt awk with his friends. As they went to look at Stirling Castle or sat by

the shore at Loch Lomond he had to
steal off to find a pub for a
short bout in which to down as much
as he could in the time. By
then he was gaunt and grim, in a
a mood of doom and gloom. It was much
more than down in the dumps. When they
made their way back to Leics all the
doubts he had thru his life screamed
in his mind. Thoughts no one could hear
roared up from out of the dark depths
of a deep ence of sile that was
more and more loud in his head. He
yearned to stay in their home and for
them to take care of him but he
knew it could not be. The fears spun
and raced in his brain but he could
not tell them how bad he felt at
the thought that he was doomed to go
back and stay with his Mam in Lon
to get a job. For a few more
weeks till his funds ran out he drank
more cans in the front room at Fleetwood
Roadd. In that time he was hurt when
Elaine asked him if he would like a
cup of tea, as if she had tried
to have a go at him. Mac loathed
him self for he felt like a leach that

sponged on them and in the end he
just had to go when one of the
kids was in floods of tears as he
had used up all of her tooth paste.
/So down to his last few pence Mac
re turned to Baird House. It felt like
a blow of ing and crush. It was
16 years since he had left to change
the world. He was lost and shamed and
in a poor state but at least it
was a home that he knew and in
a way he felt safe. The fear was
still on him a lot of the time
since he had no means and shook as
he could not drink much. In a kind
of night mare he went to the Job
Centre in Hamm. He got temp work for
a few days with *The Brook Green Laundry*
when he had to take stuff and to
drop it off from their van. For a
few Pounds Mac spent a whole day in
which he broke his back to load a
huge truck up with large cans of paint
in Latimer Rd. He tried to save from
from his low wage but was in to
ing of drink once more and found it
too hard to keep much back. He planned
to have a phone put in at Baird

House in his own name when he had
the funds. Sue wrote to ask him for
help to pay off his loan from The Bank
and could not see why he would not.
/In Nov Mac got a Temp job as
a 'Bar Porter' at Olympia. He had grabbed
at it one morn when he saw the
Ad for 'Student types' in the wind of
the Job Centre in King St. He bragged
that he knew the ropes as in years
past he had done such work in the
Vacs at White City Stadium. He rued the
way his life had gone down hill in
the mean time but when he worked at
The Computer Exhibition he was glad that at
least he was out of sight and could
not be seen by those who had known
him in the old days. In that Show
and the next ones when he donned it
the blue garb that he had to wear
veiled the way he lived from the world.
Mac had a sense that while he hid
thus he ceased to be. Garbed in his
blue smock he was gone from the world
he knew. It was the case that work
in which he had to load and push
trucks with crates of beer and fruit juice
and butts of ale from The Stock Room
to Bars took place out of the way
holed up in the depths far from the
view of most folk. If he got a
glimpse of some one from his past he
slipped out of sight. With eyes glazed and
hooked on hootch he ducked and dived
out of the way. At the same time
in his mind at times he used to
brag to him self of his past and
he looked down on a lot of men
for whom such low work was the norm.
/When Mac worked on *The Security Show* at
Earls Court it did not take him long
to see that it was the sort of
place that drew to it those who drank
like moths round a flame. He was still
shocked to find some of them sloshed out
side The Stock Room first thing in the
morns. He owned that he drank too much
but held that he was not that bad.
At Xmas he was glad to sort the
mail once more at Mornington Crescent when
some had to slave at Olympia in Bars
at the Branof Airways Tennis Show. On the
Post Mac knew that he had to keep
his drink ing well in check and found
it hard. A sole drink was no use
to him. When he met Mike at lunch

time in *The Spread Eagle* in Parkway on his way to work Mac felt soused on just a few pints and he was scared when he slurred words. His fear grew that he would lose it. Most of the time he kept out of the pub at mid day and had a few pints on the way home. On the last night when Mac bought a round of fare well drinks for those with whom he had had worked, he had to get in more for him self at the Bar as time was called. /By Dec '80 Mac had worked long hours and had the phone put in at Baird. In a way it pleased Moll but with her it was still diff for him. He spent Xmas with Mike at the house of Laura's Mam and Dad in Walmer Rd, Holland Prk. They talked a bit and played darts at at *The Prince of Wales* in Princedale Road. They drank up and down Portobello Rd in *The Sun and Splendour*, *Finch's*, *The Portobello Gold*, *The Earl of Lonsdale*, *The Colville* and *The Castle*. Mac was hap that he and Mike had a great opp for the first time to spend Xmas on their own. He had hoped that it would help them both to speak and to get close. It was a real chance for him to lear what his Bro thought of his life but Mike was piqued when Mac drank all the tins of beer he found in the house and showed no wish to stock up in their place. Mac had been irked that the cans were too small and so had drunk more. He thought Laura's pa would have had had the funds for large ones as he was a big wheel at Lloyds. When Simon Callow came to see Mike with whom he had been friends since school days Mac was drunk and rude to him. While Mike drank Scotch all the time he could more or less hold it. Mac felt shame when he fell off a stool to the floor and they were asked to leave *The Porcupine* in Notting Hill Gate. His sense of doom grew when Mike went back to Dalmeny. Mac had a dread of what was in store for him. At Xmas he had got Fran a *'Family Scrabble'*. For years he had lived with and fought the fear that he would leave her as his own Dad had left him. Now when she was eight years old Mac felt in such a bad way in side he deemed it best best for her if she did not see him at all for a while. To feel

safe for New Years Eve he went to
stay with Paul and El back in Leics.
/For a few weeks back at White City
Mac lived on the small sum that he
had built up but soon drained what he
had saved. He got a note in the
mail from Mr Orf sent on from Sue
at Kempe Rd which asked when he meant
to pay the debt he still owed him.
Mac did not know as he swigged thru
the days and lived from hand to mouth.
As a Bar Porter he found his self
at Earls Court in the strange world of
The Ski Show. In his blue garb Mac
worked in a Bar full of bronzed folk
in smart clothes. At the base of a
dry Ski Slope on which the young and
fit proved their skills, the space was packed.
In some ways Mac was quite lost in
the ness of a sphere in which he
was so out of place. On a near
Cat Walk thin girls in style each showed
off a dress more chic than the next
as well as trends in all sorts of
smart Gear to the sound of too loud
Rock. One time the Bar was so full
that Mac helpd to serve. The straight young
Bar Maid from Oz frowned but did not

snitch when she twigged as he hid in a
£5 note in his fist. On his way
to work at the Bar in the morns
in ness of need he stole small things
like cheap clips and pens from the stalls.
/In a few more weeks Mac was thrown
back in to his child hood when he
worked on *The Boat Show*. It was full
of all kinds of craft from small rafts
to the huge yachts of the rich. It
brought to mind how with his mates he
had climbed in and out of such boats
as a lad. In the Bar at which
he worked neat tots of Pusser's Rum were
sold there at a low price to boost
sales. Old Men O' War who tried to
splice the main brace but with a few
strong swigs found out but too late that
that they could not still hold their grog,
soon keeled to the right and the left.
In the midst of it Mac bent and
dodged out of the way in shame when
he saw one of Sue's old friends from
The Institute go past with his two kids.
At the end of each day Mac used
to drink with those with whom he worked
in *The Brompton* on the Old Brompton Rd.
/In March Mike wrote from Dalmeny to say

that he was glad Mac was back with
their Mam and had a place to stay
while he tried to get his life back
with a job in which he could earn
some thing. He wrote of his own bad
luck. He had flown out to New York
but not got a well paid job for
which he had hoped. Mac felt for him
but was not shocked as he knew that
by then Mike drank Scotch round the clock.
/In the short term Mac then pinned his
own hopes on what he could earn at
The Ideal Home Exhbn. He would save and
get his own flat. Such a place would
give him a base to stand on his
own two feet and sort his life out.
He got work there as a Bar man.
It was a tough world with its own
harsh Laws. The Firm let go of folk
on the spot. Just like that The Man
could say that you were 'Surplus to Requirements'.
As it was Mac worked 12 hour shifts
six days a week for six weeks. He
soon found that to make up for their
low wage and long hours, it was the
way of life for some Bar Staff not
just to bring in their own drink to
sell off but to thin drinks and to
short change folk. In a trance Mac joined
in but his skin crept down to its
pores when he heard a Bar Maid who
called to mind some one he had known
and grown up with at White City say
'He's OK. He's one of us'. In ways
Mac liked some who worked there but it
was a night mare in which he felt
lost as he toiled thru it half drunk
in a kind of trance and in which
at times he was not sure what was
ing or on go. He told her that
it was great but just threw a way
a small twist of some white stuff that
she gave him with a smile. He did
not know what it was but some thing
told Mac it would just not be good
for him. When the Bar stock was down
in two weeks he was shocked. Mac did
not feel that it was his fault but
he was sent back to work as a
Bar Porter. At the end of long shifts
he drank with those who did the same
in troughs like *The Earls Court Tavern* and
The Prince of Teck in Earls Court Road.
In the smoke it was a dark low
llfe world of pimps, thieves and whores where
you could trust no one and through which

Mac moved as if in a bad dream. It was a kind of cess pool in which to hide his fear he bluffed a lot of front and blagued a lot of bilge. At times his tone of voice was glib and took on a twang when he drawled in an off hand way as if he hailed from Perth. With pals he drank in *The Courtfield* in Earls Court Road as well as *The Barkston Hotel* in Barkston Grdns. On one night off work they drank so much that when they got a cab to *The Barons Court Tavern* the man in the Cab just drove round the block and took their fare with a big smile as that was where they were. Mac felt some guilt on his days off when he took cans with them as they went on pub crawls on The Thames Path on which he had learned to walk, from *The Blue Anchor* to *The Rutland* to *The Dove* to *The Ship* down to *The Old Black Lion* and back. At Baird House things had got worse. Mac felt trapped, for in more than six months he had drunk what he saved with which he meant to rent a new place. He felt down and drank more as Moll seethed in shent and shame that her son had sunk so low to pick up slops. He felt coshed when she cried that her 'Top boy was nowt but a Pot man'. One eve he got home drunk with a bag of booze. Can in hand he set set out to taunt Moll. He felt the need to bait her and to rouse her ire. He sat slouched on a crate by the cream shelf o'er the fire place which still bore an odd trace of the marks where his Da left cigs to burn down. When Mac gan to gad and goad her and flaunt the fact that there must have been some cause why his Dad had gone she freaked. As she ran out of the front door Moll snatched Mac's bag of cans and threw it down in to the yard. While she yelled and rushed for help Mac's first thought was that from that height she could have killed some one. His first act was to grab a few of his things and to run down to find out if when they hit the ground the cans had leaked. He spent a few nights on the floor at his friend Stu's small flat in Bishopsbridge Rd. They drank pints of ale in *The Redan* & *The Prince Alfred* in Queensway. In days Mac moved to a first floor

flat in a house out in East Sheen
owned by a friend of his Bro's. The
place was cold and bare as it was
For Sale which gave Mac good cause to
stay and drink in *The Hare and Hounds*
in Upper Richmond Rd. He kipped in a
room for weeks with just a couch that
creaked and a two bar fire for warmth.
When the flat was sold he soon had
to move on. He then had to count
on those at work who would put him
up for a night or two and dossed
on floors from Earls Court to Willesden Grn.
At times he had to ring folk from
a phone at Earls Court Station at 12pm.
/Mac then went out with a brave girl
named Di from Sydney who used to wait
on at the Bar. It was odd for
him when they slept at the house where
she stayed in Hamm Grove as it was just
a stone's throw frm Sycamore Gardens. At the
close of *The Ideal Home Exhbtn* he took
her on a trip up to Dalmeny. At
first they had a good time at Mike's
but Mac had not saved what he hoped
and went back on his own to Lon
to get a job at the next Show
in Olympia. He drank with Mike in Edinburgh
till the train left Waverley. The next thng
Mac knew was in the dawn when he
came to on a bench in Newcastle Stn.
He had blacked out and did not know
how he had come to be there. With
the last of what he had in his
Abbey National Savings Book he just had the
funds to get back to Lon. At the
end of May he got a big form
in the mail which told him that as
he had not paid the right fare and
sworn at staff on the train he had
been charged to go to the Magistrates Court
in Newcastle in July. Mac was still hurt
when Di turned to call him a drunk.
As Roxy Music sang *Jealous Guy* he felt
blue in *The Grove Tavern* when she dumped
him and went back to her boy friend.
Tho for years he had yearned for Jilly
it still tugged at his heart strings and
and he seethed as he drank in a
ness of sad for him self. He felt
poor and grudged how well paid his Bro
was as he looked in June at a piece
in *The Scotsman Magazine*. it had a nice
pic of Mike at work in Dalmeny as
he re stored a huge C18 tapes try
by R Baillie. *The Glorious Defence of Londonderry*

still hangs with *The Battle of The Boyne*
in The Bank of Ire land in Dublin.
/Mac felt pressed down as he worked once
more as a Bar Porter at Olympia. At
the end of a shift he drank in
The Beaconsfield in Blythe Rd. It was there
that he made friends with Danka who
was in The Plant at Olympia which issued
knives, forks and spoons etc. Her Mam came
from The Land of Eng while her Da
was from The Land of Po. In her
past life she had used to act. She
still took *The Stage* and looked out for
such jobs but it was hard for her
as she had hurt her back in the
last one with The Incubus Theatre. Mac
took up with a kind girl named Ewa
whom he had met on the Post at
Morn Cres. On some nights slept with her
at her place in Kentish Town but they
drank in *The Black Lion* as they liked
to walk in Kensington Gdns. Mac did not
think much of him self at the time.
His life was a mess and things could
not last. Once with her he bumped in
to an old pal named Brad at The
Serpentine Gallery. Mac had known him in the
house at Hazlitt Rd when he was at

LSE. He felt shamed and did not keep
in touch. His Mam told him that she
had heard from an old school friend of
Mac's called Rog who wished to see him.
He was now a Jesuit and taught
at a school in Washington. In his fall
from grace to the depths of Olympia for
which he jobed him self, Mac felt far
too shamed to meet him. He had heard
from it that he had been fined £50
by The Court in Newcastle which he now
had to pay off at £1 a week.
It was brought home how his life had
changed for the worse and so there was
just no way that he could face him.
/In his home less state Mac went
to Leics 'tween jobs at *Cruft's Dog Show*
& *The Smithfield Show*. Each ws an odd,
closed world of its own in which he
lived thru the days tho he felt quite
dead 'cept when he drank like a fiend
and came to life for a few hours
with those like him in dives at night.
As the folk with pride in their Breeds
split first by Age, Sex, Age and Class
vied for The Best Dog of The Year
at *Crufts* Mac barked in shame in side
and felt leashed to life like the worst.

At *The Smithfield Show* he moved in a
trance thru a large mass of scrubbed men
with crowds of their sons and heirs in
green gum boots with red faced cheeks and
necks from The Shires. As if in a
weird dream each long day he picked his
way thru a large maze of pens full
of pink pigs and spot less cows washed
clean as well as herds of goats with
beards and loud sheep and huge bulls each
with a bright round badge on its
ear won for 1st, 2nd or 3rd Prize.
Then in June Danka wrote to say that
she missed him a lot which gave him
a boost. She was ing and paint her
flat and hoped that he would soon be
in touch. Mac went back to her place
for one night from *The Beaconsfield* and then
moved in with her to Pennard Mansions, a late
Victorian Block in The Bush. The fear that
he would end up on the street was
eased. He was glad to have some where
to live and pleased that he had found
some one with whom he got on so
well. Mac had a sense that she shared
his angst as they talked of the forms
of class strife in The Land of Eng.
They were both full of wrath at Tebbit
who had told folk to get on their
bikes in the wake of the Brixton Riots.
/It was not long till they went for
tea with her Ma and Da in Wimbledon.
In the sun they sat on their deck
chairs of the sort that one hires and
strolled on The Common. At the same
time it was strange for him to live
back in Sheperds Bush. In fact Pennard Mans
were just a few blocks down Goldhawk Rd
from Sycamore Gardens. The flights of stone stps
up to her flat on the fifth floor
were like those in Baird Hse. Danka saved
his life one night when they came back
from the pub. On the top flight she
turned and grabbed him to stop his ing
and fall in which he could well have
hit and hurt his head. They used to
hear Blues Bands in *The Sheperds Bush Hotel*.
Mac got gripped by Young's 'Special Bitter' and
all the old pubs of 'The Family Brewery'.
They went out quite a lot at night
to drink at *The Brook Green Hotel* and
The Thatched House in Dalling Rd. The last
was not far from Flora Grdns Primary School
where at the age of eight Mac had
cheered The Queen to the throne in 1953.
/When the jobs at the Shows ran out

what Mac had saved did not last long. He was fraught when he could not drink. One day he said that as Danka was out at work, if she gave him some cash he would take both their things to The Laundrette. On the sly he washed them by hand in the bath so that he could buy some cans of beer with the few Pounds that he saved. He felt in the depths of shame and jumped at the the chance in Sept when he saw a sign for a full time job in the wind of the *The Bushranger* in Goldhawk Rd. He got a job on the spot and it did not take long to see why. The Head Bar man who lived in and drank halves of Stout all day and night looked like a Scare Crow. It was a loud, rough place with tough men from The Land of Ire and The West Indies on each side of the pub. On the first night Mac worked there a drunk came in and asked for a Scotch. While Mac turned to get it the man pissed gainst the Bar. One of the Staff was a Vet who had served with The Brits in Belfast. He hit him on the back of his head with a stool and threw him out.

Next morn the news was that the man who had roamed off had been killed in the night. He had been doused in oil and set a light. In the Bar not a word more was said. As Dave Stewart & Barbara Gaskin sang *Its My Party*, Mac Mac could not grasp how he came to find him self in the midst of such a night mare and how since it was a hit for Leslie Gore his life had gone down hill. He numbed out as he strived to see how he could have come to end up in side such a dump of a pub just yards from the site of his own child hood in Sycamore Gdns. The plus side of the job was that he could drink to dull the pain. The Lease on the place did not have long to run and the Stock check was loose. He now drank from The Top Shelf too and at times just helped him self to Rum and Scotch. He spent a calm Xmas with Danka's Mam and Dad in their sane world in Wimbledon but had to get back to work as Kool & The Gang sang *Get Down on It* at New Year . It was as if time had stood still while he stayed on at *The Bushranger*. When

he stared out at the arch of the
Bush Mart he just could not work out
what Mac was ing and do there at
all. As Madness sang *It Must Be Love*
he could not grasp how he had come
to be there. In a way it was
clear that he did not fit yet he
had a place there. His life had reached
a point where he was caught up in
the whole sub ure cult of ing and
drink in both Sheperd's Bush and Hamm. As
well as his ing of drink in his
long hours at work for five and a
half days a week, on his day off
Mac used to sup in near by pubs
like *The British Prince*, *The Sheperd & Flock*,
The Goldhawk and *The Wheatsheaf* in Goldhawk Rd.
They were all just yards frm Sycamore Gdns.
/At last Mac got out of *The Bushranger*.
It left him with no funds but
he could not stand it and had to
leave. In Aug the heat in Danka's small
place on the fifth floor at Pennard Mans
was too much and he spent some
nights on the flat roof up to which
there were steel rungs on the side of
one wall. Some how he got an old
mat tress up through the trap door. At

night with a drink it was cool but
in the morn he would wake in fear
in the glare of the bright sun light.
Neath the sky he felt small and in
dread as he lay six floors high with
just a low wall round the edge. When
Danka strained her back and was off work
she asked Mac to get her Sickness Benefit.
He felt shame but could not help it
as he cashed the cheque and had to
drink it. As he got back to Pennard
Mansion he crept past the door of the
flat and took his stash of cans up
to the roof. He knew that Danka lay
on the bed down stairs in wait for
him to come back with food. He felt
much guilt but in shame he slipped in
and out to the shop for his drink
and just stayed up there on his own
for the few days he made it last.
/Mac starts to act in more strnge ways
that gave him pause for thought. Though they
did not know him well, on his night
off Mac and Danka went for a drink
to *The Hop Poles* in King St with
the Bar man from *The Brook Green Hotel*.
At one point Mac went to get a
round of drinks with a £20 note which

the bloke gave him. He just walked out
of the pub and left Danka on her
own with him as he blacked out. By
now Mac looked ill kempt with flat lank
hair and scurf on his scalp that he
had not washed for quite a while. In
his worn clothes he felt like a scruff.
It still hurt one Sun morn when an
old boy in Sheperds Bush Road who
who drank in *The Bushranger* said he could
see that Mac was down and in a
bad way 'On Skid Row' and took him
for a drink to *The Sheperds Bush Hotel*.
/As time went on Mac did not know
what else to do and took a job
as a Barman at *The Anglesea Arms* in
Selswood Terrace. It stocked Real Ale but he
could not stand the place full of bright
young suits in such a smart part of
South Ken. He got a lunch but was
shamed when he found that he had to
help in the morns to clean the loos.
/He paid off the last of his Fine
to Newcastle Magistrates Court at last but in
weeks he was sacked as he drank in
the Bar and was told that he was
'in a dream'. He signed on once more
and made dole. He spent most of his

cheque for food and rent on drink. In
Oct he got a night coach up to
The Land of Cots to take Mike in
to dry out at Edinburgh Royal Infirmary. He
had DT's and Mac thought it was a
sad way to spend his Birth Day. Though
he was in fear him self as he
knew that he could not stop his own
ing of drink, Mac was glad that he
was not that bad. Mike was irked to
hear it from The Doc that the last
20 years had caught up with him. He
could not work and went on The Sick.
/In The New Year of 1983 Mac tried
to make a new start. Thru a mist
he saw Ads in *The Guardian* for an
MA in Psychiatric Social Work at Manchester U.
A full time Grant for two years drew
him. For weeks he filled in the form
but in the end did not send it.
He would have gone back to aid Mike
who had to dry out once more in
The Royal Infirmary but his ex wife Sue
went and helped him back to work while
he drank tea in stead of Scotch. Mac
had his own probs. Things had got to
a point with Danka that when he drank
she would stay with her Ma and Da

in Stoneleigh. One week end when she had
left him Mac felt low and a sense
of lack as he dwelt on the name
of the pint of Fuller's Extra Special Bitter
that he drank at *The Salutation* in King St.
By the time he got to *The Joiners Arms*
he could not bear it deep in the
ness of lin and lone. He had to
get out of it but did not have
the means to get drunk. He felt so
fraught in him self that he went next
door and just took some wine from the
shelf in Marks & Spencer. When he drank
it in a trice at home and went
back for more he was caught and charged
with ing of steal at Hamm Police Station.
Some one took his Prints and for a
few hours he was put in the cells.
As the doors clanked and clanged shut he
felt scared and at risk as he feared
they could do what they liked with him.
He had time to think too that it
was a far cry from when he had
been so proud to be in the clink
with his best friend Bill at Bow St
at the time of the war in Nam.
/At first Mac tried to treat it like
a big joke and laughed it off when

he told Danka that he had copped it
at *The Spotted Horse* in Putney High St.
With a pint in his hand he was
full of show. In Court he would rep
him self with a speech from The Dock.
When weeks passed and at the last he
had to meet a dead line to get
Legal Aid, he ran just in time down
to Owen White & Catlin in King St.
When asked by The Brief if he had
a drink prob Mac cringed in shame and
said No. He fawned and held that he
took The Hocks on a whim. The JP
was told the same when The Case came
up. Mac found him self in the same
Dock in which his Da stood when Moll
had got a Legal Sparation. When it came
down to it Mac felt great shame and
as if he had done as huge a
crime as Raskolnikov. In his mind he feared
his name in large type would be on
the front page of *The Sheperds Bush Gazette*
and that his Mam would die of shock.
In the end he got off with one
year's 'Conditional Discharge' and The Case did not
make the small print or the back page.
/When it was done with in The Spring
Mac and Danka went up to Dalmeny for

a break. At times they had fun but things did not go too well with Mike as they had not done on his past trip. Mac tried once more to get through to him but just irked his Bro who was not clear what he sought from him when he brought up their child hood. Most such times Mac was not too sure him self and was hurt when Mike griped that he was just ing and try to drag old things out of him which drained him. When drunk Mac carped o'er and o'er that he got no help at all from Mike with their Mam and still sneered at his kind of work. At the end of such a bout Mac rued what he had said. He held that it was not meant. He tried to take it back and blamed The Drink but the way he found fault left its trace and Mike said that all Mac's gloom gave him night mares at a time when the past joy had gone out of his work and he found it hard him self to go on. Mac was glad to write to him when he and Danka got back that they had been round to see Moll at Baird. She had not been hap at first as he had not called for such a long time but she cheered up when they took her with them to see *Irish Mist* at *The Hop Poles*. A lot of what they both wrote spoke of that which they could not know. /Mac took heed of Mike's ness of ill and his need to go in to The

Royal Infirmary. He was rapt as KC and The Sunshine Band sang *Give It Up* and for his part Mac tried hard to cut down his Ing of drink when he and Danka took a break in Aug. He was sworn to have less for he drove a lot on the trip to Wales which was good for him. While he vowed just to have one or two he sneaked pints at the Bar and the wait from one drink to the next meant pain. At the same time they had a good trip on which they made camp for the first time in the brack and brake on the hill side at the cliff site that looks down at the sea in Newgale. When drunk on real

ales Mac had got a tent in a
Sale. It had a small tear in the
tarp which he could not seal. He felt
a bit of a prat when it left
quite a big gap. For both it was
a time of peace once they got through
their first night which was still and calm

till the loud blasts of noise all but
killed them with fright as F111's flew low
to the Base near by at RAF Brawdy.
/In Sept Mac and Danka made a big
move from West to South Lon. She had
made up her mind to take a new
path and had got a place in Oct
to do a Part Time Degree in Psychology
at Goldsmiths College in New Cross. She then
got a paid job as a Sec at
The Institute of Psychiatry in Denmark Hill. Thru
it they found a nice top floor flat
to rent in Grove Park. Mac was full
of hope to make a fresh start. He
meant to be more resp, to pay his
share of all the Bills and to drink

less. He signed on in Brixton and went
back to his work on Marx' Theory of Value.
In June Mrs Thatcher had got back in
with a land slide win and it spurred
him back to work in The Reading Room
at The BM where he went fixed days
each week. At the same time he drank
more. He did not know Camberwell and felt
quite out of place there. He was irked
since Danka was on her Course three nights
a week. He felt lost on his own.
He drank by him self at home and
in *The Grove Tavern* or *The George Canning*.
/As Mac worked on the draft of his
planned book *On Capital* he was firm in
his own mind that he had made an
imp break thru in his own work on
Marx' Theory of Value and Labour Power. In
his own head Mac was quite sure when
he made a note that he had a
'clear view' of it while he sat in
wait for Danka at *The Brook Green Hotel*.
He pledged the book to Frances. In Nov
he did not laze but sought those who
might help to get his text in print.
When he met TC who had been on
the Board of *TP* and had pull at
RKP for a drink in *The Chippenham* he

now found him luke warm when it came
to Marx. Mac blacked out to find him
gone with his own pint still quite full.
Drunk out his mind Mac went down to
see JM in Brighton who held sway at
The Harvester Press. In Dec JS wrote a
nice note back but said he could not
print the book. In the same month Mac
asked GN to see what he could do
at NLB. He claimed that he would but
no thing came from it. As Xmas loomed
Mac lied to Danka and did not go
to stay with his old friends in Leics.
While she went to Stoneleigh he drank his
way through it in bed with a large
stash of cheap beer and wine from Sainsbury's.
She rang him now and then to check
him out as days passed in a haze.
/In The New Year Mac was pleased when
his old friend Thor got in touch. They
had not met for years. He was irked
whn Thor changed his mind and did not
ask him to crew his yacht on a
trip to France as his ing of drink
was too much and it would not be
safe on a small boat. Mac did what
he could to cut down and as Spring
came on he helped Danka to prep for

her end of term tests at Goldsmiths College.
He did his best to keep in touch
with his Mam at Baird House but a
lot of the time their rows found him
in *The Springbok* with a pint of stout
to drown his rage. He wrote to PA
at NLB and to PH at RKP but
got no where. He went to see MG
at Loughboro University and BF at Birkbeck College
but he felt let down by their lack
of zeal for his work. Some how it
came to nought as he found him self
with cans on his bench on Peckham Rye.
He felt lost on his own in the
ness of lin and lone but looked down
on poor sots who drank in groups. They
tossed back all kinds of stuff like cans
of Special Brew and Meths. He felt like
shit him self but thought he was not
that bad as he still read *The Guardian*.
/At the end of term Danka said once
more that they had a 'need to talk'.
He had come to dread it when she
said this as he knew that it meant
a probe in to some thing he had
done or not done. He was still shocked
when she made her first threats to go.
He swore that he would sort things out

or leave him self. In Sept when she went to Israel for her hols he tried to perk up. He was scared of a scene once more like the one when Sue had left but by then did not know if he was ing of come or go. When Danka got back to Lon and rang from Stoneleigh he urged her to stay for a while as he was pissed. Mike wrote to ask Mac what he was up to and to write and say what he felt a bout him but he could not do it. Mac woke up shocked one morn at Baird House to find he had lost the draft of his book. He found it in *The Hop Poles*. He tried to cut down once more when he and Danka camped in Dorset. Mac loved it as he drove round Chesil Beach & Portland Bill and showed her scenes from his child hood trip on the Isle of Wight but felt forced to drink and could not stay out of the pub. /So when they got back to Lon Mac thought up a plan to stop his ing of drink. He would get Danka to drop him at a camp site on his own with no cash for a week. A fool could see that if he did not have the means he could not drink. In the end Mac got her to drive him to a site at Henley but as she left he coaxed her to leave him some small change for things like post cards and stamps and *The Guardian*. It all meant just more pain and was no cure as through out the week in quaint old pubs he just eked this out on Halfs of Brakespeare's Beer. /Mac thought that things could not get worse but they did. At the end of Sept Paul rang from Leics to say that Elaine had died. Mac was in his ness of sad as she had been a good friend for a long time. She was the first one close that he had lost. He was shamed to meet Dons who had known him well in the past at her grave side. When he got back to Lon with just a few Pounds a new kind of shame hit when he had to walk past the men from the Mines who shook pails in the Tube with smiles and nods to those who gave as they were down to build up their Strike Fund. Most of the pits had been closed since March. He felt bad in side as he just had to slink past and drink the small sum that he would have liked to give to their cause. /Mac's fear got worse. It got so bad when he woke and had his first fag that he 'gan to put it off each hour till he stopped. One fine morn when he had some cash he went for a drink down by The Thames. In *The Rutland* he asked for a pint of beer but when it came he was so tense that he just could not pick it up. In face of The Bar Man in front of him, his fear as froth spilled down the straight glass was that it would slip through his hand or get crushed in his fist. He had to wait till the man moved a way to leave it and run out the door. Mac's shame got worse with his his debt. He felt like a leech when he cadged a drink from Danka. As she came back from work, with a lot of guile he would bribe her to go 'for one' to *The George Canning*. He made the pint last as long as he could and would press for or plead like a child for one more. Quite loud rows in the Bar came to be the norm. Once when of her friends was due to come to the flat he took mon from her purse so that he could get a way to The Pub. At times he was fraught and had to go out on his own. One time he had no thing and made mad threats to throw a chair through the wind if she would not give him the cash to get a drink. When she yelled back at him and asked what had he turned in to he heard her but did not know. At night if they slept in Danka's bed he had a dread that he would wake up in the morn to find that he had choked her. One night when they shared a bed at a friend's house in Godstone he kicked her out of it in a rage. By then Mac could not tell what he would do if he drank and at times was shocked in the morns to see black marks left from kicks at night on Danka's bed room door which she had locked when he was drunk. One time then he felt that the Land lord down stairs made too much noise it was due to their ance of for and bear that he was not hurt when he made threats to him and his Bro in a black out. Mac knew that he ought not to drink so much but did not know how to curb it. Why did not some one just stop him? In vain he wished they would. The same thought of ing and stop came back in his mind o'er and o'er. In his own mind Mac tranced that he just could not drink if he was locked a way and thought that he would get The Law to do it. He would mug some one or throw a brick through the wind of a shop in High St Ken. In the end it was Danka who helped him. As she went back to her Course at Goldsmiths in Oct, her last word to Mac was that he had to get help to stop his ing of drink or she would leave. He got her to go with him drunk to see Mr Orf, on his time with whom Mac still used to dote. Shocked at his state Mr Orf thought he might need to go in to Hosp. In a way Mac still held out that he could do it on his own but when she wrote a gain frm Stoneleigh in Nov why she had to leave him, he did go with Danka to *Accept* in W Brmptn. Mac went once but would not go back as he did not like the fact that the yong man who saw him wore just a T shirt and jeans. He did not dress in a styled suit like Mr Orf nor was he as suave. Yet at the start of Dec Mac toed the line and went up to see his Welsh GP in Camberwell who sent him on with a note to The Maudsley. Mac's shakes wre so bad that it was hard for him to walk straight so they gave him a large dose of Hemanevrin and a Scrip for the next ten days. In a way Mac felt let down as he would have liked them to take him in and to take care of him. He got drunk when the pills wore off and went back to ask for more. He felt quite hurt and scared when the hard Doc said no and put it to him that he should ring a group run by those who knew how to stop their ing of drink and how to stay stopped. It crossed his mind that the cruel bitch did not know who he was but Mac was in huge fear that he would be left on his own if he did not. He knew that Danka had one foot out the door so back at home he gave in. At the end he drank a few cans of weak beer and phoned for help.

Chapter 8

Mac's night mare did not end at once. He was stunned at the start of Dec when he went with a man from The Land of Ire who lived in Camberwell to his first Group for those who wished to stop ing of drink. It turned out to be held in the old Church Hall at the back of *Our Lady of Victories* in Abingdon Rd off High Street Ken. It made him think how his life had not at all worked out the way he had hoped. While at The Vaughan School he had gone in to the same church through the big front door. In the Group there was a mixed crowd that one might see in the street. Mac was thrown when it was led by a smart young girl who could have just stepped right out of *Vogue*. He had thought that it would be full of old men in long soiled macs tied with odd bits of string and that he would just take the pis. Pressed down it was too much when some hailed him with a broad smile but at least it looked as if they were pleased to see him. They seemed to take him for who he was and not to care what he had done in the dark past or to judge him.

/A girl who sat next to The Sec spoke of how her ing of drink had marred her life for years. At the end she had walked miles in the snow to get one. She was glad to have learned in the group that she had a ness of ill called 'Alcoholism' and had found a way to stop her ing of drink and to get well. Mac could not take in all that was said as she spoke so fast but he heard some say back to her that they too had changed and did not now need to drink. At the end of the Meet he could see that they seemed hap to sip tea out of cups and that some thing had worked for them. For him self Mac was scared that he had gone too far and got caught up in some kind of sect like The Jains. In his low state it did sound much too good to be true when told that he was on the cusp of a new life; if he did stop his ing of drink there was no thing he could not do. /Mac voiced his doubts. He had not come for 'God' which he read on wall scrolls. Some urged him not to fret and just to put it on one side for now.

They urged him to come back and he
got some small hope when they gave him
a book, *Where To Find*. He could see
there were lots of Groups each day
in all parts of Lon which he felt
at once met his needs. In that mode
next day he did not drink and went
to a Lunch Time Group at Hinde St
but drank in the eve. In the next
months on dry days he went to more
like it up in town and diff parts
of Lon. That most Ings of Meet were
held in Church Halls fed his doubts but
he was told it was due to the
fact they could be hired for low rent
and were held in all kinds of rooms.
A lot were full of smoke like pubs
which helped him feel at home. On days
when he stayed dry Mac was wracked with
fear. It was fuelled when he went back to
Baird House to see his Mam and found
a start had been made to knock down
The White City Stadium. The huge old place
had been there through out his child hood
nd as Gorbachov saw in Glasnost and Perestroika
and the old world crashed down round his
ears he felt each smashed brick that fell.
To block it out he tried hard to

read 'neath the dome in The British Museum.
/On days when he still drank Mac slid
back in to a dark place. At a
time when he had no cash to drink
he had found a way with a knife
to slide coins from the Gas Meter. With
guilt he would drink for a day or
two but then be filled with fear and
find a way to put them back. A
real fight went on in side him. He
cut right down and drank much less at
Yule with Danka. He could say yes as
Band Aid askd *Do They Know Its Xmas?*
/At the end of Jan Mac was stunned
to get a phone call out of the
blue from his daught Fran. He had not
seen her for five years. She had got
in touch with his Mam and wished to
see him. He got quite drunk that night
but had fixed to meet her the next
week at *The Place* in Euston where she
went once a week for a class at
The Lon School of Cont Dance. On their
way to it both glanced but passed in
the street. Once there they had to look
twice to hug. Mac did not have much
cash but they had a cup of tea
in a cafe and tried to talk. He

sought to tell her how he had got
ill with ing of drink and why he
had not seen her for so long. She
did not say that much at all but
it was hard for Mac to learn how
in those five years his old friend Mik
had been there at home in his place.
/With his long hair and old jeans Mac
felt that he looked like Rasputin and was
not The Dad whom Fran had hoped to
meet. He got pissed that night. He had
sworn to her that he would not ring
ring Jill if drunk, so when Fran told
him on the phone in days that he
had Mac felt he must have blacked out.

He was just sick and tired of it
and felt bushed. In a flash he knew
that if he wished to have Fran back
in his life he could not keep on
in the same old way. There was a
shift in him as his wish not to drink
out weighed the one to go on. In
The Rooms he had the strength to make
a choice to stop on Feb 4th which
was Danka's own Birth Day. In side
he felt a ness of calm and still.
/At Ings of Meet he had been told
that there were steps he had to take
to get well at which he bilked. Hung
on wall scrolls in old script they had
looked to Mac just like The Ten Cmmndmnts.
He baulked at such acts till he met
a man who used to cite Wittgenstein and
lead him to see that he was free
to scan and to make sense of them
as he wished. He might read 'tween the
lines and make of them what he would
which turned out to be a great deal.

As he had drunk his life in to
the ground for years it was apt for
him to bow to the fact that a
day at a time he should not drink.
He could not man age it on his
own but could have some faith in the
force of the groups that kept folk from
ing of drink. He was a husk of
his old self but might trust that there
was strength in them in to which he
might tap if he let go of self

will and kept a pledge to get well.
/So Mac braved the hordes who shopped in
Oxford St and went to mid day Ings
of Meet at Hinde St five times a
week as well as groups in all parts
of Lon at night time. His dole was
small but he spent a good part of
it on a Travel Card each week. Some
days he went to three Ings of Meet.
He woke up with fear each morn but

felt safe while he was in The Rooms.
He wished to take large strides at once
and sighed when he heard that it was
'a cinch by the inch' and 'hard by
the yard'. It was slow and he did
not like cliques but he got to know
a few names and made friends with some.
He met one or two cranks but on
the whole he learned to trust folk and
lost his fear that it was a cult.
He met diff sorts from all walks of

life from those who used to kip in
skips and squats in Brick Lane to the
spick and span who shone in Park Lane.
Side by side in Groups there were Lords
and Peers as well as Loords and Louts.
Once more he felt part of life as
he mixed both with the rank and file
and the Top Brass as he had in
India. He had spent so much time
on his own for years and was now
keen to hear and learn of their lives
from the strange cast, some of whom loved
their cats while some used to hate them.
/Mac bought a cheap Cassio so that he
could be prompt to get to his Groups.
From the first he had been struck by
the way folk kept time. Most Ings of
Meet would start and end on the dot.
He was thrilled like a child to buy
small things like choc that was not a
drink. At times he was in bits with
out one but held back from the brink.
His will not to take one was shored
up by those round him. Like them he
he learned to live with in him self.
/In May when Mac reached his set mark
of three months with out a drink he
thought there was a poss that he could

keep it up. He went with his Mam
to The VE Festival on The South Bank.
He took France out to hear jazz at
The Barbican and to see Peter Hyams's *2010*
at The Empire in Leics Square. In The
Rooms Mac still had doubts. It was put
to him that it would be good for
him to buy and read a big book
which set out twelve steps and told how
those who wrote it used them to stop
their ing of drink in the 1930's. As
Mac gauged its price at 4 Pints of Stout
he still asked if it was worth it.
On the whole Mac was glad not to
drink but at times would have liked to
throw it out the wind when he was
still left in pain and did not feel
well. His ing of drink left him with
much shame. When dry at times he felt
like a husk of him self as if
he would split and spalt in to bits.
He had drunk to be a man yet
with out a drink he felt a waif.
/Yet he could look down on folk as
failed. Did they not knw who He was?
For Mac it seemed as if he was
in a time warp. He was there in
the flesh but his mind was full of

the old days when he had got his
First at Leics. Years had passed while his
ing of drink had gone on but his
head was full of Joni Mitchell's *Blue* Allbum
of 1971. It was as if time had
stopped. One eve he went all the way
from South Lon up to an Ing of
Meet at Holly Wlk in Hampstead but could
not go in through the door. His peer
group at Leics were now Profs. In his
mind's eye the room was full of Dons
in wait to judge his ure of fail.
/In june Mac was 40 years old and
what had he got to show for it?

He wrote out what he could rem of
his life and when he shared it with
with a friend in The Rooms he felt
as if he had done no thing with
it. He had made a mess of his
great opps and it had all gone wrong.
The dark thought that he had failed used

to haunt him all the time. As Danka
left for work at The Inst of Psychiatry,
when he woke up each morn a part
of Mac's fear and shame was that he
still had no job and had to sign
on the dole. He had grown up with
the norm that a real man must have
a full time job. He saw Dr Pollack
once each month at The Maudsley but was
tired and mixed up and did not app
for Incapacity Benefit as he might have done.
In The Rooms Mac had learned that he
had a ness of ill called 'Alcoholism'. At
the same time in his mind's eye he

tried to think of him self as fit
for work. From May his first thought had
been to go back to what he had
done in the past. On good days It
meant more of the same as he went
to read at The British Museum and thought
who might bring out his book on *Capital*.

Mac did not feel that he had the
strength to teach and when he was dry
for six months in August he was still
not sure what to do. Each day he
sat in The Rooms with a chance to
speak but full of wrath with him self
and a life that still felt as if
it was on hold. He stayed mute as
he just did not know what to say.
/Out in the world Mac's Land Lord would
not take their rent and had forced him
and Danka out of the flat in Camberwell.
In the Spring with help from Dad she
bought a ground floor flat in Raul Road
in Peckham. Mac liked the fact that it
was near the bus stop and the shops
in Rye Lane. He cleared a big plot at
the back of the house in which she
grew lots of tall plants and fresh veg.
and where they ate out when it was
warm. The move helped thm to make a
new start for a while. They both had
need of time to sort out what it
meant for them that Mac did not drink.
He could not see why Danka got irked
at home when she asked him to take
his turn to wash up he would say
'Live and Let Live' or when she wished

to make plans for the week he would
plead, 'It's just a day at a time'.
/In Sept Mac and Danka drove up to
The Land of Cots when Mike wed Yvonne
in Sth Queensferry nr where they lived at
Dalmeny. Moll was pleased once more to meet
Lord & Lady Roseberry who helped to plan it.
Mac's shame was brought out by Moll's pride
in his Bro's ing of work for them.
Mac just held on to the fact that
while he did not have such a job
nor did he need to drink with the
help of folk in The Rooms in Edinburgh.
Held by groups back in Lon the same
held true for the rest of the year.
Tho they were not that far from the
scene on the wild Front Line of the
Brixtn Riots he felt hale and with Danka
had a calm Xmas in their new flat.
/Since he had been in The Rooms Mac
had seen quite a bit of his Mam.
Like a good son he had been to
see her once a week. He could still
be hurt by her wrath but did his
best to make up for his own ire
in the years of drink. In The New
Year she was in the ness of down
so he gave her cash to get her

hair done and took her to a group
for friends and kin of those who drank
at Southwark Cathedral. Moll felt a lot for
the rest of them in their plight but
in her ness of sad she did not
feel it could help her. On her Birth
day in Feb Mac took her to the
Christy Moore Concert at *The Ritzy* in Brixton.
With out a drink Mac did his best
to heal things with his Bro too. On
his own first Birth day on Feb 4th
he had asked Mike and his Ex named
Penny with their daught Gypsy for a meal
at Raul Road. Mike was drunk and it
was awk but at least it helped them
to meet for the first time in years.
/At that time too Mac had got thru
his fear and found a voice in The
Rooms. He had said brief things now and
then but for the first time he shared
his strngth and hope with a Group for

half an hour at The Passage Day Centre.
It had helped when a man had said
to Mac that they had come not to
see through him but to see him thru.
Mac felt as if he had got to
a new stage in his growth and soon
spoke once more to a Group in the
Hall at The Lon Oratory. He knew that
he had grown too when he loped his
way up the steep hill and went back
to the Group in Holly Walk and told
them how it was a year since he
had first tried to get through the door.

/Now and then tho Mac walked out of
Groups in great angst if folk spoke too
much of 'God'. His faith was the works
and deeds of the mass in The Rooms.
In Spring he helped to greet folk at
The Fri Group in Margaret St. In Sept
he got the great job to make the
tea on Sun at The Gordon Hosp Group
and then in Oct to sell The Lit
at The Fri Lunch Group at Hinde St.
/Thus Mac found ways in which he could
live life with out a sole drink. He
asked some from The Rooms home for meals.
His friends Bill and Mave had come to
stay in April and they all went to
see QPR lose to Oxford at Loftus Road.
He and Danka hung out with them
in Banbury and poled punts midst the chaps
and chumps up to japes and jaunts on
The Thames. Down in Rye with his pal
John he could sit in the pub for
a short while with a soft drink. The
same was true when he and a close
pal saw Wolves lose to Aldershot at Molyneux.
Nor did Mac have to drink when he
took Frances out for a trip to row
on The Thames at Twickenham. He tied the
boat up neath a tree where they had
a soft drink with their packed lunch. It
was a good day for both of them.
/It seemed like news of some one else
and too good to be true when Frances
rang Mac in June to say that she
had a part to dance in Beethoven's *Fidelio*
at The Royal Opera House in Covent Garden.
Mac took Danka and his Mam. They were

all thrilled and with pride left Frances a large Spray at The Stage Door. The next week Mac queued on his own for the Prom and took some pics from close to the stage when she took her last bow. Mac learned he could keep calm and did not have to drink when things went well. The same held true in the Sum when he and Danka walked The Thames Path in their boots and camped a week at Lechlade. He was fine on his own when she went off to Spain for a few weeks. /Frances' feat was a boost to Mac who was still not clear what to do with his own life. At the same time it was a sad truth that he got a kind of grudge that she had done so well while it had been his own fate fate to fail. In Jan it was hard for him to take when Mike had got a new well paid job with lots of scope at Burleigh Hse nr Stamford in Lincs. He and Yvonne had leased The Bothy Cottage with lawn in a glade near a copse on The Burleigh Estate. The House it self had been built for Sir William Cecil in C16 by Elizabeth 1st. Mike had been hired by Lady Victoria Leatham to re store the Vanderbank Tapestries that still hang there. It was a fine place to live on the edge of the Deer Park where herds of Elks, Harts and Stags strayed. In the Spring sheep and lmbs roamed free midst becks and brooks while hares ran here and there. Mike worked in a large old Fruit Store next to his place. In it he kept his dyes, balls of wool, hanks of yarn, skeins of thread in coils and folds of cloth. Near a bin for trash an old pair of shears on a nail hung from its shank. /His Bro lived in the grand style there but when Mac and Danka stayed with him in June and Aug his ing of drink had got worse. By then his Bro more or less drank round the clock and Mac put his wife in touch with a group to get help. In Sept when Mac was there Yvonne chose to leave Mike. Her hope

that the move from Dalmeny to Burleigh would
mean a bright new start had been dashed.
While he stayed with his Bro Mac went
to share at The Rooms in Peterboro and
then stayed close that year back in Lon.
He went each day and it paid off.

/The need to drink had gone but Mac
had lost his way in life as well
as his mind in the years of waste
and did not know if he could get
them back. For months he went on with
his work on Marx at The British Museum
which he sent to friends but did not
get much hope from them. He thought to
teach a Course on *Capital* at night class
but did not feel sure of him self.
Once a month he still saw Dr Pollack
at The Maudsley. It helped to talk for
an hour of how one copes from day
to day but there was no chance of

work at much depth so in July he
wrote to The Psychotherapy Dept. In mid Nov
with the help of a Dr Bell there
he made up his mind to app once
more for low cost therapy to The Lon Clinic.
Mac was quite close to the thought that
he might have to give up his years
of work on Marx' Theory of Value when
he was cheered by a Marxist from Iran
he met in The Reading Room. Ahmed too
worked on *Capital* and they met to talk
a great deal in the year to come.
/In New Year 1987 Mac had to join
a 'Restart' scheme at The DHSS to 'help'
him back to work but he sensed that
it would just lead no where. He was
shocked to find that he felt trapped at
The Job Centre back in a world of
low paid work with long hours at which
Moll had toiled in his child hood and
from which he had dared to leave. He
was glad to be free from drink but
yet woke up with dread each morn. He
still felt lost when it came to jobs
and in a deep ness of shame not
less but now more the norm. In Dec
in a note to him self Mac had
mused on the poss that he might end

up on his own with no job in
a small furn room or a Council Flat.
/In it Mac wrote too how he been
drawn in by Karen Horney's *Self Analysis* that
he had bought from Karnacs in March. It
had been in the back of his mind
for some time. He would see how he
fared at The London Clinic. Mean while he
stuck close to The Rooms. In Feb he
had not drunk for two years and in
March he went to a large Ing of
Meet held to mark the 40th Anniversary of
The Rooms in Lon. Mac was hap to
keep his own ties with them strong. In
April he was made Sec of the Sunday
Group held at The Gordon Hosp in Victoria
and was glad of strong bonds there. In
May he was seen at last by a
Mr Dreyer from The London Clinic but in
June was turned down for its scheme.
As Mrs Thatcher won her third term he
felt like it but did not drink. He
went on the slow List of ing and
Wait to see some one at The Maudsley.
/In the mean time at the end of
July Mac asked to be made the *Share*
Rep for the West End groups. He made
a start to guide some folk new to

groups who looked to him for help. In
June when his App to The Clinic failed
Mac had seen too that he would have
to give in and do like the rest
of those who got well in The Rooms.
They told him that to get rid of
drink in his life for good he would
have to change his whole way of life.

In a state full of lack in his
self he turned for help to a man
in whom he had some trust with whom
he could share. Strait is the gate and
as Pet Shop Boys sang *It's a Sin*
for long months he wrote down his worst
flaws and fears and all the dark stuff
in the years of drink of which he
was most shamed and which he had thought
he would take to his own grave. It
was not by chance that the man he
chose to share it with when he got

the pluck to take this step was ill
and it was thought he did not have
long to live. As it was he soon
got quite well once more and was there
for Mac for some years. At the time
Mac's fear was such, that he did not
ask him home to share but hired a
a small back room at Hinde St. In

first dream that felt sig and was the
first one he then typed. When he did
so he typed it out line for line.
It was a small but imp sign that
he was set to take new steps to
change him self. He had asked for the
help of a Therapist at The Maudsley but
knew he would then just have to wait.
/In the mean time Mac had to try and
come to terms with his past years of
ing and drink so he made quite a
long list of all those that he had
harmed and met or wrote them. He tried
to be there for Moll. On New Year's
Eve he and Danka had brought her to
a big Dance for those in The Rooms

the end it helped Mac too to list
and share the traits he steemed and in
which he could take some pride.
/As he was hugged and held in the
Rooms Mac grew and got more strength to
grasp the truths of his Self. In April
as Ferry Aid sang *Let It Be* he
wrote down a dream. In July and Aug
he scrawled two more. He kept them safe
but did no thing. In Oct there was
a shift in side when Mac penned a
deep dream that felt imp. It was the

at The Royal College of Art. They all
had a good night and he danced for
the first time with out a drink. For
Moll's Birth day in Feb he got seats
for *The Dubliners* at The Royal Festival Hall.
Frances was not keen to see him a
lot but he met as she wished. He
did not get in touch with Jilly but
chose to tear up her phone no and
let her get on with her own life.
/Mac tried to make up to Danka for
what he had put her thru and helped

where he could with her Degree. She had worked hard at Goldsmiths and in July she got a First in Psychology. When she came back from a trip with Sis to Teneriffe she had made up her mind to move and to buy a house. Mac took months to clear the back yard at Raul Rd. They had to hire a small skip to get rid of all the stuff. They still got on well but as the heir to much doubt Mac was not sure if he wished to move to the same place with her and stay as one. They still shared good times when they went for walks or just sat and talked. On TV they liked to watch *The Great Philosophers* with Brian Magee, *After Dark* and *Voices* with Michael Ignatieff. They both went up to Leics when Mac's friend Paul got wed to Polly. Mac had a grudge as he thought it was too soon. He him self still grieved for his first wife but wished to make it up to Paul for his help in the years of drink. In Sept Mac and Danka went to Mike's place while The Burleigh Horse Trials were on which gave them a rare view of Class in that world of The Rich. Mac had been up on his own in March and June to help him build a work frame. His Bro had a new girl friend named Harriet who worked for him but each time his ing of drink was worse. The next month Mac drove South with Danka to see the worst of what had been wreaked by The Great Storm at its heart round Sevenoaks. In a strong wind the leaves still swished down in swirls from The Ash; in skirls and whirls frm The Beech & Birch; in birls and whirls frm The Larch and Plane; in birrs and whirrs from The Elm and Fir; and in skirrs and whorls from The Oak. When the gale had hit Mac had walked all the way frm Peckham to Marylebone so he could set out the Lit Stall for for The Fri Lunch Group at Hinde St. In Dec he clapped as Danka got her Degree at The Albert Hall. They had a good Xmas and danced at New Year's Eve. /For Mac it was a time of change.

Through out the past year he had tried
to dev his work on Marx' Theory of Value
in The Reading Room at The Brit Mus.
He had talked a lot to those like
Ahmed and Mike Baker who were drawn to
the same work. In Nov he joined a
mixed group to read *Capital* which they set
up at Birkbeck College and then met
in the front room on the first floor
of *The Bloomsbury*. He went a few times
but still lacked self worth and found it
hard to find a voice. Some there had
fixed views but by now Mac could own
to him self that he had doubts re
what he had done in his past work
on Labour-power. He ws much less sure of
where he stood on Marx' Theory of Value.
He did not like the fact that the
group was held in a pub. It dawned
on him that he had needs of which
he was not yet clear but which such

a group just could not meet. In side
him self in a ness of deep he
felt cut off from life in a lin
of less and lone fed by all the
time he spent lost in his books in
The Reading Room. Mac knew he had to
get a job where he could do some
good but of what sort he was not
yet clear. In The Rooms he had heard
folk share how they had done all sorts
of things in the past but now worked
as Counsellors. In Sept when he had seen
an Ad for an Alcohol Counsellor Mac had
been to talk to one at *Turning Point*
in Grove Park. It was a poss he
might turn the waste in his years of
drink to some use. He got a big
shock when he found out that a lot
of folk had more exp and he could
not hope just to walk in to such
a Post. With some qualms he booked a
Course called 'Intro to Counsellng' at City Lit
set to start in mid Jan and the
same in Feb at The WPF in Kensington .
In the mean time Mac felt that he
had to get down to the roots of
his doubts and so made up his mind
to try a Surrealist Experiment in Automatic Writing.

Chapter 9

In Jan 1988 Mac got up each morn and wrote as fast as he could for half an hour. He was drawn to the words and for two and a half months he tried to put down on the page the first thing that came to mind. He got a crick in his neck but in two weeks he struck his Dream Mine. Each night he found that he used to mete a dream he put the dream thoughts down too in the form not of pics but of words. At first Mac deemed that each was a one off as he typed it out line by line and then gave it a name next day. His great fear then was that each would be the last but as they used to teem from him in the next months it turned out not to be the case. He ceased to give them names but wrote all down and tried to get their sense when he worked on them next day. Where he could not see what was meant he linked words thru sight and sound. *In the s pa ce d d ream text s he saw w or d s in side w or rds and s ought t h m out.* /As he wrote each day and night Mac tried hard to stay with what he felt but at the same time his fear spread in side such that by mid Feb he was not sure if he was on the right path. When he went to meet him Mr Orf warned that 'there was no smoke with out fire'. Mac's dread grew when at some points his great rage led him to want not to write on the page but to pierce and tear it with his pen. He wrote in the heart of each sheet for fear that he would get too close to the edge and by mid March he just had to stop. With some care he took weeks to type out the whole text. While he read *The Uses of Enchantment* by Charles Bettleheim he still wrote down more and more dreams and did his own dream work. As that grew in the next years it was clear that he had struck a rich vein which changed his whole way of life. /In June Mac had not drunk for more than three years yet felt stuck in fear. He had been to 'Intro to Counselling' at both The City Lit and The WPF but was not at all sure of his way. As he read all of *Under The Volcano* by Malcolm Lowry he knew that he had changed but as Mac sat in The Rooms and heard how some seemed to get on

with their lives he felt as if he
was in the slow lane. He was stunned
to find him self on each page in
Adult Children of Alcoholics by Janet Woititz. He
went to one of their groups held in
Notting Hill Gte. At first he had doubts
and scoffed at 'The Inner Child' but he
was drawn back and soon got in touch
with his own. Mac was shocked as he
'gan to reach and to share the deep
grief which he could not show at five
years old when his Dad had gone out of
of his young life. He found out how
deep down he had cleaved to him in
those past bleak years. He shed tears to
a tape he bought on which there was
a trad song that his Dad used to
sing named Skibereen. Mac got hold of his
Death Cert from St Catherine's Hse in Holborn
and in the end made up his mind
to find his Dad's grave. As a way
to heal things with his Mam he asked
her if she would like to go with
him. He was moved as she knelt in
he snow and shed tears in Chatham Cemetery.
/At that time Mac had found a book
f William Blake's Collected Writngs in which he
had been much moved by his short verse
in Songs of Innocence. For some months Mac
had rhymed odd words hewn from his own
dream mine. He had heaved sighs as they
struck sad chords but he now wrote out
a first short verse for his Dad called
Leaves in November. In Aug he took Moll
to The Frankie Vaughan Show at The Barbican.
/From July Mac went to see Keith Lloyd
once a week for Therapy at The Maudsley.
He was glad of his help and that
of The Rooms in a year of change.
He and Danka were still not quite sure
if they would move as one when she
found a house in Tresco Road in Nunhead.
Mac felt that in a way he was
just too safe with her. He had read
Fear of Freedom by Eric Fromm and sensed
that if he was to grow he had
to meet it and to face life on
his own at least for a while. Some
thing had made him sign on the list
of ing for those Home Less in wait
with Southwark Council. He queued a lot to
plead his case at The Housing Office in
The Old Kent Road. In June he got
a note which helped from Dr Pollack at
The Maudsley. In Aug Danka moved to her
new house where he helped to dig a

veg patch and put up a new shed
while he camped in a spare room. In
Sept he got the keys to a flat in
Queens Rd in Peckham. The freight trains
made noise as they strained past at night.
With snarls and scowls 'neath hoods like cwls
the chavs led dogs that gnarred and growled.
The Roach had bred in the flat for
months but he cleaned it to move in
and in the end got used to it.
He had done a lot of work to
make good the place in Raul Road for
which Danka got a good price so he
had funds to get stuff for his place.
Mac had to wait but got a new
phone. He joined The NFT and The YHA.
Mr Orf had moved to let his late
debt go but now in a blithe way
Mac waived his dues when he went to
pay it off. He had passed his
Driving Test frst time at Hither Grn which
gave him quite a big boost. He went
out of his way to buy *The Independent*.
Mac kept in touch with Mike but his ing
of drink made him fret as it did
when his Bro said it was Mac's fault
Yvonne had left him. When Mac had been
to stay with Mike in May he had

tried to talk to him of *Faustus* with
Simon Callow which he and Danka had just
seen at The Lyric in Hamm but he
would not join in. When Mac went back
for his Birth day in Sept Mike had
caused a fire in his flat which was
put out in time but could have been
more grim. They saw *She Stoops To Conquer*
at The Arts Centre but of late Mike
just would not go out for a walk
in the fresh air. He went in a
hired cab to buy his food and booze.
/The tale of *Faustus* used to haunt Mac

as he still felt guilt that he had
sold his own soul for drink. He had
fear that in some way he could still
lose it and his mind for the ness
of safe in a paid full time job.
When it came to ing of think on
it his mind would go blank or dwell
on low paid work in to which Mac

had sunk in his days of drink ing.
He was yet in The Restart scheme at
Brixton and had to try for jobs. In
a way he felt that he ought to
teach but Mac knew too that he ws
still not at all sure of him self.
He tried for a Post of Social Worker
with the Alcohol Recovery Projct in mid July
but did not get it. He went to
The Social Work Forum at Olympia but just
felt out of place. He still toyed with
the thought that he might yet do an
MA in Psych Soc Work at Manchester U.

/From Oct Mac saw Keith Lloyd saw twice
a week for five months. As he read
Claudia Black's *It Will Never Happen To Me*
he worked thru a great deal of raw
stuff in depth. Tho he was glad to
have his own place the move to a
Council Flat in ways forced him to depe
back in to his past and pressed him

in to the ness of down. Thru the
dream work he had done all year Mac
had got in touch with a lot of deep
child hood grief. The death of Roy Orbison
in Dec plunged him in to a ness
of sad but his songs healed and soothed
Mac too. Thru friends in The Rooms in
late Nov he wrote to Capital Clinics Ltd
to look for vol work exp in Counselling.
In the mean time he read with care
The Child, The Family &The Outside Wrld
by Donald Winnicott and saw Paula Rego's
Show of 'Adult Children' at The Serpentine Gllry.

/From New Year 1989 Mac saw Keith Lloyd
twice a week till the end of March.
He still found it hard to live in
the world, like when in Jan he went
to his friend John's in Rye for his
Birth Day. He could not stay as there
was too much ing of drink. On his
Mam's in Feb he took her out to
a Show at The Victoria Palace and in
March they met at Queensway for a short
walk at The Round Pond on Mother's Day.
In thanks for his help, when he was
seen for the last time Mac gave Keith
The Critic by Sheridan. He kept with his
groups in The Rooms and gave aid to

those who were new. As strife broke out
in Tiananman Sq Mac could still feel quite
cut off from the out side world when
he was pressed down and sad but knew
that he had grown when he shared how
much he had lacked a Dad in his
life with a close mate in his Thur
Group of ACOA at Hinde St in July.
/With time Mac saw how low his self
worth was with out a job. The lack
of one was still a source of shame.
In the New Year he had talked to
those in The Rooms who had just set
up *The Capital Recovery Centre* in Finchley Rd.
There was a poss that he might join
The Team. They asked him to their one
day Conference on The Minesota Method in April.
/But thru some one else in ACA who
had heard him share in some depth Mac
got a quick chance in May to work
part time for Bruce Lloyd's Agency in Kennington.
As Rev burst out in The Land of Po
they hired him two days a week to
train with them as an Addictionn Counsellor at
£100 per week. He was so thrilled that
when Mac went on his Birth Day to
Baird Hse to see his Mam he dropped
to his knees to ask her ness of

give for and pressed on her a wad
of notes. In four months he built up
a strong Case Load of nine but out
of the blue in August he was told
by Bruce Lloyd that he did not fit in
and was asked to leave. Mac was shocked
and hurt but when he came to look
back at it in time he could see
that he had not felt in tune with
them. At that stage he had been drawn

by Theodor Reik's stress on 'Theory & Practice'
much linked in his *Memoirs of a Psychoanalyst*.
/Mac was broke and went for a job
as a Night Guard with Centuryan Security but
was pleased when he did not get it.
Four of his Case Load chose to stay
with him and to be seen by Mac
at *The Capital Recovery Centre* where
twice a week too he did Group Work.
He took care to treat his Case Load
in the right way. For their sake and
for his own from Sept Mac went to
a Therapist once a week named Lionel Monteith
at The Lncln Cntre & Inst fr Psychthrpy

in Clapham Park Rd. In October he got
a place on its Counseling Certificate Course held
at St Thomas's Hospital run by Anton Obholzer.
He set up Therapeutic Supervision for his Case
Load once a month with Tessa Adams in
New Cross. In Nov when *Capital Recovery* shut
down through lack of funds he saw some
of them in his own flat in Peckham.
In months his Case Load was down to
just one and Mac knew that if he

was to build it up he had to
find the right place in which to work.
As New Kids On The Block had a
hit with *You Got It (The Right Stuff)*
he went to find it at a Conference
on Capital Clinics in The New Barbican Hotel
but was not at all at ease there.
/From the start of the year Mac had
still put dwn all his dreams each night.
Each day he typed them out and made
dream notes. He mergd some thoughts on a
Surrealist Show at The Hayward Gllry as he
read *Surrealism* by R Passeron. Whle he used
to scan the words on each page of

his dream scape Mac's sense of sight as
well as sound was stirred. Tho he him
self did not paint he was glad to
be asked by a friend in The Rooms
to her Show of Land Scapes in Oils
at The Albermarle Gllry. Mac had a strong
urge to write more but at that time
short tales based on scenes in dreams did
not work. He put rhymed words side by
side and got no where with out a
form in which to put them but in
May he typed out a spaced piece for
for Fran on her Birth Day named *Seventeen*.
It was the first of more such spaced
verse in the next few years. He splashed
out on a Box in The RFH but
she dropped out and he asked a friend.
Fran had joined a new dance course at
Lewisham College. In March he went to her
End of Year Performance in The Tressillian Hall.
They found it hard to talk when he
took her for a meal in Chinatown at
the end of May but then in July
they were both a bit more at ease
on a day by The Thames at Richmond.
/Mac lived a lot in side him self
and wrote down his dreams night and day
but did keep up with those close to

him. He had been to see Danka at
Easter. At The Proms they went to hear
Verdi's *Requiem* & *The Ride of The Valkyries*
by Wagner. Once a month or so he
met her to talk at The Delauncy Café
in Camden Town and in Dec they went
to see the film of *Ulysses* at The
National Film Theatre. Mac did his best to
keep in touch with his Bro too and
went up to stay with him in May
and then for his Birth Day in Sept.
Mike still drank all the time and Mac
found it hard to bear his ence of sile.
Mac had gone on his own to Swanage
where he stayed a week at The YHA.
As he walked the coast path he was
'mused to find nudes with thongs on their
shanks in the dunes. On the main beach
he cheered and jeered with the kids at
Punch & Judy. One night he went to
see *Edward Scissorhands* by Tim Burton.
/Mac had pursued his dream work thru the
year. As The Berlin Wall fell he still
wrote dreams down but did not type them
out for weeks. In Automatic Writing he went
down in to a ness of rage and
self hate in Dec but at that time
too he wrote a short four line verse

'Dear Mum and Dad/ read dum and mad
dare mud and dam/ dear Mum and dad'.
At the time in Stamford Mike was out
of work and had to sign on. He

was in debt with rent and rates as
well as RBS so Mac loaned him £50.
On Xmas Eve he met Frances to swop
gifts at The Serpentine Gllry in Hyde Prk
and next day at Danka's with out a
drink once more he could say yes as
Band Aid II sang *Do They Know It's Xmas?*
/In the New Year as Nelson Mandela was
freed and Apartheid broke down in S Africa
thru the first half of 1990 Mac wrote
his notes each Tues eve at Anton Obholzer's
Lincloln Certificate Course held at St Thomas's Hc
At that stage he was still not sure
which way he wished his life to go
work wise. In Feb he had been five
years with out a drink and to mark
it went wih Danka to Busoni's *Dr Faust*

at Englsh National Opera which still used to
haunt him as did his guilt when he
was paid his Fee by Mr C each month
and was glad to hand on to LM.

Though he still saw him Mac yet had
deep doubts as to his ness of fit
to be a Counsellor. He tried with no
luck for a job at The British Library.
His Supervisor Tessa Adams said it might help
to make his mind up if he trained
as a Psychoanalytic Counsellor on the two year
Adv Dip whch she led at Goldsmiths Collge.
In May he felt The DHSS on his
back & on The Enterprise Allowance Scheme had
plans to set up a Private Counselling Practice.
He voiced doubts to his Therapist but Lionel
was sure Mac was right for it. He
would aid him to build a Case Load
'in the £15 range'. Mac wrote to those
like his Doc who might help with it.
/It seemed as if Mac's life was on

its way when he got a place to
do the Dip Course at Goldsmiths in Oct.
On her Birth Day Frances came for tea
with Moll and Danka. In June he was
proud to see her dance at Broadgate Arena
with her own peer group frm Lewisham College.
By then she had a place to train
at The Ballet Rambert. When Mac had a
do at his flat for his Birth Day
she brought a nice young boy friend with
her and seemed to like her Dad too.
/But Mac's own mind was in great flux.
To set up his 'Private Practice' he tried
to do things by the book yet it
was a sign of his mixed ings of
feel & mock when tongue in cheek he
had *Capital Therapy* put on his Business Card.
In May he had fixed up to hire
a room at *The Lon Centre for Psychotherapy*
in Fitzjohns Ave in Hampstead but that was
as far as it went. In the end
he could not bring him self to make
it work. The crux of it was that
he just did not have the strength or
the will to build a new Case Load.
In his mind he yet had vague plans
for a PhD on Marx' *Capital*. At times
Mac still thought that he might work with

kids but when he tried Reliance Social Care it came to nought. He was still plagued by a yen for low paid jobs. He had no wish to live on % and in late May had sold at once 100 Shares sent to him from The Abbey National. /It was the case too that Mac's heart was just not in it. While he was in pain that he had not solved the job prob in the out side world, since the start of the year each night and day Mac had done a great deal of Dream Work. As he delved down in to the deep of his dark mine Mac had hewed out more and more of them all of which he wrote down and typed. As he put d ream w or ds d own t hey split on t he p age in a way t hat he co uld t hen see n e w on es in side and be t wee n t hem. If he slipped off the edge of a page Mac taped sheets up. As he worked on their texts some dream words stood out which he then looked up in his *Shorter Oxford Eng Dictionary*. For hours he wrote out terms like 'strength' and 'free' as well as 'chide', 'rage' and 'geal' to get some new takes on what such terms might mean. By June their wide range quite stunned him each day as he clipped up wads of sheets to make new 'Dream Books'. /As well as such word work on his own Mac had worked a lot on him self in The Rooms and with Lionel Monteith. As he read texts like John Bradshaw's *Shame* and *Reclaiming the Inner Child* by Jeremiah Abram the pain brought Mac to his knees but on his Birth Day a friend gave him Walt Whitman's *There Was A Child Went Forth*. which helped give him the drive to set up a new Lunch Group at Hinde St. In tears most days it was as if the split words of his dream scape spelled out how Mac had tapped in to new depths of a well of loss and ness of sad joy in his self since his Mam and Dad rived his chid hood.

At the same time when the rays of
the sun shone from a dried tea stain
on the warped page of a Dream Book
Mac saw a rare form of Art Work.
He found that the songs of Crystal Gale
and Roy Orbison helped his grief to heal.
As Christy Moore sang Mac felt that he

cried not just for him self and those
he loved but with all those in pain
in the past of The Land of Ire.
He was sad to read in *The Guardian*
that Tom Main had died in May and
Norbert Elias in Aug but was cheered when
when Frances let him meet some of her
old school friends. He was drawn to see
My Life as a Dog by Lasse Hallström
at The Ritzy in Brixton. In the out
side world there was a lot at stake

with The US in Iraq. Lots of rhymed
words and bits tales led no where and
it was a weird month as Bombalurina swam
wth *Itsy Bitsy Teenie Weenie Yllw Dot Bikini*
and Mac heard Haydn's *Creation* at The Proms.
/At the end of Sept Mac signed up
for a Course: *The Dreamer and The Dream*
held once a week at The WPF in
Kensnington Sq. In Oct he heard Judith Elkan
give her talk on *Jacob and The Angel*.
He was en tranced when she spoke of
The Text as Dream. It touched him when
she used Keats to scan through the lines
of text for sight and sound. As she
stressed the pulse of black and white space
on the page it called to his mind
The Poetics of Space by Gaston Bachelard.
/In Oct it meant a lot to Mac
on The Dip Crse at Goldsmiths to be
back at University. He found it was a
long day once a week filled with 'Theory',
'Role Play' and a 'Case Study'. In his
own time he made some Alphabetical Poems like
Rubicon based on the words in *The SOED*
from 'rubble' thru to' ruby'. By the end
of the year he had got so used
to work on his dreams each day that
Mac felt a lack on those when he

did not have one to type out. At
the same time it gave him the opp
to see a friend's Photography Show in
The Crypt at St Martin in The Fields
that had some of Fran as she danced.
He met her there and then took them
out for a steak on New Year's Eve.
/In Jan 1991 Mac went on with his
Dip Course. He had to take part in
an Experiential Group of ten. It met once
a week for two hours on Mon eves.
He was still shamed by the years of
drink and in fear that it would come
out. In the group as a whole there
was much ence of sile for five terms.
/In mid month it was a shock when
Mac was rung out of the blue and
told Lionel had died. As he went to
his Funeral Service at City Temple Mac was
glad that all the while he had help
from those in The Rooms and friends. The
Lincoln Clinic gave him the Phone No of
some one else but he did not use
it and went more in to him self.
/For Mac it was 'The Year of Dreams'.
He had dreamt a lot in 1990 and
now in the night he hewed out more
frm the deep depths and typed thm out

each day. As he tried to make sense
of them he saw The SOED more and
more as a great re source to write
out the wide range of what dream words
meant. No more a Don but as when
he saw and heard a band on Mac
did learn to look and to list en
to them in a close way so that
he could break them down and then build
them up in to a whole. By Feb
The Dream Books that he made most days
had each grown from 10 to 38 sheets.
/When his Mam came an hour late for
tea on her Birth Day Mac wished to
make things good but just could not deal
deal with her stern rage or his own as
he read *The Lost Father* by Marina Warner.
He was in pain but at such times
like those when one tires he did not
run and sat with it so to scrawl
staved clefs and notes in his Dream Books.
In April Mac flew free with Lop Lop

when he and a friend went to see
the work of Max Ernst at The Tate
and read *What Maisie Knew* by Henry James
in a stay at Mike's. With out much
work his Bro drank but they did talk.
At the start of May Mac came out
of his pain and in his dream notes
he wrote 'I could have danced all night'.
In mid month he felt poor in Peckham
but on Fran' Birth Day he sketched out
a spaced piece that he named *The Sha m an*.

/It was from that time in the notes
in his Dream Books that Mac scanned the
dreams line by line. As he did so
the sylbs sang out and their strong tones
rang through the years. At the end of
the month he read *The Man Who Died*
by D H Lawrence and *The Songlines* by
Bruce Chatwin from which Mac coined his own
term 'Dreamabout'. He had still stayed on good
terms with Danka and at The Ritzy they
went to see both Patrice Leconte's *Monsieur Hire*

and *The Hairdresser's Husband*. At home Mac found
Schumann sad but his Dream Book based on
8 dreams hewn out from the night on
June 9th was 42 sheets thick. When he
heard the *Resurrection Symphony* by Mahler on his
Birth Day Mac wrote in his notes that
as some of his rents healed in side
Dream Books could be a place of peace.
/When Boris Yeltsin was made President of the
new Russian Soc Fed and made plans to
sell off its wealth Mac was pressed down
deep at the end of his first year
at Goldsmiths but was cheered by a good
mark for a piece he wrote up on
the theme *We Carry Our Past With Us*.
In it he used Freud's *Interpretation of Dreams*
to show how split are the tiers of
both the space and time of the mind.
As Bryan Adams had a big hit with
(Everything I Do) I Do It For You
in mid Aug Mac reached a rich new
depth in his dream mine. In the morn
he saw from the way that the lines
of his dream scripts leaned that they
hd burst out in planes which sloped from
a rich seam in deep space. At a
slant they had surged with force on to
the page in a fresh poe tic place.

CHAPTER 10

From Aug 1991 Mac used to tilt each
sheet in his Olivetti so he typed on
the same plane as the dream lines he
had scrawled at a slant in the night.
He knew at a glance they had burst
from tiers in a seam of deep space.
Notes write of a *'new form of life'*
he hones & shapes which springs *'self born'*
as they cite Dryden: *'I'll tope with you.*
I'll sing with you. I'll dance with you'.
The ream hewn was so rich that each
day whn he typed them and made notes
most Dream Books were 40 sheets or so.
It was then Mac wrought some short verse
which a friend said shone like *Little Jewels*.
He got in touch with Judith Elkan. When
shown them at Coleridge Walk she said he
had made a start and liked *Remains Ascertain*.
/But there were times when Mac scrawled in
his dream notes with rage. In ways he
still felt pressed in the ness of down.
In his first year at Goldsmiths he had
not missed a class. He liked Jennifer Marsh
who taught Analytic Theory but no one to
tice him. From April to July he had
had a hard time with Ruth Porter in
her role as External Supervisor of Mr C.
He had earnd no thing frm *Capital Therapy*
and run out of funds. By The Vac
Mac thought he might just leave the Crse.
In the end it was Tessa Adams who
stressed how well he had done that swayed
him to stay on. He got Danka to
lend him the Fees and in thanks took
her to see Christy Moore at Hamm Odeon.
/So Mac stayed at Gldsmths for one more
year as Fran went to The Ballet Rambert.
He found too a three month course of
Lectures on *Selfhood* one eve a week at
The WPF in Kensington. While at Mike's in
Stmfrd for his Birth Day Mac was shocked
and scared when he writhed on the floor
with fits. His dog had barked with whoofs
and wuffs and then low yawps and yelps.
At that time Mac dreamt Mike had died
and urged him hard to write for help
to Clouds House in E Knoyle which some
folk spoke well of in The Rooms. For
him self Mac went to see John Southgate
at The Institute for Self Analysis in Hampstead.
He liked *The Drama of The Gifted Child*
by Alice Miller on which it was based
but had no funds to meet his Fees.
Mac still wrote down his dreams but his
Dream Books dropped off as he had to
start his Dissn for the Dip Course on

Winnicott's Theory of The Good En ough Self.
He wrote down just one dream or so
each night but did not type them as
he read thru Winnicott, Fairbairn, Stern et al.
At Xmas he felt hurt and raged when
his Mam just did not turn up for
lunch but at New Year he had a
good time when he went with Fran to
look at the work of Lisette Model in
The Photographer's Gllry and that of Paula Rego
at The National Gllry. With some friends from
The Rms he danced in The Camden Centre.
/As M Gorbachev fell with The Soviet Union
in Jan 1992 Mac was glad to know
that at long last Mike had seen that
his life was on the line and had
got help at The Ferdowse Clinic in Sleaford.
Mac wrote each month in the Spring and
urged him to get well. Mike seemed keen
to grasp the first steps to take when
Mac sketched them in lay terms. The clear
and formed way his Bro used to write
it self changed when he did not drink.
/For the first six months of that year Mac
still dreamt most nights. He wrote them all
down but spent much less time on them.
He typed out the odd one and made
a few notes but most of his time
was spent on course work for The Dip.
By mid March Mac was glad to get
his Diss on Winnicott done but fell in
to a ness of down and made up
his mind to see a Counsellor at Clouds
for him self. There was a part of
Mac that wished for them to take him
in but he was told that his kind
of pain was the norm for one from
his type of split back ground. He did
not need to be there but to press
on with his group work in The Rooms.
He had no funds for their Family Week.
/At the end of March Mac was shocked
when his wife rang to say that at
home Fran had downed some pills. Jill had
gone with her to The Accident & Emergency
at The Westminster Hosp from where she had
been sent to The Gordon Psychiatric Hosp in
Vauxhall Bridge Rd. Mac was stunnd as Fran
had seemed well the last time that they
had met. When he went to see her
the next day she told him that she
did not want to go on with her
ing of dance. The pills were a cry
for help to bring it to a halt.
/In April Mac made 4 prints from some
of h is ty ped d reams in w hic h s wat hes of

s paced and s plit let s had b urs t out on
to n ew p lanes. Blown up and backed on
black card these prints based on dream words
were the first ones he dared to make
which in a way were more than just
texts to be read but Works of Art
to be seen (297x420mm). As it was Tessa
and Jennifer saw ing and mourn in them.
While John Major won well at The Polls
and The Cold War thawed out at the
start of May, Mac spoke to a group
in The Rooms which met at the Conservative
Club in Stratford Rd in Earls Crt whre
there were large pics of old PM's like
Hume on the walls. Tho one did not
take sides in The Rooms Mac was not
at ease there. When he spke Mac made
sure to cite Engels that to be Free
one must do what one needs to do.
/At Gldsmths till June Mac ws then glad
to write up *The Case of Mr C*
whom he had seen once a week for
two and a half years. His script was
based on some of Mr C's dreams and
Freud's *Intrpn of Dreams*. In July Mac got
his Dipl with a Distinction and Merit. He
had hoped that the Course would help him
to make his mind up if he wished

to be a Counsellor or not but the
ploy had not worked. In mid Feb he
had versed *Is This All?* and sent off
a job App to *The Dictionary of Art*.
It failed but gave him time to read
Hardy's *Tess* and to sketch out long rhymes
like *Corridors of Stone*. He had gone for
a job at Quitline but found him self
in *The Canterbury Tales*. Mac had thought he
might work as a Counsellor with kids but
that was not how it had turned out.
He had tried for Posts of Alcohol Counsellor
with ARP in New Cross and Student Cnsellr
at Thames Poly but with no luck. In
Spring he had hoped to have a break
and get a job in a Book Shop.
/As his last year at Gldsmths drew to
a close it was hard but Mac had
to face the fact his daught was ill.
He found him self on his way to
see Fran back in The Gordon Psychiatric Hosp
where she was said to have Paranoid Schizophreni
Mac was shocked. She had lookd well at
the start of May. They had been to
see *Major Barbara at The* National Portrait Gllry.
She had seemed in good health on her
20th Birth Day but then downed more drugs.
/At the time Mac wrote notes for a

planned verse *Little Father Time* based on a
small boy in Hardy's *Jude The Obscure*. On
his own Birth Day a friend drove Mac
and Fran to see Mike. They took him
back to Ferdowse Clinic as he had spent
the week end on his own at his
bare new Council Flat in Wittering. By then
Yvonne had filed for a Divorce. While still
at Ferdowse his Bro had moved in May
as his lease at Burleigh had come to
an end. He had worked on his last
Aubssn Rug & lived on Benefits. He owed
large Bills for Gas, Rates and Tax as
well as a huge debt to The RBS.
/Back in Lon Mac found him self once
more at The Westminster Hosp. He had gone
to see his friend who had fought with
AIDS for two and a half years. Mac
saw him on the Ward a few times
and at home where he said that he
wished to die. It was the first time
that Mac had seen a corpse. In a
few weeks he did his best to join
in chants for him as he breathed in
and out at a Buddhist Temple in Clapham.
/At the end of the month Mac was
glad of a break at Ulverston in Cumbria.
A pal had a job as The Cook
on a Roman Dig at Stephenson Ground run
by The Archeology Dept at UCL. Till he
sprained his left foot he dug for two
weeks and went for long walks at Coniston.
/In July Mr C came to see him
for the last time but Mac still met
up with Tessa at least once a month
for the rest of the year. By then
she was a good friend and there for
him at a time when Fran, Mike and
his Mam were all ill. He had seen
too how it had helped Mr C to
get well when he picked up his flute
and Mac liked to talk with her of
Art as well as Psychoanalysis. In Aug when
they went to his Memorial Service Mac
gave his Bros the verse *Carlos Is Still*.
He sketched out some steps to write more
but found no form. He tried to use
Robert Graves' *In Broken Images* but it did
not work. He felt that in a way
with his prints and verse he had made
a start in art but when he went
to share at Arts Groups in The Rooms
it still did not sit well to call
him self an 'Artist'. Since child hood days
it had been not his but Mike's realm.
/In Aug Mac went to The Proms with

a friend to hear Mahler V. He wrote to his Mam whom he had not seen all year and sought to heal their rage. He took Fran to Mahler's *Resurrection* but at the end of the month she downed more pills and was back in Hospital for a third time. At first Mac did not rec the scalped girl on the Ward with shaved head who clasped an ash tray full of dog ends. Mac was deep in the ness of sad at the start of Sept as he made a sketch of a sloped poem *The Edge of Life*. Mike wrote near his Birth Day to say that he now called in a lot to *Mind* and he was ing and learn to cope with his drink at The Ptrbro Alcohol Project. While still at Ferdowse in July on a day out in Stamford he had 'just had a few Beers'. He had been told for the first time of a Scan in Edinburgh that had showed brain dam age in 1983 but had yet gone back to drink when he left Sleaford. With the help of friends in and out of The Rooms Mac him self some how did not need to drink. He felt new strength in side as at last he wrote a fare well verse to his girl friend

Jilly frm Leics days called *The Morning Chorus*. He tried lines based on dreams such as *Love Bites* but got no where as he went on to ask *Is it long enough?* He had read Prufrock by Eliot and in his rough dream notes in mid Nov he asked *Do I Dare (Disturb The Universe)?* At the time he wrote too *Somebodaddy* based on Blake's own verse *Nobodaddy*. He was glad to feel safe to read it one Thur Eve in the ACOA Group at Hinde St. /In mid Dec Mac was turned down by The Lon Centre re their scheme for low cost Therapy. At Xmas he was tense as Fran was back in The Gordon Hospital. For a while she had seen a Therapist named Mrs Duffy at The Tavistock once a week but then just ceased to go. Jill had got scared that she would take more pills at Xmas and her put in the Ward to keep her safe. On Xmas Eve Mac went to see Fran when he had talked to Danka who worked by then as a Forensic Psychologist in The NHS. He tried to get Frances to go with him to a Nw Yr dance with Eric Clapton in Woking but in the end she just would not. /At the start of 1993 Mac was still

tense when it came to jobs. In the
Autumn term he had done the odd Class
to fill in on the Diploma Course at
Goldsmiths. He still did not have strength to
teach or to build up a Case Load
but at the end of Jan he did
help to set up a new step Group
at Hinde St for those with work probs.
His dream notes at that time kept in
mind *To Thine Own Self Be True*. At
the start of Feb when Mac saw Danka
for her Birth Day he had not had
a drink for 8 years. He was pressed
down but worked on some lines he called
The Heart of Darkness based on words which
moved him in Conrad, while in notes he
made a sketch of *The Flame of Life*.
/Out of the blue Mac's frnd Paul rang
from Leics to say that both his old
Prof and a good pal Bill had died.
He got a note from Bill's wife but
felt so lost in his own life that
he did not know what to say. When
he went up to Leics for Ilya's Funeral
he was pleased to see old friends but
found it hard to face Dons he'd known.
One said that he had been the best
in their year but he still felt shame

that he had spoiled his opps and on
the out side. Nor did it seem he
could do much for his Mam, his Bro
or Fran all of whom were not well.
He could not write a verse for Ilya
but tried to keep his mind fresh. In
March he heard Edward Said speak on the
Arts at The Gustave Tuck Theatre in UCL.
/At that time Mac took Frances to hear
Jeremy Reed speak in Mile End Rd. He
made tea for her and his Mam at
his place. At the end of the month
he ws fraught when once more Fran went
back in to The Gordon Hospl. It stirred
old fears in him for her like those
he had for his Mam in years past.
He rang The Tavistock who said they wld
get back to him. In April Dr Anderson
wrote that he would speak to Mrs Duffy,
Fran's Therapist. At the time Mac was much
moved by Di Middlebrook's lfe of *Anne Sexton*.
Moll was in the ness of down her
self but Mac took her to see Frances
in a new Psychiatric Hostel in Cambrdge St.
Mac wrote to his Bro that he had
found life hard and read *Wuthering Heights* to
keep sane. With Danka he had been to
see Clint Eastwood's *The Unforgiven* as well as

Camille Claudel by B Nuytten & A Comeau's
Tous les matins du monde. He had made
a sketch for a sloped spaced verse named
I N T E R P E N E T R A T I N G M I X U P
basd on Michael Balint's term in *The Basic Fault*.
/On April 6th Mac felt low when he
signed on but went to hear a Lunch
Time Talk at The Tate on William Blake
and liked his use of 'Word and Image'.
He got no where with a verse called
My Soul is Dry but drew a sketch
of a word wise owl. In the next
few years the free Lunch Time Talks at
The Tate played a huge part in Mac's
growth as he learned of works by Arp
Blake Claude Dine Ernst Freud Gris Grosz Hals
Hoch Johns Judd Klmdt Moore Mnch Nolde Oud
Prince Ray Scott Taaffe Velde Wols and Yass.
As they spoke of Modernsm (Pre- and Post-)
he could not but be struck by the
real depth of some like Mark Gisborne and
Michael Grossbard. Their words brought Fine Art to
life for him in a whole new way
as did those of Justine Hopkins, James Malpas
and Sarah Towig O'Brien. Quite oft en Mac
heard Laurenc Bradbury twice at the week ends .
Then in April Mac was whelmed by the
Works of Georgia O'Keefe at The Hayward Gallery.

/At that time Mac him self still tried
in vain to write more rhymed verse. In
the next months he would start long works
like *The Goldhawk Road, The Holy Trinity* and
The Nursery Curse based on his child hood
but could not find a form. In mid
May he made an 'élan plan' for his
linkd works based on twelve steps but found
it led no where. At Marble Arch he
spoke at a large group in The Rooms
on Raskolnikov's need to work thru a lot
of pain to make things good and to

get well. !t was worth it but one
paid a high price for a new life.
He was cheered up when he went to
The South Bank to hear Paul Durkan in
The Purcell Room and then Ian Sinclair and
Roy Fisher in The Poetry Library's Voice Box.
/As Fran's Birth Day neared Mac was down
in the ness of dark and went back
to The Hoy Trnty Church at Brook Grn.
He had no wish to find 'God' but
he liked to sit in ence of sile.
He knelt down and wept in the pew.
He was moved when he saw a faint

rain bow on the side of the Altar
cloth as light came thru the stained glass
wind. In days he was drawn back once
more to the scene of his child hood
in Sycamore Gdns and spoke that eve in
The Rooms at St Augustine's in Hamm. He
still went to groups each week for help
him self and to aid those who wished
to stop ing of drink. In Peterboro Mike's
Course on 'How To Cope With Alcohol' had
let him sip on. On her Birth Day
Mac took Fran to hr Mahler 7 at

The South Bank and in that week he
tried diff forms of a piece *Know Hope*.
He felt good when at the end of
words like chant, lant and want his '-ants'
sang out. On June 1st when he looked
a street sign for 'Peckham' read 'Mecca'.
In that week he saw a rain bow
round his bare Night Light and once more
drew a sketch of *The Flame of Being*.
/Near his Birth Day Mac met Fran at
The South Bank; and Danka took him out
to hear Bob Dylan and Van Morrison at
The Fleadh in Finsbury Park. On its eve

he met friends at The Tate to hear
L Bradbury give one of the Talks on
Paris Post War: Art & Existentialism 1945-55
which meant a lot to him just then.
At the time a close pal gave Mac
The Slctd Poetry of Rainer Maria Rilke. He
felt good and as one does looked up
the sense of 'mirth' in The SOED. He
made a friend in The Rooms from The
Land of Ire who read Eng Lit. They
went to Mozart's *The Magic Flute* at ENO.
The man urged Mac to write and sent
him *The Days of Wine and Roses* by
Ernest Dowson. He read a pal's *Irish Ways*.
/At the end of June Mac made some
notes on the words Wit and Inwit. For
months he wrote 'it' words down for a
verse called *Witches*. He was thrilled whn he
found new 'its' in both short and long
words. He could see the poss of our
hum but with out a form he 'quit'
and put them to one side. He met
his daught for tea at The Tate and
next day saw Dr Anderson at The Tavistock
who told him that Mrs Duffy hoped Fran
would soon go back to see her. Mac
too wrote to Mike of The Fleadh and
asked how he was as he had not

heard from him for such a long time. /In July Mac was made the Sec of the step Group for those with work probs. For weeks he worked on a verse called *The Tin Man* but he was not hap with the form and put it to one side. On lots of sheets he played a great deal with both the pre- and the suf- fix of words. He sketched two spaced works *Prefix* and *Suffix*. He made a dark work *Slaughter* but then with Fran wrote a joint light piece called *Tippex To The Top*. /At a time when he read *Twelth Night* and went to hear Mozart's *Cosi fan Tutte* a slight sketch of a small Wizard Child just popped up from one of his dreams. In it Mac The Mage waved his wand at dawn. His Aufs and Elfs were game as well as his Imps and Ants who tried to keep it simp. His stick looked a bit like a mace or a club with a knob on one end to bonk hard some mite like The Tsar if he tried to beat time or to tick him off if he got on the wrong end of it. When he waved his vare lots of Elves like The Rats who loved Arts were keen to take a bow. The Clods had colds but chased their Star and The Clots did not rave or scold them. The Dope oped his heart and in Erse said to The Seer "you reap what you sow" as he laid by The Dail. With a Throw of the Dice The Pup spoke out in Erse v The Cuts. As Sylb and The Brat did dares they sang Bart to The Scut. He curbed his sharp wroth tho The Harps seemed to blast and blare. Tom got self worth when he made a small jeu de mot on old names that were 'rased just like that' by means of a deft bit of sword play to pare his nails. His heart was slain but his eyes did not blear or blur when The Twat read Watt and The Twerp had a nerve to read Verne to Old Dears and say "who reads wins". As he looked at Pope's *The Rape of The Lock* and Ovid met a morph to fill the void The Twit risked it with a pear from one of the bins. With his guilt on the wain The Gink was made King and held out that The Prats were right to state that "a whole is more than the sum of its parts". On his head His Nibs had a Crown of Gold with Gilt that shone.

In his search to find and fill his
full at the end of The Dream it
ws The Louse who found his Heart and
Mind twined to fay and fit his Soul.
/Mac made long alphabetical lists of words with
odd cleffed mus marks and sketched out yet
one more plan for linked works. It came
to nought but in mid Aug while he
saw Fran twice and took her to the
Proms he made new works like Breadth and
Rhapsody. Fran sent him the verse she had
done since June. Mac got some hope when
he read in Goethe's Faust, 'This world will
not be mute to him of worth' (Act V).
/At the end of the month when he
and Fran went to Rye to stay with
John, Mac's notes show that at times he
now thought of him self as a 'poet'.
Back at home he wrote long lists of
an a grams and words with one sylb.
As he saw and heard the eye in
sigh he did rough drafts of spaced works
like The Curiologist and The Weird. In Sept
he was moved to hear Terry Frost speak
on Painting and Photography at The Tate. In
notes Mac's mind raced with lists of '-ions'
found in words with diff no's of sylbs.
/At that stage Mac felt tired but on

Sept 6th he sketched an out line of
a new spaced poem which he first called
A Gestatory and then An Oratory. For some
time the sounds of -ory had rung in
his ears as when he looked up a
sense of this or that word hewn in
his dream lines or heard Lunch Time Talks
at The Tate on The History of Art.
In Gov The Tories led by john Major
had then ruled for more than a year
and he had thought to call it Lavatory.
On Sept 12th he made a start to
look for words with the suf fix –ory
in The SOED. When he had found
a few he made up his mind on
the spur of the mom to go on
and to search for all he could find.
He now chose to set out on his
own and like Vasco de Gama to make
a long trip through both thick Vols of
of the large work. In side a loud
voice raged tht he should not dare
to try to go all the way from
end to end or just could not but
he was thrilld to take a chance. In
the way of it the risk paid off
f or as Mac pre s sed on he r each ed a
w hole n ew s pace of abs t ract poe try.

Chapter 11

Wth out a drnk Mac mre thn once felt like Sisyphus that he too had a huge steep hill to climb. He would soon read *Cezanne: A Man and His Mountain* by H McLeave. In the mean time there were chinks of gold light at which he could gasp as a bright sun shone dwn thru the gaps in the leaves of the trees edged in fne gilt by The Clre Gllry at The Tate. On Mike's Brth Dy in Sept 1993 Mac set off once more on a new trip through both large Vols of *The SOED* to find all words with the suffix -tor frm 'actor' to 'zelator'. Thy were classed in terms of their no of sylbs and typd out in shpd frms on his Olivetti to make a set of Fifty Two prnts. Thy wre blwn up to 297x420mm & nmd *The T-or-i-ad*. Their name was bsd in part on Pope's *The Dunciad*. For Mac they were a new form of Abstract Poetry. In the Lunch Time Talks at The Tate Mac hd bn struck by the link from Blake to Hgrth & Trnr of Poetry & Pntng. In his prnts the fnd wrds are typed in dff planes wth spcd gps. The sgns on the keys of The Olivetti are used both to mark and to fill some of them.

All the wrks are linked in a set by a crvd red line bsd on Hogarth's Line of Grace. Each print too is placed on top of one of Mac's typed dreams the black 'dream lines' of which can be seen through it. In sight and sound the sure look and sense of the work found on its face and in its depths shows the need to choose this or that ing of mean in all forms of dis course. /In that time Mac heard P Brook give The E Jones Lecture on *The Empty space* held at The Middlesex Hosp in Cleveland St whn he askd *Does Nthng Cme frm Nthng?* For a while Mac linked all the 0's in the drm wrds each day with mrkd crved lines tht mde thm flw. In Oct he ws awed whn he saw M Hopkins' Tran Beams whle he std on Vxhall Brdge. With sken and squint of the eye bright rays of sun shine flshd and trned to drps of ore to melt in The Thames. /Mac had mixed ings of feel at a Two day *Squiggle* Cnfrnce on The Self hld at Jacksons Lane in Highgate. He was still drawn to such Talks but his mind was else whre still at wrk on *The T-or-i-ad*. He wrote to Mike and his Mam of

the hope that in some good way it
wld chnge their lives. He flt sad for his
Bro who still went to *Mind* and his
Mam in the ness of lone as well
as Fran who ws still up and down
on drgs at the Psych Hstel in Pmlco.
As Mac grieved too for Ilya the black
pen strokes neath each line of the dream
texts he scanned each day took on more
and mre the dnse look of pckd tiers in
a deep mine but at times they seemed
too like curved staves on a score sheet.
/When Danka rang to say that she had
met some one else Mac felt lost at
first but not in the same old way.
At a Lnch Tme Tlk on D Bomberg
at The Tate for the first time he
had the pluck to speak to M Grossbard
who said he knw his face. Mac ws
mvd to tears whn he gt hme. In
Nov he ws plsed to get from Moll
a piece in *Irish World* on Eddie Linden
the 'Poet of the Oppressed'. As he put
the last tch to *The T-or-i-ad* Mac heard
Prof Renata Gaddini give a talk to The
Sqggle Fndn on 'Lullabies & Rhyms in the
emtnl life of Chldrn and no-lngr chldrn'
at the old Cmmnty Cntr in Jcksn's Lne.

In Homer's *Iliad* Mac hd fnd Hector and
Nestor et al and hung on to them
in a lte Pst Fce to The T—or—i-ad
as Fran got up set when he had
tea with hr and Jill at Rossetti Hse.
/Mac used to fret when his Mam said
that she had not heard from Mike but
he fnd peace in The Poetry Library whre
he read all sorts like Barnes Brecht Burns
Flann Graves Mao Poe Stokes Swift Wilde
and Yeats. The tier lines in his dream
notes were hard and clear as his smooth
cleffed curves that linked the mus o's in
drm words came bck. On a clear Xmas
Day at Peckham Rye he saw The Sun
and Moon in the same sky just like
the one Terry Frost hd tlked of so
wll at The Tate. The sme eve Mac
saw too a drk Rain Bow round the
whte Mn. The nxt nght at Rsstti Hse
with Fran and Jill they all laughed a
lt at the film *Crms & Msdmnrs* by
W Allen. As the old year drew to
an end a fresh trawl on one more
trip thru both Vols of The SOED led
to a new print *The Poetry of Line*.
/In New Yr 1994 Mac kpt up his
drm wrk. He still went to his grps

in The Rooms bth fr him slf and
those in need of help not to drink.
He ws gld whn he sw *The Cavalcaders*
by Billy Roche at The Royal Court. He
had thghts just thn that he might do
a PhD on *'The Adult Child in Dickens'*.
In stead he mused on verse from Bly
to Verlaine as he hrd tapes and read
books in The Poetry Library. In mid Jan
Mac wrte thre to M Enright and askd
If she might like to put a few
of *The T-or -i -ad* prnts in its Show Space.
When she said that she liked them but
it ws 'too exprmntl' he flt sprned. At
such times he just held on to the
hrd rad in his hll. Whn S Lfbvre
askd him in The Tate why he ws
at such a lot of Lunch Time Talks
Mac said he was keen to learn. He
flt tht he now knw what was meant
whn he heard it said tht at times
the way of art was a lone one.
/Mac flt prssd whn Mike wrte to say
he hd *Lumbar Lordosis* and Fran wnt bck
on Mulberry Wrd at The Gordon Hosp bt
at the end of the month once more
he saw the ring of a Rain Bow
round the night light at his bed side.

He knw tht Fran lkd Phtgrphy and urged
her to app to Cmbrwll College of Art.
In a lett Mac told Mike what his
wrk with prnts mnt to him. In Feb
he was up with the birds to make
a fourth trip through The SOED to trawl
for -o -tic and –up words. He sketched
plns fr *Poetry of Wit* and *The Growlery*
which cme to nowt bt crd wth tears
of joy as his dream notes ran on
the pge wth ease and he re calld
how his pen hd flowed in his Fnls.
He spent whole days on them as he
had for months in which time too he
rd D Sweetman's *Life of Gaugin*. He rhymd

-um lines for his mum's Birth Day and
mde a search in The SOED fr all
wrds wih the suf fix –um whch he
used in a st of prnts *meum millennium*
that he hoped to put in book form.
He wrote that he had plans as well
to pt *The Poetry of Singing Bread* and
Tu Whit Tu Whoo Poetry in a small
book or set of books. At the end

of the month Mac asked him self if
he wished to do Art to be like
Mike to plse his Mam or him slf.
/In March Mac nerved him self and spke
to M Gisbourne at The Tate. They got
on well so he sent him his short
'Nts on *The T–or-i-ad'*. Whn he sw wrks
bsd on *The Iliad* at Kenwood House by
Sir A Caro Mac felt poor since he
did not have the price of a seat
to hear him speak but rich when he
saw the wealth of his own dream work
and more Rain Bows in rings round the
flame of the night light. Mac wshed to
make the best use of his time yet

in the less and ness of hope with
out a job some days he was full
of wrath with him self. His tears asked
'what's the point?' as he broke down at
a Group for those with work probs but
at the end of March he faced the
fr and mde a trp thru *The SOED*
to find words with the suff ix –try.
He used them to draft an alphbtcl poem

for a set of prints named *Try Poe try*.
/Mac knw tht his Mam ws dwn as
Mike still drank and hd to go to
Mind in Ptrbro whre he hd mvd to
a new flat in Cumberland Hse in Eastgate.
With love Mac snt Moll *Leaves In November*
which he wrote at the time when they
had been to his Dad's grave. He tld
her hw he hd re called the prssd
Ives in the old Ox Dctnry she hd
used to tch hm to rd and wrte.
In Aprl he wnt to stay with hs
frnd John in Rye for a few days
but could not wait to get back to
type the prnts tht mde up *Try Poetry*.
He heard a tape of the verse by
DH Lawrence and sktchd bth *Poetry of It*
and *Poetry of The Id* for Edward Said.
/At the time Mac splashed out on a
Day Crse on *'Drms in Clinical Practice'* at
The BPS in New Cavendish St. His notes
at the time say the spce tween letts
and wrds in dreams is not no thing
but full pre verb al ing of feel.
He rd *The Art of Spiritual Harmony* by
Wassily Kandinsky bt ws tired at the end
April and did not write his dreams down
at night. He felt gd when he showed

Judith Elkan and a fw mre clse frnds sme of hs nw *T-or-i-ad* prnts bt in in the ness of down in May he wnt bck to sit in The Holy Trinity at Brook Grn. For ten days he wrote up drms but no nts. He did rd *Malevich* by LA Zhadova and then once more he wrt wrds shpd to the crvd edge of a line of grace on the page and he trcd out *The Ptry of Spce*. On Fran's Brth Dy Mac wnt to hr Cse Cnf at The Grdn Hsp. She did not turn up but he talked with Jill at home on how they might help her. Nxt day Mac made *The Poetry of Form* and *The Poetry of Time*. He wrte to Moll and urged hr to gt sme aid at an An On Group as he could not cope with her ness of down and in days made *The Poetry of Line*. Like the rest of his works at that time it ws bsd on Hogarth's Lne of Grce used by hm too to edge his drms. Whn he looked at all his works of Abstrct Ptry in whch he hd used bth black and red strght lines Mac sw just hw much he had done and thought at tmes he mght gt in tch wth *Bkwrks*.

In May on the day whn Mac typed out Mayakovsky's vrse on ence of sile he had fixed up with Maureen to go and see Mike in Ptrbro. At the start of of June they drove up to his nw place. He ws nt well. Tho Mac got an odd glimpse of the old Mike his mind nor hs speech ws clear and the the Bro he had known had gone. Mac had strong ings of mixed feel when he shwed him some of his new prints. He was not sure what to make of the wld stare which cme frm him with a strnge knd of grin. He hd hoped it mght be a way to shre sme thng and to get close to his Bro but he flt tnse too with shrp tares of guilt swn since Art hd bn Mike's sole realm in the years snce thr child hood. At home that night Mac was in tears. /At the start of June Mac took Frances to see Mrs Duffy at The Tavistock and then back to his place for tea. Fran had sent him verse called *Love 1*. He said no whn she asked to stay for the wk end as he did not wnt her to lean on him too much. It ws the case too tht he hd booked

a place on a two day Course held
at The ICA on *Analysis and The Image*.
/On his Birth Day Mac went to talk
to Roy Trollope who taught part time at
St Martin's. He cld see the care tht
Mac tk with his wrk and sd thre
ws a place for it in Fine Art.
At a tme whn Mac's steem of slf
was quite low and he still felt that
hs drnk pst ruld Roy's vw cheered hm
and helped him to push on. The nxt
day he had fixed to meet M Grossbard
at The Tate where Mac showed him a
thck sheaf of his Abstrct Ptry. Mac ws
a bit irked when he seemed to flick
thru it too fast bt was buoyed up
whn he urged hm to prss on and
to try for a plce at Art School.
On sme days of fr thgh Mac stll
went back and sat in the sme old
pews in The Holy Trinity at Brook Grn
where he felt safe for a while as
he did in The Rooms. He now helped
a young nurse from the Land of Ire
who cme to ACOA at Hnde St. On
July 6th he hrd Prof M Main gve
a talk at The BPS on *'The Level
of Repn in the Stdy of Attchmnt Orgn'*.

/In the next months Mac wrote down his
dreams but no notes as he spnt mst
of his time on spcd poems. He mused
on *The Poetics of Reverie* by G Bachelard
as he sent off *The T-or-i -ad* to Bookworks
who wrte with thnks but trnd it dwn.
As he hrd a tape of Gertrude Stein
Mac thght his own wrk std up wll
and as he made more prints he still
dwlt on a Book of his 'Abstract Poetry'.
At times he had a break from work
and went to The Lmbth Cntry Show in
Brckwll Prk. He styd in Rye with his
friend John but in a few day he
had to come back to Lon to join
'Freshstart' at The DHSS. It was then he
wrte *Free Poetry for The Singing Ringing Tree*.
/On Aug 4th Mac mt Maureen and they
drve up to Ptrbro once mre to see
Mike in his flt at Cmbrlnd Hse. By
thn his Prphrl Neuritis hd gt a lt
wrse. It tk its toll & mnt tht he
cld nt wlk strt. Whn thy wnt fr
tea in twn he wnt frm sde to
sde and he flt rbbd of his Bro.
It filled Mac with dp pain to see
his Bro in that night mare state. He
took flight to stay with his friend John

in Rye where he read James Ellman's *Joyce*.
Back in Lon Mac went with friends to
The Sthwrk Irish Fstvl tht is hld each
yr on Pckhm Rye. He did nt knw
what to think when in mid Sept his
Bro wrote to say that he might move
back home to their Mam's at Baird House.
/Mac cld stll brwse shlves in Gldsmihs Lbry.
In Aug he had searched for works which
used 'Word & Image'. In the Concrete Poetry
of E Gomringer his piece *Silencio* rang loud.
Mac hit too on S Bann's *Concrete Poetry:
An Intrntnl Anthlgy* as wll as wrks like
Alphbtcl & Letter Poems by P Mayer. In
The Poetry Library he found a sheaf of
B Cobbing's work. Mac worked on a long
alphbtcl poem nmd *Ions*. He had mde lists
of words suf fixed with -ions at least
since Mrs Thatcher wnt at the end of
Nov 1990. On Mike's Birth day Mac was
glad to see friends in The Rooms wed
at Langham Plce. Fr days he ws trapped
in the deeps and dwelt on probs but
he wrote a note with his left hand
to his hrt chld in sde which hlpd.
At the start of Oct at The Tate
he hrd B Morrison on *Art and poetry*.
He read the Intro of William Boroughs to
Poesie Sonore Int by H Chopin in which
thre is no clear line tween the ing
of poe try mu writ and paint sic.
Once mre he sw a Rain Bow ring
round the live flame by his bed side.
/Mac tried to get Frances to go back
to see Mrs Duffy at The Tavistock but
at the end of Oct she broke down
and had to go in to The Gordon
once mre. As they wre short of rms
she ws mvd to The Royal Masonic Hosp
at Rvnscrt Park. When Mac went to see
her near the site of his child hood
he flt swathed in the mems of thse
days and wrapped in ties of time. He
mt with Jill and Dr Nathan and then
too wnt bck to see Dr Andrsn at
The Tvstck but all hd to own tht
none wre sre hw to gt Fran well.
At a Lnch Tme Tlk at The Tate
Mac hrd S Bann on Cncr Ptry. He
was moved to seek out P Meyer at
his home in Hither Green who then in
turn put him in touch with Bob Cobbing.
In days Mac mde a spcd wrk *reproduction*.
He wnt to hear Jerome Rothenberg read at
The East West Gllry in Blenheim Cres and
J Whittacker speak to a Blake Soc Meet

in Greek Street on *The Ancient History of
Albion*. At the strt of Dec Bob pldgd
he wld prnt *The T-or-i-ad* the nxt yr.
In the mean time he urged Mac to
jn his grp nmd Writer's Forum which mt
each Sat in *The Victoria* off Mornington Cres.
/As Fran wrote to Mac from her Ward
in The Royal Masonic tht she hpd to
write mre vrse in the Nw Year of
1995 he mde a strt at Bob's grp.
In three month he wrote a set of
Abstrct Pms bsd on wrds frm *The SOED*
each of which closed with a diff lett
of the Alphabet. In the midst of thse
too ws one nmd *The Poetry of It*.
A grp like Bob's ws all quite nw
to Mac and at first he just sat
and tried to grasp how it wrkd. In
Jan he md a spcd piece s t e p h e n for
the son of Robert Sheppard and he wnt
to hear Bob in 'Birdyak in Concert' at
The Samuel Pepys next to Hackney Emp. He
Mused at a Wake for Eric Mottram by
'Sub-voicive' at *The Three Cups* in Hlbrn.
He wrte a piece nmd c u r n with one
sylb words like b u r n and t u r n.
His drm notes shw tht at times Mac
ws in the ness of dwn prssd deep

but he rchd nw grnd whn he fnd
his own voice and spoke some of his
Alphbtcl Works out loud. At the same time
he wrte *Specific Poetry for The White City*.
For five parts it was first read out
in the grp by Bob Cobbing, Robert and
Jen Sheppard, Lwrnce Upton & hm slf. All
bets were off and they had fun with
sme of the long wrds as they rd
parts out in turn. Mac sent it to
Mike who hd bn in Ptrbro Dist Hsp
with Liver probs. He wrte to Moll too
and told her that he was fed up
wth hr veiled thrts to do a wy
with her slf. On Feb 4th it was
10 yrs snce Mac hd stppd his ing
of drink and he had made up his
mind to make the best of it. At
Wrtrs Frm he rd *T'Othr Poetry* & nxt
day asked close frnds to his flat. In
Jan Fran hd mvd to a Psych Hstl
at Lexham Hse in St Charles Sq &
cld not go but wished him well. That
wk he wrte *A Mnfsto fr Abstrct Poe try*.
The nxt he made a shaped poem m l rt h
with spcd one sylb words like health and
wealth as wll as earth dearth and death.
/In Feb at Bob's group he read out

the frst prts of *The Poetry of F*.
Mike rng hm up frm Ptrbro to say
that he was back in The District Hsp
wih 'Excess Fluid'. Mac did nt und wht
that mnt. He and Maureen hd fixed to
take Moll to him on her Birth Day
but in the end wnt on their own.
Mike st and grnnd by his bd wth
a swlld Liver and a nw girl frnd
whm he hd mt on the Wrd. He
tried to jke in the old way as
he nw lnt on hs Zmr frm. Mac
saw thru it that he was not at
all well bt did not grasp how ill
he was. Back in Lon he went to
a small Arts Group but he still felt
dwn as he thn played *Hmcmng* on a
tape which he hd lnd of J Bradshaw's.
/In March Mac wrote notes on the poss
of a new ing and o p en up of
C las sic al lines of v rse to give t hem a
new f or m. He learnt from Moll that Mike
hd bn sent to The Fairview Nursing Home
in Lincoln Rd in Ptrbro, 'to keep him off
the drink'. At Writers Frm Mac rd out
The Poetry of I. As The Beatles once
more had a hit with *Baby It's You*
he wnt to a Day Confrnce on the

thme of *'Identity and Cont Poetry'* led by
R Sheppard in The Centre of English Studies
at Ryl Hllwy. Whn Mac rd *'Diapason Son'*
at *The Victoria* L Upton said he would
pt the piece in *Radical Poetics* bt it
came to no thing. As *Let It Rain*
by East 17 ht No 1 Mac's Mam
rang at the end of the month to
say that Mike had been sent back to
The District Hosp. Mac phnd up the Wrd
to chck hw he ws. On April 1st
at Wrtrs Frm Mac rd *'Ship of Fools'*
and *'Cobbing Bob'*. On 3rd he mld Mike
phots of each of them from his trip
to see him at Ferdowse. He sent his
Bro too *The D ays of W in e and R os es*
in the hope that it might move him
not to drink and to get well. He
snt the sme to Moll who rng him
on 6th to say Mike was back in
the Nrsng Hme. On 8th Mac phnd hm
in the morn to see if he'd got
his lett. Mike ws plsd to hr frm

him and said he liked the phots and
Poem. His Bro ws gld to knw that
Mac wld cme to see hm at Eastr.
That ing of eve Mac ws tuned in
to The 10pm News on Radio 4 when
his Mam rang out of the blue to
tell him Mike had spat blood and was
on his way back to Ptrbro Dist Hosp.
In a short time she phoned bck to
shout tht he ws dead. Mac heard her

voice full of wrath as if it was
his fault. He was in shock as the
nws wnt round and round in his head.
The next day he went to Baird House
and thn with his Mam and Maureen
to The Holy Trinity Chrch at Brk Grn.
As it was The Stations of The Cross
were on. In those hours the rite held
them. The next day they drove back up
to Ptrbro to reg Mike's death. When asked
his Prfssn all three said at once: 'Artist'.
The date for The Funeral had to be
put off with The Co-op as it was

Easter. When Mac went home for it he
fnd tht his frnt dr hd been smashed
in. At Pckhm Police Stn he was told
they sght a child of ing and miss.
He did nt go to Writers Forum bt
mt Moll at Dino's in Sth Ken near
Mike's old schl at The Oratory. In a
blur he took her on to hear Laurence
Bradbury at The Tate tlk on Kandinsky whse
work Mike had liked. Back in Ptebro he
went to see Mike who had been laid
out at The Co-op Fnrl Prlr and sat
with him in tears a bout two hrs.
They clrd his flat up fr The Wake.
Mass was at St Peter's and All Souls.
Wth the nec aid of The Social Fnd
in a sad ness of grief and fear
and rge all thse who lvd Mike dr
lft him in a plot at Eastfield Cmtry.
/It took Mac five days to sort out
Mike's stuff and clean ou the flat with
help frm his girl friend Annie. Most eves
he wnt to Evensong in The Cathedral nr
by from which he cld hear the slow
set sound of the bell ring as it
was just a stone's throw a way frm
Cmbrlnd Hse. He had no God or wish
for one but the ing of chant in

the huge bare spce in which he sat
more or less on his own helped a
grt dl to clm and to soothe hm.
One eve he flt mch ness of knd
frm thse in The Rms. On one he
wnt to see *'Remains of the Day'* at
The Film Soc hld in Ptrbro Library. Hs
frnd Paul drove from Leics to take what
he kept of Mike's stuff bck to Lon.
/In May Mac grieved. He still drmd sme
but made few notes. He tried to write
some verse for Mike but could not. He
heard sme wrks by John Keats and the
Poetry of War and Peace rd at rooms
in The British Library by C Herbert and
G Benson. He went to a Symposium on
K Patchen at The Tate. At that time
Mac was held by those in The Rooms
and clse frnds. One gve hm a piece
by Lorca on hw art can heal wnds
in the fght wth the *duende* of dth.
For Fran's Birth Day he gave her a
spcd poem Fran McGreal. Whn he tk
his Cousins frm Galway to Mike's grve he
typed out *'A Haiku for Anne and Alma'*.
In June Mac took three days to sift
-*mic* wrds frm bth Vls of *The SOED*
for a draft of *Ogmic Poetry For Mick*.

/As Clock thn sng *Whoomph! (Thre It Is)*
on his 50th Birth Day Mac went to
see Fran who ws still at Lxham Hse.
Tessa gve hm *The Ofrd Dctnay of Art*.
Tho he felt dwn and dead at times
Mac ws gld to mke the spaced poem
Microcosmic. He shrd rge in The Rms whn
he felt stuck in Peckham. He saw a
friend in *Talk to me Like The Rain*
by T Williams at Kings Collge. He wnt
to chck out Cntrl St Mrtn's Deg Shw.
Lts of *Wrd and Imge Evnts* wre hld
fr six months at The Tate frm July.
As Danka made it clear tht she just
wished to stay friends he went to the
Shw *Rites of Passage* on Chnge and Idnty.
Whn Mac sent Faber hs spcd pce called
Poetry To Diddle Daddle he did nt knw
If he wished to laugh or to cry
as it came back in the next Post.
Wth frnds he wnt to The Wlthmstw Fstvl
and thn to The Southwark Irish Festival on
Pckhm Rye. He grieved for Mike. And whn
he met his Mam at Queensway and they
wlkdd The Rnd Pnd in Kens Gdns Mac
told Moll of his Bro's love for her.
/Mac ws mvd on his way up to
stay wth a frnd in Mull whn hs

coach to Oban clld at Inverary whre Mike had lived and worked. While in Mull he read *The Necessity of Art* by E Fischer as wll as bth *Art and Revolution* and *Ways of Seeing* by J Berger fnd on his Bro's shlf. Wth lts of swms and walks Mac flt fit and well whn he cm bck to Lon. He hrd Grieg and Mahler at The Prms. Yet In his nts he wrte that he was in fear as Fran and Moll wre each in the ness of down. Pressed in to the deep part of him self Mac wished to live and and nw thght tht art might be the way to free hm self. For yrs he hd flt shmd on the dole bt it hd lnt hm the tme to rd and wrt and to thnk hw he cld be rsp and true to hm slf. Wth the the shck of his death one of his frst thghts hd bn tht Mke hd pvd the way for him to go whn his turn came. At the sme tme Mac ws then 50 and it left him with the ing and feel that he had no thing to lose and he now thought that he mght try and go to Art School. He would gt a job at night as well to kp hm slf. Whn Mac wrte to tell Moll he said he did not thnk Mike wld mnd. He trd to mke pce when he met her at The South Bank. /From The Land of Ire Mac wrote to Moll for what wld hve bn Mike's Birth Day. He had gone to stay with his Csns in Kilkerin frm where he told her hw mch Mike hd loved her and knw what she hd done for him. For a while he fr got his ness of sad and had a lot of fun with his coz whn they tk trns to rd out a drft of his *Poetry to Diddle Daddle*. /Back home in Lon don he made a print on a Photocopier of a phot of him self on Mull whre he hd styd wth his frnd in The Lnd of Cots. From the tones of it as he sat in the curved wind of an old walld fort he was struck there and then by hw it seemed in black and white as if he too was made of stone and and as if both it and he were mde of the sme hrd stuff. Frm the the fresh way it looked out to him in side Mac sensed that for him he had made art in quite a new form.

Chapter 12

Frm a dark seam of deep grief for his Bro Mac made Prints in black and white which he called *Art Noir*. For the nxt six mnths thse 'Photo Prints' of him self and a range of fam and friends wre all mde on the Phtcpr. He blw sme up and chngd the scle bt thy wre all mde first in the sme A4 size. As he mde a strt on thm Mac felt the hole in his life left by the loss of Mike but filled it as bst he cld. He saw M Grossbard speak at The Tate on Christian Boltanski. Wth a good friend he heard M Cousins tlk on *'Damage'* at The AA in Bedford Sq. They signed up too for Rchrd Wells' Course hld once a week on *'Psychoanalysis and Art'* at The Mary Ward Centre. At The Royal Court he wnt to see *The Stwrd of Christendom* by Seb Barry and hrd Rob Creeley read at The Voice Box in The Poetry Lbry. /On each side of a short trip to Mike's Grave in Eastfld on his Birth Day Mac spke once more with R Trollope. His new *Art Noir* Prints with out words had helped him some how to feel that he could now make 'real' art. In Oct he then made two Prints *Piettas I and II* for The Sthwrk Opn. In frmes thy wre the first works of art which he made to show. From Nov 19h they were on view at the Café Gllry in Sthwark Prk. As Bjork thn had a big hit with *It's Oh So Quiet* Mac saw a Show pt on by The Male Identity Group clld *'A Space for Reflection'* and a day of tlks on it at The University of Wstmnstr. At the time he blew up new phots as well as some from his child hood. While thre wre shades of light and dark the Prints from them cme from the black ness of down deep in side him self. He did the sme wth phots of Mike as wll as sme of his Dad which he hd gt frm his Aunt in The Land of Ire. At first it was a way to get in side and touch him. At the tme Mac heard T Eagleton and C Toibin on *Ireland: History and Hunger* in The Chelsfield Room at The RFH. He used his Minolta to take phots of frnds and playd with Prints of them too. It ws then that Mac made his first black & white Prnt by 'chance' nmd *Another Rilke*. At Xmas he gve one to Laurence Bradbury. /In New Year 1996 Mac did more of his *Art Noir* prnts. He still wrte dwn his dreams but did not type thm and made few notes. At The Tate he went on with Lunch Time Talks and wrkd thru tapes of all types at The Poetry Library. Each week he wnt with his frnd Michael to his Course on *Psychoanalysis & Art* at The Mary Ward Centre as well as to the talks on the *Philosophy of Art* at The Slade and M Cousins at The AA. Mac still mde dole and ws nt sre what to do. In mid Jan he wrote a new CV and tried for a job as an Addn Cnsellr wth The Drg & Alcohol Fndn. In Feb he made a call to The Lon Res Centre and tried to get through to St Luke's Centre but kept at the wrk on his *Art Noir* Prints one of whch ws *The Death of Capital*.

/As Lunitz sang *I Got 5 On It* in Feb Mac wnt to an Opn Day at Cntrl St Mrtn's. He gt on wll wth M Peel in the Prnt Std whch lead hm to thnk he mght app thre to do a prt time Fine Art Degree. He ws moved to sign off at The Job Cntr to jn a schm clld *Jobwise* which trained him to do Mrkt Rsrch.

The pay was quite low but Mac could chse his shifts each wk and do his own art wrk the rest of the time.

/At The Tate in mid Feb Mac went to the *Art & Power Symposium* as well as *Beyond Prhbtn of Images* at The Slade. As Ocean Colour Scene had a hit with *You've Got It Bad* in March he sent off his App Form to Cntrl St Mrtn's. Gina G sng *Ooh Aah... Just A Little Bit* as he then got a part time job wth Taylor Nelson in Frrngdn. He wnt to tea at Maureen's with his Mam fr her 80th Brth Dy. On Mther's Day he mt hr at The Irish Cntr in Hamm and wnt wth hr to Eve Mass at St Aug. In April she was not well and went in to Charing X Hospl. Fran was still in the Psych Hstl at Lexham House and Mac too ws pressed but he made a fw *Art Noir* Prints with rnd and sqre shapes. He did sme based on phots of Cezanne and Van Gogh as they looked you straight in the eye. With some he used trad masks and mvd a few prints on the Copier to blur them. In drm nts specks of dust shone in the sun light for him. He was scared when Moll and

Fran were ill but still kept in touch with bth of thm. Whn his Mam wnt back to Baird in May he got her a new gas fire and wnt for tea. /It mde a chnge for Mac to hve a wage but he could not stand the job at Taylor Nelson. By then he did quite a few long shifts each wk for NOP as well but it was the same kind of wrk in which one mde cld calls on the phone and a chore for him. In mid May he was turned dwn for a part time Post as Student Cnsellr at The Lon School of Economics. As he hung on to hear from St Martin's Mac kept up his Course at Mary Ward and Lunch Time Talks at The Tate. He still went to those held at The Slade and The AA in Bedford Sq. He made a trip to hear a talk on Chagall at The Steinberg Cntr up in Fnchly and on Freud at The Mus in Hmpstd. He laughed at Tony Hancock on TV in *The Rebel*. With friends in the last week of May he heard Dr Maggie Gee at Birkbeck ask *'How may I speak in my own voice?'* Next day on May 24th Mac went for an Int wth P Eachus & P Weston at St Martin's in Charing X Road. When quizzed on his art work Mac felt that he had spoiled his chance as he went to see *Portia Cghln* at The Roayl Crt. /Fr hs main crse wrk at Mary Ward in june Mac put text with the print of *Another Rilke* and wrte nts on it. As he wnt to Fran's Rvw at Lexham House where she had moved to a lat on the ground floor he made a print of the sme knd he nmd *Another Kandinsky*.

While Moll was back in Charing X he took her out to Richmond Park. As she was moved to The Royal Masonic he went to the *Art of Paranoia* at Chelsea College and too to the Deg Show at Camberwell School of Art. On June 18th Mac then learned that he had got a place at St Martin's. He tried for jobs as a Cnsellr at The Brk St Agncy and as a Night Guard at First Security bt hd to stay at NOP. As his Mam came out of The Royal Masonic he felt in the ness of fear full and went twice to see a Student Cnsellr at Davies St. As he had gone on with *Art Noir* Prnts Mac hd ct & pste fierce msks on phots of his Dad's face. In his own chld mnd's eye he trnd hs Da in to the drk fiend who scared him. /In Aug Mac and a friend camped at a site in Axmouth where he mt Dawn

who lived in Bristol. He liked her smile and the way she wre her light blnd hair in a whorl. They got on well and cmpd on their own for a wk in Devon. As Cheryl Crow had a hit with *If It Makes You Happy* Dawn cme to stay with him for a week end in Lon. Nr his Birth Day Mac shed trs at Mike's grave in Ptrbro. Fran was still in and out of St Charles

Hsp and Lexham Hse so in mid Sept Mac took her to his Aunt's in Galway. Family Therapy had come to a halt as Jill hd bn tld she hd Esophageal Cncr. Whn they had wed she got a cyst on hr brst but the grwth hd bn hrm less. For a wk he and Fran got on well in The Land of Ire. Dad and Daught wrt lts of jnt vrse till she ran off to stay with her Boy Friend who was in Belfast. Back in Bristol for a week end with Dawn Mac wnt wth hr to see L Bourgeois' wrk in hr big nw shw at The Arnolfini. /In Oct Mac made a start on his Deg in Fine Art at Cntrl St Mrtns's. The Part Time Course was one and a half days a week for five years. On the frst day in his Std Prctce he ws quite lst in his nw role so he sat and read a bk. He had to be urged to pick up a paint brush and join in with the rest. As Blacksheet sang *No Diggity* he ws in a state of shock at home when out of of the blue Dawn rang to say that she ws wth chld. For a whle they were not sure what to do as weeks

went by. Mac would have tried to make things work. In the end all he could do was to be with her whn she md the chce nt to kp the babe.
/At the strt of trm Mac hd gt a full time job on a night shift at Dbnhms. He hd hpd to stck it out and to do his Art in the day but he got much too tired and chose to sign on the dole once more. At St Martin's whn he 'gan to make work he did not do what was then in vogue. Nor did he make art to sell and did nt care what it wld fetch. In days he sn mvd to work in 3D with *The Poetry of Space*. It ws an 'Abstract Mobile' mde of 6 crvd A4 sheets on which hung spaced vrse by Mayakovsky & sme lines by him self. Thru more text on the top page looked down the fce of Apollinaire. He md sch Mbls too with curved bits of card in diff cols which frmed and re frmed as they moved rnd in spce. His *Abstract Head* was mde with curved black, red and white card. Such works were shaped in part by Naum Gabo whom he read at The Tate Library fr a pce on his *Revolving Torsion Fountain*.

At that time in his notes Mac sketched a spcd wrk *K no w Hope*. In Oct Fran hd gt a flat frm The Peabody Trust in Holbein Plce nr Sloane Sq bt she found Xmas hard and went back in to The Gordon Ho. Mac him self got on a list fr hlp in The Psychthrpy Dpt at The Maudsley. He ws nt sre hw he felt at The Hayward Gllry whn he wnt to see *Bynd Reasn: Art and Psychosis*.

/In the Nw Yr '97 at St Martin's Mac still asked him self if he shld be thre. Did he want just to mke his own work or did he wish to prove that that he could make art to best Mike's or wht? He still mt wth Dawn quite a bit but in fear that he would lose her. On Feb 4th he hd nt drnk fr twlve years bt at tmes cld still feel pressed in the ness of deep.

When he saw Fran at The Gordon Hosp
she shared some of her pain with him.
In mre Automatic Writing Mac wrte that at
times his word work gave him self worth.
Thru the term he tk dwn his dreams
bt with fw notes. At St Martins he
mde 4 Mbls wth Art Pst Crd Bks.
They tried to shw sme thing of the
form in the work of each artist so
Mondrian's ws square whle Miro's hd lts of
shapes in our col. Kandinsky's was sharp in
diff plnes while tht of Modigliani ws crvd.
In March he put the last touch to
his txt pce on *N Gabo's Torsion Fountain*.
In a Work Shop with S Johannecht he then
learned hw to make lrge prints in black
and white on a Press. As The Globe
oped on the Sth Bnk & Boyzone sng
Isn't It A Wonder in the Spring he
shwd sme lk *Anthr Rilke* and *Fcng Freud*

as well as his Mobile Pst Crd Bks.
/In his third Term Mac did a Sculpture
Class wth Naomi Dines. It hd a Surrealist
Brief 'to make things strange'. Out of the
blue Mac shocked him self when he made
a piece with Baby Bottle, Sheath and milk
which he clld *Open Closure*. He had to
chck frst with T Adams that it would
be seen at St Martins as Art. In
thse wks he had fun as he used
a range of milk botts, teats and pots
to make works of babe and child hood.
One sch 'Aftr Picasso' ws nmd *Three Dncrs*.
By then Fran had moved to a new
Psych Hstl at Beaon Mews in Vctria frm
where she sent him lots of her verse.
/As Depeche Mde sng *It's No Good* in
April Mac and Dawn wnt to see the
wrk of T Emin at South Lon Gllry.
He did nt wtch hr Vid on Abrtn.
At the time he felt in the ness
of dwn and thght he might give art
up but when he got a high mark
fr wht he wrt on Gabo's *Torsion Fntan*
he made up his mind to press on.
He sktchd a spcd txt *pure sculpture*.
/In May Mac hrd Rbrt Bly speak at
St Jms's in Pic on *The Sibling Soc*.

205

Whle it ws hrd to rd *Postmodernism* by
F Jameson Mac had a wish to grasp
and work thru *The Logic of Late Capitalism*
as Blair formed the first New Labour Gvrmnt.
He felt it was worth it and thought
mre of *Material Culture* at The Hywrd Gllry.
In the Workshop Review at St Martin's in
May he showed with the rest a wrk
Untitled. It ws mde up of four clear
shths flld wth rain. On a white dish
each one in side hd the neg Print
in black and white of a smal babe
at a stage of growth in the womb.
In the trd of S Davies' *Untd (Odol)*
by then Mac had made a start on
wrk with Toxic Plstc Cntnrs of stff like
blch which to hm hd an 'anthrpmrphc' lk
lke hs *Meditation, Plstc Spce & After Capital*.
In June he went to a Day Conference
on *Cncptlsm & The New British Art* at
The Tate and for his Birth Day one
hld by The Freud Msm at SOAS on
What is an Objct? At tms Mac saw
his art ws wrth while bt whn he
flt lw and in the ness of down
he cld not spk to M Kelly whm
he knw frm the pst whn she gve
a talk at The AA in Bedford Square.

/As The UK gave Hong Kong back to
China in July Mac sw Dr Francis Keaney
fr Thrpy once a wk at The Maudsley.
He was prssd in the ness of deep
snce hs Mam hd mde mre thrts to
kill her self and Frances was still up

and down in Beacon Mews. At times he
then found it diff with Dawn. He and
she had seen lots of Rain Bows when
they hd cmpd once mre at Easter in
Devon. He had been to Bristol for good
wk ends whn they saw *Rhapsodies in Black*
at The Arnolfini and Dickens' *Hard Times* at
The Theatre Royal in Bath. They had gone
to see *Michael Collins* by Nl Jordan. She
hd dragged him on to the dnce floor
at an Irish Caelih in a Church Hall
bt as M Brooks sang *Bitch* at the

end of July Mac found it hard to
be with her. At the time he made
a spaced text *Mind The Gap* and sketched
out an Instlln called *M in d T he Gap e*. As
All Saints sang *I Know Where It's At*
in Aug Dawn told him she hd met

sme one else. Mac tk it hrd, in
prt since he felt low as he still
had no paid job. He had just tried
fr a Cnsllng Pst at The Redcliffe Prjct
in Earls Court. He had been to see
Dr R Lefever at Promis. He had sent
Apps to The Lon College of Fashion and
ACAPS in Brixton bt with no luck and
he fnd it tough each week just to
buy sme fd and to pay his fares.
While Mac hd lnch wth hs Mam at
The Dove in Hamm on Mike's Birth Day

he had mixed ings of strong feel as
he let her help and give him £50.
/In Sept back at St Martin's Mac did
a class with Gary Perkins. The brief was
'Measurement'. For it Mac mde a sculpt clld
*Waitng to measure wth aplomb – a gross punnet
for Apollinaire* with a plumb line, some fresh
fruit (an app, two plums and a pear),
two thin tapes and a light cane tray.
For the Painting Show at end of term
in Dec he mde *Immaculate Misonception*. It ws
done with Black Board Paint on phots of
sculpts wth babe botts & sheaths. He mde
too *One Canny Sound Painting* wth *Imagine* by
John Lennon and vrse by him self slowed
down in a loop on a Sony Walkman
in a 5 Litre Can signed R. Matt.
At the end of Nov he had done
a sketch for a spcd piece *re ad y ma d e*.
In the hope that it would be a nice
Xmas Mac asked a frnd frm The Rms
to share it with him, Fran and Moll.
In hs car they picked up his Mam
frm Brd Hs & Fran frm The Grdn
but whn they got to Mac's flat a
row blew up and they just had to
take thm straight bck. He saw Lib the
next day when she lent him *Duchamp* by

C Tomkins. At Lunch Talks at The Tate
Mac hd bn drwn to The Douche at
once as he had not just found a
nw frm of art in The Rdy Mde
but had done it with a light touch
and our hum and wit he shared. On
New Year's Eve Mac and Lib went to
St James's and thn on to see frnds.
He liked her as she was keen on
her wrk and full of bns. She crd
for her art as well as for him.
/In Jan '98 they gt mre clse and
bth wnt to stay with his old frnds
John & Anne dwn in Wilts whre they
hd the use of a smll carvn with sft
shp skin rugs & a wrm coal fire.
In The Nw Yr Mac ws asked by
P Eachus to mke a pce of wrk
fr a bg Pblic Shw *Drctns* tht ws
put on each yr by thse from all
Dpts of St M's in The Lthby Gllry.
For it Mac honed the work that he
had done in Dec the name of which
strssd a light play on words and things:
*Waits nt to msre guillaume wth aplmb a
grave punnet for Appolinaire*. Fr it Mac rd
up on his Calligrammes & Ideograms as well
as The Srrlst Poème-Objet. In the nxt mnths

while Will Smith sang *Getting Jiggy With It*
Mac made Montage prints in blck and whte
of Duchamp and his Rdy-Mds whch used
ing of space to pun on their names
lke *t he g lad fly*. At that time too
Mac wrte hs txt on *Cmmdty Ftshsm &
Aesthtcstn of The Cmmdty-frm*. In it he
looked at Duchamp's *Fntn* (1917) as wll as
Warhol's *200 Dllr Blls* (1962) & Koon's *The Nw*
(1980-86) in the dev of Capital in C20
/In thse days Mac stll wnt to Groups
in The Rms four or five days a
week. He still wrte dwn hs drms tho
with fw notes. He sw Dr Keaney once
a wk for Therapy at The Maudsley. In
March he sent Moll a crd with love
on Mthr's Dy. Fr Fran's ske he and
Jill mde a start with Fmiy Thrpy at
The Grdn Hsp. All 3 of thm went
once a mnth till Jill got ill in Nov.
/In md March Mac and Lib wnt to

see a Show *Meridians* by Avis Newman at The Lissn Gllry. They sw thr frnds Adrn & George and then spnt a few days just them selves in St Ives but as Run-D.M.C. v Jsn Nvns sng *It's Like That* thr pasts weighed whn they gt too clse. Tho they tried to make things work they just could not. Tiffs turned to spats of pain whch gt wrse as tme wnt on.

In the Easter Vac as Busta Rhymes sang *Turn It Up* they made Prints wth herb and tea stains. As The Tamperer hd a hit with *Feel It* Mac made *Head Dance*. While he put white matt paint on his Bottles and took lots of phots of them in big and smll spcd groups he read up on bth R Ryman and G Morandi. He mde six Prnts he nmd *Still Art*. On May 8th Mac went to a *Cnfrnce on Cinema & Archtctre* hld at the AA. At the Stage 1 Degree Assement in May

he showed *The Blues*, *The Whites* and *Tricolour* in steel frms wth hs Duchamp Mntge Prnts lke *Red Dee Made*. As Garbage hd a hit with *Push It* in his space Mac too hung a red E made of wood named *Red E Made* and an old Last nmd *The Last Rdy-mde*. Whle he did mre Prints based on the work of Duchamp like *si lent s po kes ma n* and *mot e f or mar cel* he had to plan an External Project for the nxt year. At first Mac thght he might mke of thm an Artist's Bk but faced the fear of a Public Show in the Studio he shrd with Lib in Cmbrwll. /When Lib had found out in June that she would have to give up her flat in W Nrwd Mac asked her if she wld like to live wth hm. It took mnths to clr hr plce & to cln up his as well as to get rid of lots of their old stuff at chp cr bt sales. At the sme tme they kept up their art work. By the end of Aug Mac hd mde *The Trinity Formula* and *Al mo st An Oct a gon*. It was not all work though and they wnt to stay wth her frnd in Lewes for a week. They spnt hap days on the bch at Sfrd 'neath the chalk cliffs. Mac read D Harvey's *The Conds of Pstmdrnty*. Fr a fw days in Sept they camped at a site on The Thms at Hrly. In Ckhm thy hd fun at The S Spencer Gllry and the scne of *The Rsrrctn* in the Chrch Yrd. They called in at Larne to see the hse whre D Thomas and Caitlin lived on the way to Wst Wales. While they cmpd at Newgale Frm they wlkd the cliff path and swam. When Lib took grt phots of the land scape he took adv & learned to view it in quite a fresh way. They lghed a grt deal whn they rd Freud's *Jks & Thr Rln To The Uncns* but in the end Mac felt the joke was on them as he found that he hd gt used to hs own spce and their plns fr hr to mve in and to lve wth hm did nt wrk out. Nor wre his hps fr Fran mt. He had spnt quite a lot of time with her at Beacon Mews as well as in Fam Thrpy each mnth at The Grdn Hsp. With its aid he had fixed up for hr to see sme one at *The Cassel* which hd dne a lt for him self. in mid July bt in the end they did nt think tht they cld help her. In Sept she dosed hr self with mre pills and was back in St Thomas's and thn on Ebury Ward at The Gordon Hsp. /At the time Mac worked on his Duchamp Prnts lke c al l to a r m s and thr o n e. Back at St Martins's in October he got dwn to his text *avante garde n* which traced the use of the trm avnt-grde bck to Saint-Simon. He used the wrk of Duchamp, Magritte & Broodthaers to look at its role as a pol site in which the fight of art for art's ske hd bn fght out with the dev of Mdrnsm. Nw in his third year Mac lrned to silk screen and made a start on his black and white Duchamp Prnts (420x594mm) fr his Shw in the Spring. In Dec he hrd Thierry de Duve speak on his *Kant Aftr Duchamp*. He ws mvd mre by the vrse of Galway Kinnel in The Prcell Rm on The Sth Bank and he wrt a nw wrk fr *Libby Shearon*. Jill sent him a nice card at Xmas. He rd M Polizotti's *Lfe of A Bretn*. As he put the last touch to *avnte-garde n* in Jan 99 Mac rd C Becker's *The Sbvrsve Imgntn*. Wth plte glss he mde a Mobile nmd *throne weird* (47x53cm). As he

did his ing of print at Sthmptn Row
he wrt dwn hs drms in whch frms
of rev rose up more than once. In
mid Feb he had some fear but went
to see Jill in The Royal Marsden Hospital
whre she had an Op fr Esophageal Cncr.
They hd hd to brk off Family Therapy
at The Gordon Hsp in Nov whn she
had got ill. As she ailed thru 1999
he spnt tme each mnth at Rsstti Hse.
For The Small Wrks Show at St Mrtin's
in md Mrch he used a Jameson's Bottle
set at a slant to make *unsteady made*.
/From March 19th to 21st Mac then held
hs frst Shw *du c ha m p du p r int em p s* at
the shared Studio in Cmbrwll Rd. When he
hng his 20 prints (420x594mm) Mac ws in
tears for Mike but proud of his work.
He was irked whn none of the Staff
who tght him at St Mrtn's hd the
time to go and look at them. He
wrte up the Show in the frst two
weeks of April. It w as a new f or m
of 'Be s pke Art' in whch t he see r
w as as k ed to ta ke a fresh loo k at
t he set of Prints bot h of The D ouch e
and hs Read y Mad es. They wre nm d so
t hat he w as c al led on to h ear t heir

diff mu (sic) al so und s & thus to
thin k on t hem in quit e a frsh way.
At the end of the mnth Mac him
self felt the sharp shock of the nw.
On April 29th in The Viewing Theatre at
St Martin's he went to a slide show
by F Banner of her large Prints which
she namd 'word scapes' or 'still films'. Bck
at home in his head he found the
thought of all the dense text in her
hge wrks lke *Top Gun* (7'x15') too mch.
He could not bear all the words piled
up on such a scale. They were far
too loud and he had to get rid
of thm bt they hd lft their mrk.
He jst wipd the wrds a way bt
in his mind sme hw kpt a strng
snse of the lk of the punct mrks.
On two sheets of A4 with his Olivetti
he typed out just the punct marks from
a pge of *Capital (Vol 1.157)* by K Marx and
one frm *The Uncns* (CW 11 191) by Sig Freud.
He called the works *Punctigrams I and II*.
In thse Prints which seek to shw wht
is not there as much as what is
the drk mrks are stil clr bt he
flt at once in a new spce no
mre of *art noir* bt of *art blanc*.

Chapter 13

Mac sensed at once that the new form
of The Punctigram ws imp for his art.
He did not know what it meant or
wht it ws worth bt felt that he
had to try and find out. In this
he ws bckd by his Tutor M Rossi.
At the end of term when he showed
bth *Capital 1 157* and *The Uncons CW11 191*
(bth were 59.4 x 84.1cm) their diff from a fig
Prnt lke *A van t gard en* ws plain. In May he
trans posed a code of punct marks for
letts to make *What Is To Be Done?*
In those weeks of much dbt he made
too Pnctgrm 3, *The Fetishism of Cmmdities &
Its Secret* (*Capital I*, 163-177). At the tme he hd
fnd *Pause & Effect: Punctuation in The West*
by WB Parkes filed and shelfed near his
desk in The British Lbry. As he plngd
in to read the role of punct marks
in the Hist of Art and Sci he
fleshed out a field quite nw to hm.
He lked at thse like Tschichold as well
as Adorno, Barthes & Blanchôt on thr prt
in the marked space of ing and write.
In J Derrida's *Acts of Literature* he read
of S Mallarmé's lck of mrks and use
of the blanks on each page in the
ence of sile in *Un Coup de Dés*

an old trans of whch he fnd in
The Lbry at St Mrtns. He lkd at
the use of 'neg space' in art from
the vrse of Apollinaire to the sculpts of
R Whiteread. In Barthes' *Empire of Signs* he
found the white ness of empt in *Mu*.
To void a spce not to fill it
was a new way to show its form.
On Frn's Brth Dy he wnt to tea
with her at Jill's bt on his own
in mid June he fnd hm slf on
his way to see his ex wie at
The Tr Hsp in Clm. It ws hrd
to see her so ill bt he got
hlp frm pls in & out of the
rms. It still mnt a lt to him
tht he cld hr L Bdbry twc a
week at The Tate. He gt a big
bst whn he sw the lrge wrks of
J Pollock at his show there. As he
thght of wrk with Braille and Morse in
July Mac saw the work of H Klingelholler
on Art & Language at The Whtechpl. He
tried to keep in touch with his Mam
but when the old rage of one or
bth blw up it led him bck once
more to sit in the calm ence of
sile at The Holy Trinity in Brk Grn.

/By the end of July whn Mac and Lib spnt a week at the hse of a friend in Stroud he felt a need fr his own space to give his whole Self to his work. The more he looked the more he fnd punct marks like the dot used in Art works from G Seurat to R Lichtenstein & J Latham. Jst thn Fran was in and out of The Charter Clinic and The Gordon Hsp. It ws clr that there ws no chnce Jill wld gt well. He hrd Poulenc at The Prms bt flt the need of a break in Aug & in mid month he went to camp in Nwgle on his own. Whle thre he rd the poetry of J Clare and James Joyce On his transtsr rad he heard The Proms and *Elctve Affnties* by Goethe. It raind bt when he walked and swam he felt free. /In the first three weeks of Sept Mac wnt to *The Bcktt Fstvl* at The Brbn. He saw a range of his plays on stge and scrn. On R 3 he hrd K Laws and M Esslin *et al* speak on his marked mu (sic) al style. By thn Mac hd read *Damned to Fame* by J Knowlson and *Who the ?* by B Whitelaw who stressd the strict way Beckett used to pnct his txts and wrte thm lke scores. As he rd thru *Fair to Middling Women* in Spt Mac mde Pnctgrms (4-10) whch wre bsd on his txts of *Godot, Cascando, Monologue, Hppy Days, Words & Music, Endgme & Play.* He gave them the nme of Rhtrcl Pnctgrms as they all came from the ing space of breath and the voice. The comp of pnct mrks in each *blanc* spce brght out at once the spec form of each one. /In Oct Mac typed out the mrks of *Come & Go.* He got a boost to see hw A Boetti had used pnct mrks in wrks shwn at The Whtchpl Gllry. He was thrilled to find the way in which Art and Language used marks of punct in *Dialectical Materialism (Drk Grn) 1975* as he rd M Baldwin's *Art and Language in Practice*. He was shocked by the rate at which Jill lost weight when he went with her for Radthrpy at The Ryl Mrsdn. In tht mnth he wrote no dreams but looked out and went to ENO three times to Der *Freischutz* by Weber, *Orfeo* by Mntvrdi and *King Priam* by M Tippett. He sw too N Hawththorne as *King Lear* at The Barbican. At the close nw Public Lbry in Pckhm des by Alsop & Stormer he fnd S Beckett's *Trilogy*.

In Nov he made Punctigram 11 based on a age of *The Unnamable*. He used the Lttr Prss at South Row to mke Prints of pnct mrks frm the frst Pnctigrms as well as to print *K no w Hope* and *Mnd The Gap e* (21x16cm) in Eds of 31. When he was still not at all sure of his wrk a talk by Mchl Renton on the spce of txt in Mdrnst Art at The Slade ws a great hlp. At The Royal Crt he hrd H Pinter rd *Old Times* and was moved in Dec to mke Punctigram 12 bsd on his shrt piece *The Blck & Whte* (29.7x42cm). At the tme Moll had a bad stroke and went in to Charing X Hsp. Mac mde Punctigram 13 *Mrks For Mgritte* (42x59.4cm). In it for the first time he used punct marks from diff fonts. As he wnt to Trinity Hspce each week thru the month to see Jill he ws shckd each time at hw thin she got. At New Year's Eve he then wrkd on Pnctgrm 14: *Dancing Air (for Hogarth)*. /Mac was not there when Jill died on Jan 9th 2000 at Trinity Hospice but he went at once when he was told. He was stunned by hr frail form and felt down but when he came out on to

the Cmmn and saw the thin curved arc of a cold white moon that hng low in the ness of black he ws mvd. In days he pt the last touch to *Dancing Air*. Jill's Obit in *The Grdn* did not touch on the role of Marxism in their lives whn they hd met bt Mac was glad that at least it said she hd wd hm & hd Fran wth hm. /As Oasis sang *Go Let It Out* in Feb he had not had a drink for 15 yrs. Cheerd by Mzrt's *Magic Flute* at ENO he then sketched a nw work called *A Respect is Haunting Europe*. In dbt so whn he saw Y Kusama at The Srpntne he mde www.where to begin?//.com (42x59.4cm). 'Gram 15 ws bsd in prt on 1915 Sup Comps whch used Mrse. As he went to see Fran back at St Mary once mre he mde Pnctigrams 16-18 ea with qute diff fonts: *Rolling Oval* (fr Fonta *Spiral* (for Smithson) & *Dble Spiral* (fr Joh /In the mnth Mac had made a start a new artists' book bsd on S Mallarme' *Un Coup de Dés*. Whre M Broodthaers *Un Coup de Dés - Image* hd subbed strai black lines for Malllarmé's text, in his ov *Un Coup de Dés – Espace* Mac trns psc

a code of pnct mrks. Mac hd learned
both from Duchamp's *The,* in which a star
re placed each word 'the' and from Miller's
lines of mrks in hs *'Poetry of Punctuation'*.
He was urged on in this quest as
he rd J Drucker & C Phillpott on
the role in Art of The Artists Book.
Mac had worked a great deal too on
Words & Music bsd on Beckett's play. At
a prompt in Jan from Mario Rossi he
hd used the pnct mrks on all eight
sides of the txt to mke two Prints
of the whle play in blck & wht
in both a pos and a neg form.
As Fran wnt bck in to St Mary's
he shwd the rk in the last week
of March and thru April at the first
Irish Cmmnty Opn Arts Exhibn hld in the
UK at The Irish Centre in Hamm. Based
on Beckett's short text in which he used
marks of punctn like mu (sic) al notes
the pulse of the marks in black and
white was to be read like a score.
In a grp phot for *Irish World* Mac
cn be sn in his Bro's brwn jackt.
At the sme tme he & two frnds
got a temp job as Curators in the
Directions Show at St Mrtns. He set up

a small Visitor Survey tht he wrte up
in May and for which he was paid.
Mac hd made a sktch for a spcd
vrse *sighed* bsd on a suf fix –ide.
He kpt his hopes for his work up
as he then wnt to hr R Townsend
ply the Orgn at St Mrgrt's Lthbry and
made a trip with a friend to look
at H Moore's sculpts out in Mch Hddn.
He tried to learn from old works as
wll as the Cncptual Art of S Hiller
in *Live in Yr Head* at The Whtchpl
and those like Bob Cobbing *et al* at
347 minutes, ideas and exp'n in Cnwy Hll.
While he read *Point and Line to Plane*
in Apr he mde *Leaping Moons* (for Kndnsky)
and *Climbing Frame* (fr Mondrian). As wll as
thse 'Grms (19/20) he mde *Mind The Gap e*.
(42x59.4cm). Whn Moll hd a wrse strke Mac
went to see her at St Mary's. As she
lay on her side she could not move
or speak much but said she was sorry.
They both cried. He mnt to kiss her
on the fce bt slppd and gve a light
kiss on the lips. Whn Mac laid hs
cheek on hrs he flt mre clse to
hr thn he hd dne since he cld
rem in his whole life. At the end

of the month he then went to hear
The Pearl Fishers by Georges Bizet at ENO
and mde *Mind The Hap*. Frm Wncntn whre
he had a break with friends he wrote
to Moll hw Mike and he loved her
and knw wht she hd dne fr thm.
/Then in May as Bon Jovi had a
hit with *It's My Life* Mac made a
plan for The Deg Show in 2001. As
Britney Spears sang *Oops!...I Did It Again*....
the song called to mind that by chance
at St Martin's in March he had left
the neg form of his print based on
Words & Music by Sam Beckett on a
flat Light Box. When the small white marks
of punct had shone and stood out from
the drk bck ground like the stars in
a black sky he had thought at once
of S O'Casey's *The Plough & The Stars*.
(He had notes on the play in a
dream book as far back as Aug 91).
As Mac read through the text of the
Play and saw the dense marks of punct
used to grasp the fast clipped speech in
Dublin 1916 he thght of a scheme to
make a piece in a wind and then
a large Light Box (8'x6') bsd on the
whole txt in which the mrks wld shne

out lke brght stars. By hs Birth Day
in June he had typed out all the
mks of the Play on A4 shts. Sm
of the keys on his Olvtti hd gt
so wrn tht he hd gt scrd they
wld nt last out but they did. He
lrnd hw to square up smll sheets in
the cmptr at South Row and to make
a lrge ink jet prnt on Plyflm (59.4x84.1cm).
/On Fran's Birth Day in mid May Mac
had found out that she was back in
The Ptrsn Wing at St Mry's. He hd
bn shckd as they hd plnnd a trip
to Hmptn Ct. He hd flt prssd dwn
but wrkd on the punct marks in the
text of *The Plough*. The next week he
saw *Valley of Hell* by Ahmad Rafiq Alrawi
at The Royal Crt. As Sonique then sang
It Feels So Good in The Crse Rvw
of Year 4 at St Martins Mac shwd
slides of his Pnctgrms as well as a
fw nw text prints mde tht mnth sch
as *This Is Not a Snipe* (42x99.4cm) and
This Is Not A Hype (42x99.4cm). He had
sktchd out too a spcd pce *Post Capitalism*.
As the month drew to a close Mac
mde a pln fr hs Diss'n on *Appunctuation:
A Med'n on Punctuation*. He hd dne wth

most of the first part in the past 12 mnths. He lookd at the worth of The Punctigram as an art frm bsd on mrks dis placed frm the rlm of ure Lit er. With devs in the space of ings of writ and prnt in The Wst the mrks of pnct frmd the wy txt is read from left to right and from the top down the page. At the same time they wre thre to be seen through. At bst they were mskd and veiled. With 'The Rev of The Word' in Modernism the word was freed in a way at a cst to the mrk which was lft out. In the art frm of The Pnctgrm the mrks are thre to be seen. They are there to be lookd at, not seen thrgh. At the same time the space of the Pnctgrm asks wht it means to see. Does the see-r read the marks in space or look? Menander The Attic Poet in C4 said 'Thse who can read see twice as well'. In space the eye is more or less wde of the mrk. For a poet the *blanc* it self may nt be just a gap or lack. It is nt no thing bt fll. In the dpths nt a wrd is lost if it sings out in white clouds and flecks as light as snow flakes. /Out of the blue at the start of June Mac hrd tht Moll too ws in St Mry's Hsp. She hd bn on her way to see Fran whn she hd a wrse strke at a Bs Stp and hd thn to be kept on a Ward her slf. He flt quite dwn whn he sw thm both on the sme day in diff Wards bt wrkd on his Diss'n. He flt trapped but let his mind roam as he read Lectures on No Thing and Some Thing in *Silence* by John Cage. It was like old times when he heard Tom Nairn give a tlk on *Farewell Britannia* in The Old theatre at The LSE. He went to an Int Cnf on *Peace in The Blkns* at The Cnwy Hll. On a Sun mrn in the same place he hrd a talk on *G Bruno & Free Thght* at SPES. At the end of the month he went to see *The Country* by Mtn Crimp at The Royal Court and hd a break with his frnds who frmd the peace of Wlts. /Through the nxt mnths fr hs Diss Mac sought out works of art whch had marks of punctn. In July he found Pol Bury's *Pnctn (Points Blanc)* frm 1965 in a Shw

clld *Force Fields* at The Hayward Gllry. He
saw C André's txt wrks at The Whtchpl.
At St Martin's he tried to weigh up
glss & matt prints of pnct mrks in
the text of *The Plough & The Stars*.
As he rd wrks lke *Art Aftr Philosophy*
by J Kossuth who brght punct dwn just
to form Mac gt strssd but was less tense
when he worked in The Poetry Library. He
felt calm when he heard R Townsend play
Bach on the Org at St Margaret's Lothbury
and Copland's *Fnfre Fr The Cmmn Man* at
The Proms with Lib. Less so when he
went to see Fran who was now on
a lckd wrd in The Ptrsn Wing at
St Mary's. His Mam hd bn out fr
a fw weeks whn Mac saw her at
hme in Aug bt she ws dwn and
spke of death. He felt thre ws nt
much he could do but gave her a
prnt of *Dancing Air*. Whn he cmpd in
Rye Mac was thrilled to see the black
night sky still full of stars. While there
he rd *The Rescue* by Joseph Conrad and
The Waves by Virginia Woolf. Back in Lon
he got down but it cheered him when
he put his framed *Words & Music* up
on wall. At the end of the month

Moll was back in Charing X with a
wrse stroke so tht she cld nt spk
or write. She ws in the ness of
dwn but Mac urged her to hve hpe
as he hrd Shostakovitch 7 at The Prms.
/A t times when he went to see her
thru the mnth of Sept he felt pressed
and trapped him self but he went to
The Rms and shrd his pn. He trd to
live a day at a time glad that
he did nt hve to drink. Whn he
felt low he hng on to sme self
wrth bsd on the fct tht he had
nt drnk. He rd *Ulysses* by J Joyce
and workd on the end of his Diss.
Based on his vrse of the sme nme
from 1994 he mde a new Artists' bk
nmd *Poetry To Diddle-Daddle*. He urgd
Moll to get well so that next year
she could go and see his Light Box
of *The Plough & The Stars*. At The
Real Irish Book Fair hld in Blacks Rd
Mac heard *I Could Reach The Sky* read
by Tim O'Grady. When he went to see
Moll the next day on Mike's Birth Day
she said that she wished to get well.
In The Purcell Rm Mac hrd T Paulin
spk on The Sonnets in his tlk on

Shkspre fr the Mllnm. In it he tchd on his use of wrds with one sylb. /At the end of the month Mac took a shrt break wth his frnds in Wncntn and went back for his last year at St Martin's whre he now had his own Studio spce at Chrng X Rd. With Paul Eachus as his main Tutor for the nxt 8 mnths he worked on a Light Box bsd on *The Plough & The Stars*. As he rd *Sn O'Casey: Politics & Art* by D Greaves in tht Autmn trm he mde a first rough Light Box with just a smll light blb & crd brd bx (59.4x84.1cm). With Karl Baker he worked on the draft of his Diss on *Appunctuation* & mt the dead line in Dec. In Prt Two of it hs Thry of Pnctism hld tht Frm in art can nt be grspd with out the Mark as a thrd trm wth Wrd and Imge. It is the mld whch casts thr spce. /Snce he hd gt bck frm Wltshre in Oct Mac had been to see his Mam each week in Charing X. Sme days he went drssd in Mike's brwn jackt. In Nov she raged whn it seemed like she wld be sent to a Nursing Home as she was not yet in a fit state to go back to Baird Hse. At times Mac asked him self if he tried to be like Mike to gain her lve. If so it ws clr by then that the ploy jst did nt wrk. At The Brbcn he wnt to see *I Could Read The Sky* by N Bruce. He was ired him self at Charing X whn a yng Doc stppd him in a full Ward and out of the blue voiced his dbt tht if Moll got worse and fell uncns it would be wrth while to brng her rnd and to go on with her care. It was hard at Baird Hse to go and gt Moll's clothes for hr to mve but he wnt bck once mre to The Barbican to see *The Golden Bowl* by Jams Ivory. In Dec he heard P Blake at The Cochrane Thtre and was much chrd up by Sean Rafferty *In Tune at Home*. In The Radio Theatre at The BBC in Portland Place Simon Callow read from *A Christmas Carol*. Whn he wnt to see The Stamford Nursing Hme with a view to Moll's move thre Mac felt quite strange when he found out that it was clse to Qn Chrltte's Hsp whre she hd first brought him in to the world. In the Hme the tmp ws high and thre was a stale smell of food. It seemed weird as thre wre no chairs in the hall whre folks ate. They did nt nd thm as they sat in wheel chrs. He ws glad to go to The Xmas Concert hld by R Townsend at St Mrgrt's and too to read up on Joseph Cornell's life and wrk in *Utopia Parkway* by D Solomon. By New Year's Eve Moll could move her hand and leg mre and still hoped tht she could soon go back to Baird Hse. The Leics Grad Rvw 2000 had jill's Obit. /In The New Year 2001 L Bradbury at The Tate thanked Mac fr *M in d T he Gap e* (21x16cm). It was a year since Jill had died whn Mac went to see Moll 'fore she left Charing X. In mid Jan France came out of hosp while Moll moved to The Nursing Hme at Stmfrd Brk. For a few weeks he called in most days as she was down and he him self felt in fear and pressed. At the end of the mnth tho he fnd tme to fill in an App Form for a Bk Arts M A at The Cmbrwll Sch of Art. /For The Review at the end of Jan 2001 Mac thn mde a cheap Light Box wth sm rgh wd (45x33x15cm) and an 8

Watt Ftzgrld Strip Light. It shwd one of four large prints that he had scnnd frm *The Plough & The Stars*. Whle the mrks did look like stars in the dark Mac had to ink in the Polyfilm prints to brng out thr light and lt thm shne thru. Whn he ran it by the Tech N Wells it ws clr he had thght on too large a scale. He did nt hve fnds or mns to bld one bg Light Bx bt wld hve to sprd the txt of the scrpt on 10 prnts each with its own smll box whch he cld then fit to mke a whle. At that stage Mac still thought of it as a wall pce. Frm Whttn's Tmbr in Pckm he gt two lrge shts of 12mm MDF (8'x4'). When it came to St Martin's at the start of Feb it was still not clear if Moll could go back to live at hr flt in Baird Hse at sme pnt. As Mac took in The Celtic Art of L Kearns at *The Cross of Change* in The Irish Centre he flt quite torn. In a way he hoped tht she would bt he felt guilt since he could not tke care of her him self. While he read of the gold braid of *Godel, Escher, Bach*

by D Hofstadter Mac found it hard by
then on Suns just to see her once
a wk. She shared a rm with sme
one nr death and it ws a strain
on hm. By mid mnth he hd mde
a slow start to clear things up at
Baird Hse. As his Mam neared her 85th
Birth Day he fell down in the street
and raged whn he hurt his eye brow.
/With Nick Wells' help the sheets of MDF
had been cut to size to make a
st of prts fr each Lght Bx (45x33x15cm).
By the end of Feb Mac had scnned
in the last print of pnct mrks from
The Plough & The Stars & frmd up
up his plns fr the work now called
The Plough & The. For The Show he
thought too he might use the Sterling Box
fr a Collage piece à la Cornell (60x40x14cm).
/As Mac worked on *Un Coup de Dés*
in March he saw more and more how
mch mu (sic) mnt to Mallarmé who sd
in his Preface to *Un Coup* how its
clew ws to be read like a thread
tht rns thru the frm of a score.
He used to write a grt deal to
to the sound of or gan mu (sic).
On Thurs Lnch Tme Mac hm slf oft

went to hear Richard Townsend and his guests
lke H Reinertz play Bach & Buxtehude on
The Org at St Margaret's in Lothbury.
As he rd wrks like *Sounds and Signs:*
Aspects of Musical Notation by H Cole, Mac
mde 3 *Musigrms* (30x42cm) in whch the pnctn
and the texts were re placed by mu
(sic) al notes. *The Latent Clew* ws bsd
on the Preface to *Un Coup de Dés*.
The Music of The Spheres I and *II*
used txts frm the bk of the sme
name by Jamie James on the way both
Boethius & Guido frst wrte neumes fr pln
chant and or gan in C9 and C10.
As he then read H Weinfield's trans of
Un Coup de Dés Mac learned that the
lay out of 'The Septentrion' in the txt
in code is a form of The Plough.
He snsd at once the clse link with
O'Casey and grspd tht in sme way his
own *Un Coup de Dés – Espace* cld be
brght in as a part of his Installation.
He made a new Print of it (29.7x42cm).
/Tht mnth as Shaggy sng *It Wsn't Me*
it was a shock for Mac to see
hs Mam in a Wheel Chair fr the
frst tme. Each Sun he used to psh
her from the Home to a small Green

near by to get out of the place for gulps of frsh air. He wld park her next to a bench on which he sat as he tried to cheer her. He felt dwn whn he lft bt ws well hld as he stll wnt to The Rms. In md mnth Fran st fire to hr bd at the hostel and ws sent to a lckd wrd at St Mry's. Mac's drms were torn wth rage and strife. At the same time he went to an Open Day at Cmbrwll School of Art. In wks he ws seen by S Johannecht and gt a frm plce on The MA Bk Arts Crse. At the end of the month in the AHRB Form he set out his plan to learn the craft skills to make a real Artists Book of *Un Coup de Dés – Espace*. /In April Mac used Braille marks to make Prints *Double Blind I and II* (30x42cm). He called hem Brailligrams I and II. He made up the parts of each Light Box for *The Plough & The* and with a nw drill scrwd thm tght. He used Matt to paint them black on the out side and white on the in side which was then lined with tin foil. An 8 Watt Fitzgerald strip light was fixed in each as well

drk leads & plugs as they wre stored. /At Easter Mac went to see Moll at Stmfrd Brk and pshd hr out in the Whl Chair to the grn. Fran ws in St Mary's and he took her out fr a wlk at The Rnd Pnd in Kn Gdns. At the end of April he tried to keep his mind free and went to the *Verbal Inter Visual* Shw in The Lthby Gllry and to T Kemp's *Wayward Writing* in paint at The Rivington Gllry. When Blair came out on top with most votes once more in May Mac lrned that his spce for The Degree Show would be on the 8th Floor and made a start to clear and paint it. In the next wks he worked too on the Prnts fr his Artists Bks. It felt like a big step whn he let go in the end and made his book bsd on Mallarm∅ *Un Coup de Dés – Espace* at its full scale and right size (42x59.4cm). /As G Haliwell then sang *It's Raining Men* on mre Sun trips Mac whled his Mam in her chair out to the same old bnch on the grn. He had asked for the tyres to be pmpd up but they were still sft. On her Birth Day in mid month he went to see Fran at

St Mary's. In days she was moved to the Hnry Mdsly Scrty Wrd. She pt the phne dwn on him when he rang up. /The Deg Show lmd so Mac gt the Prspx fr his Lght Bx frm Anmar in Bthnl Green. While he st it up in the drk spce at the end of May a nw pm askd Wht Do U Thnk? On one Prnt at the lst he inkd in the thn crvd arc of a Moon. As DJ Pied Piper had a hit with *Do You Really Like It?* he typd out a list of works in the past years. At the lst he mde *Ogmic Elegy* (73x53cm) bsd on his poem *ogmic poetry for mike* which he first wrote in June 95. A fw dys pst his own Brth Dy Mac had to sign on with *Job Links* at The Elphnt & Cstle. He tld thm tht he hpd to do an MA at Cmbrwll. It gave him the time to get on with his work and to have an odd break to see the art at Tate Britain. /By then Moll had to let go of Baird House. It took weeks for Mac to sort things out. He kept what he could. One thing he had found and kept was an old School Bk from inf ant days aged 6 at The Sacred Heart. In it he had put down a list of short words to learn: *'us yet if bee wail see sod some fleet ill blush flock gray may sheep aim sun well wet mill just nd saev (sic) will hope nxt rag free buzz flax pie ate waill (sic) gray If need print ran car jar cow hen cat dog cow plum pear fish sun lug box pan cot end teeth duck chin'*. Mac sold the new gas stove but gave the fridge to sme poor folk who lived on the grnd flr. He tk last phots and left. /Mac's Deg Shw tk place in June. He clld his Instln *The Plough and The ( )*. It was made up of The Light Box *The Plough and The*; The Sterling Bx Cllge; 2 Artists Books (*Un Coup de Dés – Espace, Ptry To Diddle Daddle)*; a Prnt *Ogmc Elgy* as wll as 7 bxd trays of Documentn. He had thght to try and get Moll thre bt in the end he flt drained and it was too much. At the time he read *The Man That Was Used Up* by Edgar Allen Poe. At Tate Britain he saw A Manguel's view of the world as a bk in *Rdng Pctrs*. Whn the Show hd cme to an end and he put

The Plough Light Box on the wall of his bed rm Mac was cheered to have got a First but felt sad and pressed. It would nt bring his Bro back. He asked him self if that hd been his aim. Whn he sw *Dnce Hll Days* at The Rvrsd Stds it dwnd on hm tht it cld not make up for the loss of Baird Hse. Nor wld hs First cure Fran or Moll. As he rd Robert Musil's *A Man Without Qualities* he ws in the ness of sad but the book held him. /He was thrilled to see mre Tran Beams from Vauxhall Bridge at the end of July. He lkd the wrk of Arte Povera 1962-1972 and GiorgioMorandi at Tate M and was cheered in md Aug to hear frm RHAB that he had got a Grant for a yr to do his MA at Cmbrwll. He cmpd for six days on his own in Newgale and thn wth Lib fr a wk in The West of The land of Ire. At Doolin in Clare they wlkd The Cliffs of Moher and heard trad pub mu (sic). /Back in Lon at the start of Sept at the Prms Mac wnt to hr Schumann and thn Rach. While he made time to go and see Moll, he rd J Drucker's *The Century of Artists Books* and ws kn to get down to work on his own *Un Coup de Dés - Espace (38x57cm)* fr his MA at Cmbrwll. As al-Quada thn hit The World Trade Centre hard in New York he heard from Fran that she was soon to be sent to a locked Ward in Shrwsbry Crt Prvt Hsp in Rdhill. At tht tme he chngd tck & bsd on Mallarmé Mac chose to mke a nw Artists Book he nmd *Un Coup de Des – Musique*. The Musigram wld tke the frm of two sails hung on the wall. Each would bear six sheets of Mallarmé's text on which mu

(sic) al notes would take the place of his wrds. The seeds of sch a pln hd bn in his mind snce Feb. At the end of Sept Mac flt lke ing of in give but based on a page in whch a rnge of fonts ws used to shw The Sptntrn Mac thn mde prnts on 2 lrge shts (42x59.4cm). He prssd on as they looked like the night sky but when he learned of the role of ence of sile in *Mllrmé - A Thrw of The Dce* by G Millan he sw they wre mch too loud and in your face. With the frsh white dawn of Mdrnsm the Poet hd used words in space on the page as a score to make mu (sic) as ence of sile in the mind. In Oct Mac grspd too tht the notn hd to be in code and that he had to use white in the cmp. A sht of Toshashi whte wve frm Falkiner's wld be plcd on top of each print. 'Ticed by iced seas of white in Mallarmé by mid Nov his plan was for two sails in the air. As Mac did re srch on the piece and wrte that Term he learned of the strng lnks in Mallarmé's wrk with tht of Wagner. At the time he went to hear Rchrd Townsend play the Orgn at St Mgrt's. As The United States launched a war in Afghanistan he saw *Time of The Gypsies* by E Kusturica at The Rvrsde Stdios as wll As S Prokoviev's *War and Peace* at ENO. In his drms The Book of Books cme and went at night in to the air. /At tms Mac flt prssd as he wrkd on Mallarmé and went to see Moll. He wished to live more and liked a trip with thse on his Course to MOMA and The Pitt Rivers Msm in Oxfd. On Xms Eve Fran did not want to speak to him when he went to see her in Redhill and he was glad of help in The Rooms. He was thrilled to hve fnd *Aspects of Wagner* by B Magee who tght him how closed his own mind had been whn it came to Wagner and his work. /In the Nw Yr 2002 Mac was asked to spk to his Mam who hd been rde to Stff at The Nrsng Hme. He ws gld of the chnce wth thse on his crse to be shown by M Duff sme of the Artists Bks at Tate B. In work on a draft of his text *Un Coup de Dés – Musique* he found more like The Cubists who used notn of mu (sic) in their art. He saw Klee's wrks in *The Nature of Creation* at The Hayward Gllery. At the start of Feb he took a trip with the rest on his Crse to The Ryl Obs in Grnwch. It took his mind off the fact that the Hme in Stmfrd Brk was due to close. He now went to see Moll twice a month. At that time Fran set fire to hr bd and spoiled hr chnce of a mve to a Hostel in Oakley Sq. /At the end of Feb Mac had made his first mock up with a short mast of plain bamboo and 6 smll shts (21x29.4cm). He saw John Latham at The Queel Conference and the art work of Richard Artschwager at The Serpentine Gllry. While he rd *My Life* by Wagner he hrd *The Valkyrie* at ENO. He put the last touch to his text *Un Coup de Dés – Musique: A Med on a Musigram*. By mid March he saw the Installation in terms of a Mobile with two linked sails which danced in the air. As he bght eight 7' lngths of bamboo and made a new mock up on a mast with six A1 shts Mac thght he might do a PHD at Cmbrwll or Drtngton. In The Music Library at Victoria he looked at the score of Wagner's *Longherin*. He used the score of Beethoven's *Fidelio* to make a nw frmd Prnt wth the sme nme (60x49mm). By the time he heard Victor Burgin at Tate Brtn at the end of the month he hd hng two sails frm one arm of bamboo in the Studio. As he hrd L Bradbury at Easter it struck him that

it ws 7 years since Mike hd died. He felt down when he went to see the work of Boltanski at The SLG and fr mnths no dreams cme to him. There were long dead siles of ence on the phne whn he spke to Fran in Redhill.

Mac had dbts re his PhD as he cld not rd mu (sic) and thght he might go bck to his wrk on punctn. He hd to get help from a Counsellor at Davies St whom he saw once a week till the end of his MA Course. He was cheered when he went to *Paris: Capital of The Arts 1900-1968* at The RA. /Whn Mac sw his Mobile in the Sclptre Studio at the start of May the scale lked too small. He tk what felt lke a huge risk to blow the sheets of hs sails up to 59.4x84.1cm & in the nxt wks mocked up a full size Mobile. In those weeks at Tate Britain he saw *Art Since 1960* and thn at Tate Modern *Matisse Picasso: Dncng Wth Art*. He mde Prnt *Leonore I & II* based on Beethoven's score and *Avante-Grid I & II* based on Krauss'

Originality & The Avnt-Grde. As he thn rd *High Art Lite* by Julian Stallabrass he went to hear *Return(s) to Marx* at Tate Modern. /Once Mac learned that he had a large spce for his MA Show he worked on on his tall masts (7'6"). As he typed bits of text to put on the walls in June he made the last large Prints for the sails and bought white cord to tie them to the arms and mast. For thse he got black gloss. In time he swthd the spce in whte pnt as wll as two old desks whch he found to use for his Dcmntn. He took phots of thm to mke a nw wrk *Tablature* (A2). At the start of July the print was then hung in the space wth *Leonore* and *Avante-Grid*. With those on the wall the sails of *Un Coup de Dés – Musique* wre launched to keel frm side to side and to list in the flux and flow of the sea. They wre free to flt up in the air and soar to the heights as they pitched and rolled in a dance then plunged to the depths of the deep.

In the week it was judged Mac went to see *The Silver Tassie* by S O'Casey at ENO. He ws proud of the work in his Shw frm 10th to 13th July and at the lst ws gld to mke a good Vid of it with B Royal. /In the next days Mac felt at a loss. He wnt to hr *The Creation* by Haydn at The Prms and with J Morgan to see hr *After Jenin* scrnd at BAFTA. He stayed with frnds in Wncntn fr a few days. He ws glad to shre with thm tht he hd gt a Dstnctn fr his MA bt whn he cme back to Lon a gain he felt prssd in the ness of dwn. He stll wnt to the rms & did not drnk bt a strng prt of hm yt ws prne to lse hpe. He went to see his GP as hs Cnsllng as wll as hs Grnt ws at an end. The Doc gave him a sick nte for 'Dprssion' bt he cld nt bear it once he had been to The DSS in Lordshp Lane. In fear he signed on once mre at the Job Centre in Pckhm. In his notes at the time Mac felt as if he had lost his voice trapped in a gulf btwn low life &High Art.

Chapter 14

Out in the wrld once more now his MA had cme to a close Mac held on to wht he cld read. When he took a tent to Newgale for a break in Aug he rd *Underworld* by D Delillo. At The Job Centre in Peckham at the end of the mnth Mac joined a CLAIT Crse for 6 mnths with Pecan 4 days a wk to lrn the ABC of Computing. Not sre how to app The Art Wrld or wht to do whn he cme back to Lon, he thn wrt to N Crwfrd whm he hd mt at his MA Shw. Mac hd a hpe tht he might prnt *Un Coup de Dés – Espace*. In the mn tme Mac trwld *The SOED* fr 'or' words. In a short list of one sylb wds a phrase says, 'the story is born'. At The BL Mac was thn thrilled to find *Ma(r)king The Text* ed by J Bray et al which holds that sense in Lit is mde as mch by spcd pnctn and marks as by words on the page. In the nxt mnth he fnd too *Reality* by J Kozlowski in whch jst the pnct mrks on the page are left in a part of Kant's *Critique of Pure Reason*. He hit on *Moi-Meme* by Charles Nodier in whch a whole part of the book is a *blanc*. /Whn Mac rd *Victor Hugo* by G Robb in which he said that words on the page have a life of their own he ws gripped. He ws still kn to lk at Art and lkd the lrge wrks of B Newman at The Tate but a lot of the time he read all he could. To kp his mind free he browsed the shlvs and jst picked up bks by chnce from *The House of The 7 Gables* by N Hawthorne to *Alias Grace* by M Atwood. At Cmbrwll School of Art he searched out the joint space in *Fluent: Painting & Words*. /Since Octbr Mac had gone each Fri to hear Mark Cousins once more at The AA in Bdfd Sq. As he rd *Unlocking Mallarmé* by G Robb he signed up at Birkbeck for a Course on *Lit, Phil & Abstrn* wth C Gill and T Gough. He sgnd up too fr *The Mng of Mdrnsm* run by C Gill in which the class was to read the text of *Ulysses* by Joyce. In Oct he wrote a small spaced poem *True To Myself* and some short notes fr a tale set in Alexander's Brbrs in Hamm. At the end of the month Mac met Nei Crawford in Tate B. He put him in tch with R King at Circle Press but when they met in Nov he could not print *Un Coup de Dés - Espace*. Wth D Gordon at The Hayward Mac askd *What Have I Done* as he pressed on in md Nov to The Poetry Libry Frm. He wrkd on a prnt nmd *Hppy Dys*. At the end of Nov Moll was sent to Chrng X Hosp. He had kept in tch and sn her twice a month in in the Hme. Mst tms she hd bn rt dwn and sd she wshd to die. Now it ws fr real and she was in fear for her life. Mac went to see her most days in the few wks that she ws still cons. He drppd out of the Crse at Birkbeck which ws thn due to read 'Mlly's Mnlg' in the last chptr of *Ulysses*. He ws thre fr Moll as mch as he could be. At the sm tme he wnt to Shws lke Fluxus at Tate Britain. As Moll slppd in to the deep ness of un cons Mac chrnd in side but was held by the groves and vales of *Swann's Way* as he read Proust at her bed side. Whn she did die he made plns for her to be laid out at The Co-op Fnrl Prlr in Hamm and fr a hearse to tke thm for a Requiem Mass to St Aug's. At Mrtlke Crem he thn spke of wht she hd done for him and Mike. Through thse days he got help in The Rooms. Once each week he went to a Men's Group. He hrd *The Rhinegold* at The Brbcn whch mvd him. Mu (sic) was a salve that soothed him. On Nw Yr's Eve he read more Proust. In its own way it was a balm whch clmd hm. In the wke of Moll's dth he snsd tht his wrld hd chngd fr gd. In The Rms he cld shre tht he ws sad at her loss bt in a way he flt free and a slve no mre. With out guilt he could be him self. At the same tme whie on his Crse at Pecan Mac was not sure what to do. He still thought of a PhD in Fine Art but hung back. In Jan 2003 he put the lst tch to a Prnt nmd *Molly's Monologue* (84.1x118.4cm) bsd on the lst 36pp of *Ulysses*. It showed their marked form of spaced punctn. He made Prints too based on rare punctn mrks in sme pp of Sterne's *Tristram Shandy*. He had been touched at once by Sterne's wit which had won his heart when he

hd rd hm and thn fr mnths in
1993 hd mde a list of 'wit' wrds.
/He was still not too clear what he
hrd at The SLG whn W Furlong urged
hm *To Hear Yourself As Others Hear You*.
He stood on the fringe as Tony Benn
led a small Vigil in Traflgr Sq 'gainst
war in Iraq and then went to see
Lee Miller at The NPG whre he hrd
too R Hansell & G Benson rd Byron.
In Feb Mac's pen flowed as he wrte
dwn his dreams. On 6th he ws due
to get Moll's urn from The Co-Op in
Hamm. He wke up with thghts of how
in parts of a tale in The Land of Ire
by Joyce called *The Dead* Dublin pales as
the soft white snow falls that comes from
The West. He was moved to blank out
those parts of the text in a print
named *Distant Music*. He mde a strt too
on a wrk bsd on S Beckett's novella
How It Is in which a man fights
for brth as he crwls thru the md.
In the wrk in whch thre are no
pnct mrks Mac tk note of a lot
of one sylb words as in the line
'good good end at last of part three'.
/That month Mac saw *1984* at The Lyric

as well as *Max Beckmann* at Tate M.
He mused on a PhD bt still thght
twce as he re read and wrkd thru
Ma(r)king The Text by J Bray et al.
Whle he mrnd Moll in Mrch he did
mre 'Instant Writing'. It was in the form
of loose verse shaped down the page. As
he read *Camera Lucida* by Roland Barthes he
plnnd a prnt bsd on Joyce's *Finnegan's Wake*.
In March he saw *The Threepenny Opera* at
Tate Modern. As The US went in to
Iraq he tk Moll's urn to Ptrbro. While
he rd *The Double Helix* by J Watson
he had a lapse and took the wrng
train to Cmbrdge. Still un sure of hs
Art Mac rd *Atnmnt* by I McEwan. He
hrd M Taylor spk on Giorgio de Chirico
at The Freud Museum. He sw as well
Painting Prsnt: Art & Language at Tate M.
He planned a Print based on Part One
Bk Three of *The Hunchback of Notre Dame*
in which V Hugo writes of The Cathedral
as a 'Book of Architecture'. As its bells
pealed out loud in his mind Mac read
Lrng from The Ptnt by P Casement. He
did mre Autmc Wrtng in a shpd frm.
In his notes he splld out a page
of one sylb wrds & wrte lines lke

'I dare to read oh do/At last
it is to time/The tale tot tell
leaps out'. In Invrnss on a wk end
brk he rd *Kidnapped* by RL Stevenson. In
Lon he saw *Victor Burgin* at Tate Britain.
He hrd A Renton at *The Translator's Notes*
in The Café Gallery. On the blank page
of the walls it had works based on
J Ortega y Gasset's pleas tht mst of
speech is made up of siles of ence.
/In April Mac got his CLAIT Cert from
Pecan. He signed on once more and felt
down but saw Cy Twomly at Tate Modern.
As he read Joyce he made *Fine Again*
and *K no w H o p e* in a nw frm. Mac
hd scnnd hs drms fr mnths and he
now dreamt a lot of his dad. He
mde a trip to put his Mam's ring
in his grave at Chatham. In the sun
he read *Music & Silence* by R Tremain
in the Grave Yard. At home with his
left hand he wrote a first joint let
to his Mam & Dad. He still wrkd
on his Print based on *How It Is*.
At tms he clld it *Wit – How Tis?*
or *How Wit Is*. As he rd Beckett's
pared dwn wrk once mre he tk nte
of those lines with one sylb words like

'how it is vast tracts of time' (p18).
In May he was stnnd in his flat
whn he rolled out *Wit – How 'Tis*.
At hme he had jst cut and paste
the prts & ws nw mazed to see
all its spcd whtes fll sze. Tho he
still felt some guilt with out a job
he thought it could be an imp wrk.
In the month he heard R Hamilton on
Duchamp's Lgcy at Tate B and L La Feuve
on *The Spce Btwn – G Matta-Clarke* at
The AA in Bedford Square. At The BL
he wrkd thru Bray et al once more.
/Mac hd kpt in tch with Fran and
in mid May he went to see her
on her Brth Dy at The Ptrsn Wng.
He took her home for lunch and tea
but she left irked. He cheered him self
when he saw *Billy Liar* at Tate Modern.
He got the chance to stay with friends
for a wk in Marbella whre he lghed
a lot at the *Comic Plays* of Lorca.
/Out of the blue in Lon Mac was
brfed in June tht Fran ws with child.
Five months gone and still on a locked
Ward in The Paterson she would not say
who the Dad was. It helped Mac when
he tlkd to Dr Anderson at The Tvstck

but there was not much he could do. Mac heard *Tristan & isolde* at ENO and saw *On Being John Malkovitch* when it was shown at Riverside Studios on his Birth Day. He sw *Kirchner* – Exprssnsm *and The City* at The RA and *Brdgt Riley* at Tate B. At the end of June he had set out with a nw plan to make some mon with 2000 *K now Hope* Pst Crds he had made but in the end Mac could not bring him self to sell them. The whle schme failed but at The BL he read Image on *The Edge – The Mrgns of Mdvl Art* by M Camille. Thn at St Mrtn's in July Mac mt P Eachus & shwd hm *Hw Wit Is*. He ws nt sre which way to go wth it and Paul cld not tell hm. In the nxt wks Mac hrd N Rsnthl spk on *Kirchner* at The RA. At hme he worked on a nw Print based on *Portrait of The Artist as a Young Man* by Joyce while in The BL he read *The Work of Joyce & The Visual Arts* by AK Loss. In *The Widening Gyre* by J Frank he read of 'Spatial Form' and 'Simultaneity' in the Art & Lit of Mdrnsm. /At the start of July at St Mary's Fran learnd from Dr Bher tht she wld hve to hve the babe thre. Tht mnth she would not see Mac or speak to him when he phoned. At the time he went to see the Independence Show at The SLG and hrd Shstkvtch at The Proms. As he read *A Serious Man* by D Storey he worked at The BL on his PhD App.

In hs own nts he wshd to wrte for hm slf bt was lost in ence of sile and cld nt see the way. Whn a frnd st up hs e-mail Mac flt as if he hd joined the C21. /With no nws from Fran at the start of Aug Mac saw *Waitng fr Godot* twice at The Southwark Playhouse. In an Ing of Meet at The Paterson Centre it was still not clear if Fran could take care of the babe or if she wished to keep it. Mac him self felt lost and was nt sure what to do. Thru the month he wrkd on a Print called *Index* (   ) bsd on *Art in Theory 1900-1990*. At the time he read *Dr Jekyll & Mr Hyde* by RL Stevenson & *Lghtr In The Drk* and *The Gift* by V Nabokov. While he read *The Man In The Iron Mask* by A Dumas at the end of Aug Fran ws mvd to Clrnce Wng in Praed St. /As he read Beckett and wrkdd on his PhD App in Sept Mac felt torn as it smd Fran cld nt kp the babe. Whn it ws dmd that she was nt

fit to mind it he was shocked to be askd if he wshd to raise the child. In a way he wld hve lvd to bt as he read *The Years* by V Woolf he just flt too old. On the bs he usd to blenk & blink at tots: he liked to wink at them and say Boo! but he knew no one close with yng ones. By thn fr him the wrld of babes and bibs had gone. It hlpd to shre doubts with Dr Anderson. /Mac usd *Mdrnst Fctn* by R Stevenson and *The Symb Aesthtc in Frnce* by A Lehmann when he wrote out his PhD App on *The Punctage: A Medn on Appnctn*. The rle of punctn in Mdrnst Art ws the thme he set out. The Punctage ws

a nw form of Print diff from Collage and Montage. In the field of punctn he had set out 3 types: The Punctigram with mrks in spce (*Hppy Dys)*; The Punctiglyph wth marks and words in space *(Dstnt Music)*; The Punctigraph wth wrds in spce (*How Wit Is*). /At the start of Oct he signed up at Birkbeck for *Mdrnsm & Lit II* with C Gill. In *Mdrnsms – A Literary Gde* by P Nicholls he ws thrilled to rd of a Ftrst lke Khlbnkv who tk hs cue frm Fine Art to find ing of mean in The Look of hs wrk. In this tme he scnnd his drms in dpth. He spent hours at *The Book Show* in The Nunnery by S Morley & T Peixoto. /On 13th Mac was on his way to tch a Clss on *Mallarmé & The Book* fr the MA Bk Arts Crse at Cmbrwll when he gt a call on the bus frm St Mry's to tll hm tht Fran had had a boy and bth wre wll. As he rd V Woolf's *The Vyge Out* Mac wnt to more lngs of Meet at The Paterson. He still felt torn as he wrkd on his new large Print based on *A Portrait of the Artist as a Young Man* but in the end while he read *Rubicon*

by T Holland he had to say that
he just could not bring up the babe.
As a Foster Care Order was made at
the end of the month Mac worked
on a Print based on Beckett's short tale
nmd *The Calmative*. He mde use of the
page it self as a point of punctn.
In Nov he met more with the Staff
at The Paterson bt thn as he read
The Book of Disquiet by F Pessoa he
found that he just had to stand back.
/As he read *The Captive* by Proust Mac
was asked by Nick de Ville at Goldsmiths
to make clear his Appn. He wrote back
that he wished to inv mu (sic) al
ntn & pnctn in Mdrnst Wrks of Art
to dv a 'Thry of the Psychcl Sbjct.'
In the mn tme at the end of
Nov in The BL he read F Budgen
on *J Joyce & The Making of Ulysses*
as well as *Silence in Dubliners* by JM
Rabaté in *Jame Joycs* ed by C McCabe.
While he read too *Music & The Mind*
by A Storr Mac dwelt on mu (sic)
in Joyce and Proust. He wnt to hr
Lucia de l'Amr by Dnztti at The ENO.
At tht tme he saw *H Sugimoto* at
The Serpentine and *Dcdnt Art* at Tate B.

Askd by Fran to tke care of her
and Dylan Mac ws in pain whn he
told her that he could not do it.
/At The BL he rd *Wagner & Literature*
by R Furness. In Mac's ntes mre rhymed
words tried to take shape but with no
form. In text with no vowels he wrote
a verse *Th P d P p r f H m lyn* based on
Browning's wrk. In md mnth he sw *Richter*
at The Whtchpl. Whn thy mt at Gldsmths
he tried to make his Appn yet more
clear whn asked by Prof Nick de Ville.
That Xmas Mac spent it with frnds. In
New Year 2004 he read *The Odyssey* by
Homer. At The BL Mac read E Dujardin's
The Bays are Sere & Intr Mnlogue (1888).
He ws thrilled to find Wagner's great inf
on Modernists such as Joyce thru the
mu (sic) and poe try of his prose.
Mac scnnd his drms in the dp seam
of his mine in mre dpth. Shrt bits
of vrse cme frm his heart bt hd
no form. In a way he felt that
he hd lst hm slf once mre whn
he swppd e-mls wth N de Ville as
he ws brd wth pnctn. He was mvd
more when he wrote half a page on
the time Moll brought him home in a

cot frm Qn Chrltte's Hosp. It ws hrd
to bear his own ence of sile as
he flt pressd to srve his time; to
sift thru sch stff to knw hm self
to find a form in which to write.
He was not sure what it meant on
the 7th when a man in his dream
asked 'how to spell tu wit to woo'.
In ntes on The Talking Cure Mac wrte
that what is thought and felt is put
in to words and thn shared out side.
In 'The Writing Cure' they are seen on
the page and hrd in side. That mnth
at NPG Mac cght J Calder's talk on
V Woolf and saw too B Bazell in
J Clare – Rflctns frm a Mdhse. Mac
him self gve a slide tlk on Mallarmé
to hs Mdrnsm Class at Brkbck. As they
mde a strt on *A Man Witht Qualities*
by Robert Musil at the end of Jan
his PHD App to The Lon Inst was
trnd dwn as they cld fnd no Sprvsr.
/In Feb Mac saw *Battle For Music* by
Donald Taylor at Tate Britain. At Tate M
he saw *L'Inhmnie* by M L' Herbier & too
The Fgtve Ftrst by G Quinbet. They wre
the first of a lot of such films
he sw in the nxt mnths. He hd
not had a drink for 19 years but
flt dwn. He still hd no job. He
flt pr & trppd in the flt. Fran
ws lckd up in The Ptrsn. At tms
he trd to wrte vrse on hw Mike
had died but he just could not do
it and used to rase it. Once more
in 'Inst Wrtng' as wrds flwd and each
phrase tk shape in the woof and weft
of the weave dwn the pge Mac knew
that he did not want to die but
felt that to live he had to write
and he ws nt sre hw. He felt
lst a gain at The Rnd Pnd as
he wrkd thru *Int Mn* at The BL.
At The Royal Soc he was all ears
at *Hvnly Music: The Snds of The Unvrse*
made by both A Fabian and C Crawford.
/On 19th Nov hs Mdrnsm Clss on Beckett
rd a shrt late wrk nmd *Lessness* (1969).
In notes nxt day Mac mde mre lists
of one sylb words. At the close of
the mnth as he rd *A Cmpsr's Wrld*
by P Hndmth on mu (sic) mde frm
the spce and tme of tones. He hrd
Wgnr's *Rhngld* at ENO. In his nts at
that time there are more shrt lists of
one sylb wrds like least/tales/stale/steal.

/Mac was seen by Nick de Ville and J Hand at Goldsmiths in Mrch and ws asked to App fr a PhD whn he ws mre clr. He flt snubbed as it ws nt hard to hurt his pride bt in a way he did not mind. His heart was not in it. Tho he did not knw how Mac ws sre nw tht he wshed to wrte in the first plce not for them but for him self. One ing of morn he wrote dwn a dream in which Mike smiled at him wth lts of bits of dried fruit Mac diced by hnd wth a knfe & trnd by chnce in to letts. Mre notes tk a shpd frm dwn the pge. As he wrkd thru *Intr Mnlgue* in dpth at The BL he was told Fran was to be sent to a 'Med Scrty Unit' at Ealing Hsp. In the next weeks he flt held as he rd *An Intro to The Ring Cycle* by WO Cord and thn wnt to Acts II and III of *The Rhinegold* at ENO. As he rd *The Unnmble* ed H Bloom on Bcktt Mac flt dwn whn he dwlt on the fact that he was next in line nw that his Mam had died. At the sme tme wth scenes in tales frm his past life words flowed dwn the page in shaped form some with short sylbs like 'my mine/deep down/the space/in me'.

At the end of March when he read *Lve's Lbr Lst* by Shkspre he tk nte of lines in which the owl hoots and coos in the eaves: 'Tu Whit Tu Whoo'.

At the start of April he made short lists of one sylb words and then a strt on the vrse *Tu whit Tu whoo* wth lnes of 8 shrt one sylb wrds the first one of whch rn like this: 'A don be band ye hope her rent'.

/In the nxt wks Mac mde mre odd notes with 'it' wrds. By mid April he changed to lists of words with a 'wit-' pre fix lke 'withhold' & 'without'. As he read *Night and Day* by V Woolf Mac grasped it when she said of Lit Form that if one were free one could set dwn what one chose to shw in the flux of life. As Eamon hd a hit with *Fuck It (I Don't Want You Back)* Mac flt glad not to be bound by strict rules of a PhD. At Tate B whn he sw *Chldrn & Lng* Mac lkd *Poto & Cabengo* by J- and J-P Gorin as wll as *Messages* mde by G Sherwin. Thru April he still searched for a form.

At the end of the mnth he hd plans for a work in 4 parts based on wrds wth one, two, three and four sylbs but thn fell back on short ones. When he got hold of a print of the txt of *Lssnss* at Brkbck on 6th and heard it read out in a low tone in clss he ws strck by the no of short words in such lines as: 'no sound no stir earth ash grey sand'. At hme Mac brke sme of the wrds down in to 8 sylbs per line. He did the same to a page and a hlf of *Ulysses*. He hd the thght tht he could try and write a whole work with words of just one slyb. On a qst from 5th-9th May he mde a new trip thru *The SOED* to fnd all one sylb wrds. He thn mde a strt on a work he clld *Tu Whit Tu Whoo*. /On her Birth Day Mac went to see Fran who was still at The Ptrsn. The sme day he saw *Ticket of No Return* by U Ottinger shown at Tate B. In *John Keats: A Life* by S Coote he read vwls shld not clash to mar the sound bt flow like notes of mu (sic). At the start of June Mac went to *The Valkyrie* at ENO but still found it hrd whn he saw Fran once mre at St Mary's on the eve of his first Ing of mt wth hr babe. Whn he told his GP in trs tht he mght tke care of the child Dr D sd that at his age he shld not but if Mac had some thing to say he shld write it. On 10th June Mac met Dylan for the first tme wth the Fstr Nrse at the Brunel Fmly Centr. In the same mnth he saw *Le Sang D'Un Poete* and *Le Tstmnt d'Orphée* by J Cocteau at The Rivrsde and wrte *Tu Whit Tu Whoo*. In July Mac sketched a plan for a land scape lay out like the one in Un Coup de Dés by Mallarmé. He hd a 7 part plan based in a way on The 7 Ages of Man speech of Mlnchly Jacques in Shkspre's As You Like It. Whle Mac rd Coleridge by R Holmes he pt the last touch to a typed draft of Tu Whit Tu Whoo in July. As he rd The Wake Fran ws thn mvd to a lckd Scrty Wrd at St Brnrd's. Mac wrte to the Soc Wrk Dpt at St Mary's to say tht he could not tke cre of Dylan. With in weeks as he saw Msre For Msre by The Bard at The Cor Fndn Mac was told a pair had been found who wre a good match for the child. Some what clmd Mac wnt too to see G Orozco at The Serpentine.

/By the start of Aug Mac had come to the end of Fnngn's Wke. He hd read it at speed as he did not wish to be plld right in to it. He felt the ness of sad in the dps of Joyce fr hs dead Dad. He kept in tch with Fran in St Brnrd's on the phone as he filled sheets with lines of short one sylb words and part wrds fr Tu-Whit Tu-Whoo. In it he hd come to close off all vowls at the end of wrds wth cons in the nxt ones. Fr a long tme he hd seen nw trms 'tween the wrds thus tk frm.

/When Mac took a tent to Newgale he rd Buddenbrooks by T Mann. In Lon he went to a CPA for Fran in Ealing and then stayed on his own for a wk at The YHA in Wndrmre. He tk wlks and wrte lts of shts of vrse. As he workd on TWTW bck in Lon in Sept he heard a great deal of good mu (sic) at The NPG. He saw The Chnse Op thre and heard the Qanun playd by A Chhadeh from Syria. In that year and the next one he liked the wde rnge of typs of mu (sic) thre.

/In the lst wks of Sept Mac made Prnts of the frst two prts of TWTW but he was still not sure how to go on with Art in his life. He did not want to stay signed on at

The Job Centre and he wrote for a
2005 Prspcts to Drtngtn Collg. As he sw
An Avant-garde Twist at Tate Britain in Oct
he joined *The Meaning of Mdrnsm III* Crse
with C Gill at Birkbeck but dropped out
when he found it too much like the
class he hd dne. A friend had jst
died. He did nt hve time to lose.
/Mac had bn gld to mt Angela and
Ptr wth Dylan at The Brunel Fmly Cntr
at the end of August. It was strange
whn he sw Fran at St Bernard's as
she cld not see her son. Mac felt
that in sme way as time wnt by
he mght act as sme knd of brdge
fr them. He ws glad to see Dylan
once mre in The Coram Cntr at the
end of Oct. As he trawled thru the
loose shards and shoads in his lode of

one sylb words in Nov for the odd
ones he'd missed they smd lke old frnds
a bit like *P Robeson & British Miners*

and *Gwen & Augustus John* at Tate B.
As Eminem sng *Just Lose It* he ws
glad that he had not and by mid
Nov he had typed 7 prts of *TWTW*.
/Mac lkd the way in whch BS Johnson
stalked new forms for his books in the
60's. At the mnth's close he bought *Like
a Fiery Elephant - The Life of BS Johnson*
by Jonathan Coe. For two days Mac went
to Films and Talks at The Irish Centre
in Hamm fr The Pat Kavanagh Cntnry. At
St B's Mac ws pleased but dazed when
Fran seemed well and bck to her self.
As he read in *Zeno's Conscience* by I
Svevo tht words have to be a 'vent
in thm slvs he hrd *Siegried* at ENO.
/At the start of Dec Mac took note
of the txt wrk of Langlands and Bell
who won The Turner Prize at Tate B.
As Pussycat Dolls sng *Stickwitu* he wnt on
with notes for 'The prole logue' of TWTW:
'Red owld min ode from are to ream
His owls mine lode from mare tor eam'.
As Band Aid 20 had a hit with
Do They Knw Its Xms? Mac ws nt
sure whn he sw Fran in the midst
of the lost souls on the Ward in
Ealing. He spent it wth friends at home.

As the yr clsd the nme of hs wrk ws chngd to *my it to you*.
/At the start of 2005 Mac had a drm in which the strs of The Plough turn to dull gold that spin and whirl in the sky. As Elvis Presley had a ht once mre wth *It's Nw Or Nvr* Mac prssd on with *my it to you*. In Jan he saw *Faces in The Crowd: Pctrng Mdrn Life frm Manet to Tdy* at The Whtchpl. He hrd T Arthur's Trio at The NPG whre he wnt twce a mnth for the rest of the year to hear a rnge of mu (sic) lke *Nw Nse*.
/The frsh typd drft of *mity* ws an Alphbtcl Pm wth pro nns tht gve it life and the first line now ran thus: 'my ow l is wi t o lo his o y' Its new shape was based on the form of Brancusi's *Endlss Clmn*. It hd 7 spcd *blancs* in each line. The work was set in 7 prts. It stll used Mallarmé's two pge 'lnd scpe' sprd. At the end of Jan he hd typd 14 pp in Part One.
/By md mnth Mac hd thght he mght use the work for a PhD at Dartington. In mid Dec he had bn shamed whn he signed at The Job Centre near Lant Street with a yng Grd from Leics. With friends in The Rms Mac shared that he was not sure what to do. In a way he wshd to wrk at *m I t y* on his own. He mght get a tmp jb and tke a Lap Top to The Lke Dstrct to work on it there or try for a PhD in 'Theory'. In the mean time he hrd a Lunch Time Piano Recital of Bthvn and Schmnn at St James. At the end of Jan he had a walk with friends nr Chchstr Hrbr. At the start of Feb he was 20 years with out a drink.
/As he then heard Slyvic Paskin talk on *The Pleasures of The Text* at The NPG he ws well but felt trapped. He snt off an App to Dartn with the aim tht he wld mke an Artst's Bk thre based on his work *my it to you*. At the time Mac rd *The Double* by José Saramago. He went to see a film

on *Lee Miller, The Language of Love* by
Anne Harvey and *Frida Khalo* at The NPG.
He saw *Turner Whistler Monet* at Tate B.
As U2 had one more huge hit with
Smtms You Can't Mke It On Your Own
he ws held in The Rooms. While he
wnt on with his own wrk on *m I t y*
he rd *A Drm Play* by Strndbrg and
A View From The Bridge by A Miller.
At NPG A Penrose spoke on L Miller.
On a day out in Bournmouth Mac read
K Ishiguru's *An Artst of The Floatng World*.

/As Easter cme Mac flt sad and dead
when he thght that a draft print of
mity cld not brng bck Mike or Moll.
He chrd as men like Shaw, Wilde and
Yeats from The Land of Ire took Lon
by storm at *License to Ceilidh* in NPG.
He hrd MA Caws spk on Lee Miller
at the same place. At the end of
March he ws back in The BL to

look once more at Khlebnikov. As he read
A Miller's *After The Fall* at Tate Britain
he sw *Rivers of Time* by K McGahan
as wll as the wrk of *Anthony Caro*.
In April at The BL S Gilbert struck
a chord in *J Joyce' Ulysses – A Study*
whn he strssd Molly's prf fr mon sylbs.
Mac felt kin ship too with 'Atomism' in
the Lettrism of Isidore Isou which he fnd
in *Modern Visual Poetry* by Willard Bohn. In
Space Btwn Words – The Orgns of Slnt Rdng
by Paul Saenger he learned that with the
the slw brk dwn of *scriptura continua* in
The Land of Ire from C7 to C15
wrd spn mde pss mod ern ing of
read in ence of sile in The Wst.
/On the eve of his trip to mt
J Hall and M Leahy at Dartn Mac
sw *W Blake: Mn Wtht A Msk* by
R Rosen at The NPG. He was glad
of an opp to show some of his
work but left cold by John Hall's talk
of 'Prosody'. It irked Mac as he was
still not quite sure what he wished
to do. In Lon he hrd John Caldar
spk on H Pinter and P Durcan rd
his vrse at The Irish Centr in Hamm.
He heard *Twilight of The Gods* at ENO

while at the month's end he then read
N Schaeffer's *Life of The Mrqs de Sde*.
/At the start of May Blair won a thrd
Term bt the pain ws eased fr Mac
whn The Dpt of Pnsns wrte to hm
tht frm his 60h Birth Day in June
he had a right to Pension Credit. It
wld free him from The Job Centre. It
helped him to let go and while he read
Poems & Shrtr Wrtngs by Joyce and wnt to
see *August Strindberg* at Tate M from mid
month he looked at the form of one
sylb words in *mlty* once more. On her
Birth Day Mac wnt to see Fran who
had bn mvd to Mott House. It was
a 'Half Way Hse' in the grnds of
St Brnrd's Hsp bt stll wth lckd drs.
He took her out for tea in Hanwell
and did the same at the end of
the month. Wth frnds he spent a day
in Calais and had a walk near Alfriston.
/At the start of June as he read
L da Vinci – The Flight of the Mind
by C Nicholl he felt more free to
tke sme rsks in hs wrk wth *m l t y*.
On his Birth Day with Lib he heard
M Macleod on cello & M Sturfalt on
piano play Poulenc at The Prcll Rm. He

asked friends round to eat at his flat.
In Newgale he read *Kafka* by N Murray
as well as G Flaubert's *A Sntmntl Edctn*.
/In July on two sheets he typed more
alphb lists of one sylb wrds he wshd
to use but was still not sure of the
strict form or length of the work. In
the mean tme at The Cohrane Theatre
he saw *The Thrpnny Opera* by B Brecht.
As Mac rd the *Cmplte HC Anderson* he
had a clear dream in which his Dad
hld him. At Tate M he saw scrned
The Life & Death of F Kahlo by
K & D Crommie. In mid month he
hrd *The Valkyrie* by Wagner at The Prms.
He still felt guilt at the lack of
a job as he rd JP Sarte's *Nausea*
& *The Dwarfs* by H Pinter. As he
went to one mre CPA for Fran at
Mott Hse he read F Kafka's *The Trial*.
/At the end of July Mac went back

to see Fran at Mott Hse. Thn for
10 days or so in The British Lbry he
trwld a gain thru bth *The SOED* (2002)
and *The Oxfd Dctnry of Mdrn Slng* (OUP
1992) ed by J Ayto and J Simpson fr
one sylb words. He rd T Davies' *Hmnsm*
(1996) which at times cites *The Rise of
The Indvl in Ren Italy* by J Burckhardt
/Thnks to a friend in Aug Mac had
the use of a place to stay near
Blrgwrie in The Land of Cots. He flt
guilt but free to work as he read
W Scott's *Rob Roy* & *Waverley*. Whn he
came back Mac found Fran still full of

rge and he heard Bthvn's *Ode To Joy*
from The Proms on R3 with mixed ings
of feel. He was clmd by Verdi's *Requiem*
and then saw *Julius Caesar* at The Lyric.
/As he rd *Stanley* by Frank McLynn in
the first week of Sept Mac made yet
one mre trp thru *The SOED* fr wrds

of one sylb. It ws the 3rd sch
trek. It was as if he had to
wrk thru the whle lst of wrds yet
a gain to make a fresh start on
mity. Its nw Alph Frm now wnt frm
'o' to 'p' and its first line ran
'my ow is on as it is owned'.
As he rd *Chekov* by R Brtltt &
A Brkn's *JM Barrie &The Lst Bys*
he used No 7 to shape the lines
of the txt in a new stepped form.
/In Oct Mac had a break and went
to The Land of Ire. He stayed with
kith and kin in Galway and Conamara fr
a week. He flew with The Wild Swans
at Coole. Wth frnds in Dublin he wnt
to The Writer's Mus in Parnell Sq as
well as a Show on Joyce at the
Nat Lbry. They sw *The Bldy Sndy Enq*
at The Abbey Thtre & *The Wrong Man*
by D Morrison at The Tivoli. They went
to Klmnhm Gaol and saw whre the men
who led The Rising wre shot in 1916.
Back in Lon Mac worked on a fresh
drft of *m l t y* with a first line thus:
'my owl or ow a lows i sow'.
He sw *Toulouse Lautrec* at Tate B and
tk his coz to *The Carmelites* by Poulenc

at ENO. As he rd *Hide & Seek* by W Collins he was glad to see 2 yr old Dylan at The Coram Centr. /In Nov Mac rd *Byron* by F McCarthy and sw *Brontë* pt on by Shrd Exprnce at The Lyric. As he workd thru *m l t y* in mid month Mac heard on R3 that it ws S Beckett's Cntnry Year in 2006. His wrk on Beckett came to mind and he rng Ros Scanlon at The Irish Cntr in Hamm. Whn she hd seen sme of his prints she fixed up for him to hve a Shw in June and July. Wth sch a big bst Mac sme times gt up at 4am or 5am each morn to get on with the work on *m l t y*. At The Blake Soc he heard D John speak on *Creation & Imgination*. At the end of Nov he read *Marcel Proust – A Life* by WC Carter. He hrd *Siegfried* at ENO and at Tate Modern he went to see *The Mthr & The Whre* by J Eustace. As Mac went on with *m l t y* in Dec he rd *The Gd Soldier* and *Prde's End* by F Maddox Ford. He sw Prof Heard's *Mgc Lntrn Show* at The NPG and then wnt to the Xmas Shw at the sme plce. With pals he went to a Carol Service at *Our Ldy of Vctrs* in Abngdn Rd. It was 21yrs since Mac had gone to The Rooms at the back of the Church there for the first time. On Xmas Eve he called to see Fran in Mott Hse. He wnt to a frnd's on Xmas Day. /In the New Year 2006 Mac hd a brk for a few days. Whn he stayed at The YHA in The Duddon Estuary nr Barrow he rd *Effi Briest* by T Fontaine and B Dylan's *Chronicles*. Back in Lon he saw J Latham's Obit in *The Guardian*. He went on with Part 7 of *m l t y*. As he worked out the ing of space for Prts 1-7 he rd *Dscrts* by A Graylng as wll as *The Rogue* by A Tournier. At a lrge CPA Mtng at Mott Hse

in mid Jan Fran hit out at Mac in frnt of the Stff. It ws thght by all that it was time for her to mve on bt no one knew whre. It helped Mac to keep calm when he hrd the *Cmbrwll Cmpsrs* and mre of the same at NPG in the next few months. He sw *Fuseli, Blake &The Rmntc Imgn* at Tate B and thn pt the lst tch to a frst drft of *mlty* and mde a prnt out. The frst lne rn 'my owl o r ow a lows i sow'. At the tme Mac ws drwn by the name of P Hbsn's *The Crdle of Thght*. As he read *Murphy* by S Beckett he saw *Mister Scarface* by F Di Leo a Tate M and *An Amrcn in Prs* by V Minnelli at Tate B. At the end of Jan he saw L Bradbury end his last Talk at Tate Britain with a slide of Trnr's *The Fghtng Tmre*. He thn wnt to size up the walls of the space for his frst Show at The Irish Cntr. /At the start of Feb Mac had not hd a drnk fr 21 yrs. At ENO he

sw *Rigoletto*. On a whte Inv crd he called his Show *How Is It?* For it he had nw prnts mde of *Mlly's Mnlg* and *The Calmative*. In mid mnth he pt the lst touch to a Print based on a page of *Watt* by S Beckett he nmd *What Centre?*. He drw on two Book Slips frm his work in The

BL then to make *Recent Beckett*. As Mac used his text of the same name to do a Prnt *Lssnss* (42x60cm) he rd in *Sm Bckttt & Music* ed M Bryden hw the ence of sile and sound of its mu (sic) in blck and wht ws tund by maths and stats. Mac thn mde Print clld The *7 Ages of Sam*) bsd on phots of his fce splt and splcd frm each stge of hs life. As Mac drew up lists of works for the Show he hrd *A Shrpshre Lad* by AE Housman at The NPG read by V Underwoood. He read *Dead Souls* by N Gogol and went to *Drwngs of Mchlnglo* shwn at The BM. /In the first week of March Mac read *The Phil of S Beckett* by John Caldar. At The Conway Hall he heard Dr JH Arnold tlk on *The Plitics of Medvll Unblf*. As Chico sang *It's Chico Time* he read in The BL *The Origins of English Nonsense* by N Malcolm. From it he learned how J Brooksbank in C18 mde lng lists of all the mon sylbs in Lish of Eng to teach his Syllbry in schls. In tht month Mac rd *A Bend In The River* by JS Naipul and *The Painter of Signs* by RK Narayan. He rd *Deomns & Angels:*

249

A Life of Jacob Epstein by J Rose. He got a boost when he watched his MA Vid of *Un Coup de Dés – Musique*. /In April Mac dwelt a lot on Beckett. He wnt to Shows like *Rhrsng Beckett* and *Words & Music* at The Chelsea Space. He hrd J Tilbury speak on *Beckett as Music* in the same place. At The Barbican Mac was there for the wide range of Films, Plays and talks held at *The Beckett Cntnry Fstvl*. In md mnth he hrd John Caldar speak at at The Thtre Bkshp and The Godot Cmp rd Beckett's *The Lost Ones*. At that tme he chngd the nme of the Artist's Bk for his Show to *my i to you*. He hrd S Barratt in *Wtng fr Gdt* on R3 and thn mde a print that he clld *How Wit Is* whch plyd on the nme Go/dot. As it ws said in lte April at Mott House tht a plce for Fran to move on might be found he heard Peter Hall at The NT tlk on *The Coming of Godot*. Mac liked the strng wood cuts frm B Deacy's Artists' Bk *A Life in Relief* based on Michael Davitt. He read *The 7 Pillars of Wisdom* by TE Lwrnce as he saw *Shapng The Real: The Art of Elsworth Kelly* at The V&A.

/On 2nd May Mac hd a dream in which whch once mre 'time' plyd a sig prt. As he hd done fr years his mite tk note of it. As Mac mused on Bcktt and hs use of the 'it' wrd in bth the names of hs wrks like *How It Is* and through out his txts, Mac thought of a poss book of 'it' he might write based on all the 'it' wrds he could find in The SOED. Not just short ones with one sylb like 'bit' and 'fit' but those of all lengths with more sylbs like pity and witty. Each sent ence in the book would have at least one such 'it' word. He had mde short lists of such 'it' terms at least since 1993. On 4th May he set out on an imp trip thru both Vols of *The SOED* to trwl fr all 'it' wrds. He mde lsts of 81p and pt thm to one sde as he worked on the Show. For this In May Mac had a Print mde of his Artist's Bk he called *my i to you* (29.7x42cm). He thought of

it as a nw frm of Abstrct Ptry
the first line of which now ran
'my ow is lw w hen ow a lows'
At the front there was a quote from
W Shkspre's *Msre Fr Msre* 1V. 3. 125:
'Mark what I say, which you shall find
By every syllable, a faithful verity'. At the
small Book Shop Theatre in The Cut Mac
saw P. Marinker and J. McManus in *Embers*
and P. Pacey in *From an Abandoned Work*.
At the same time Mac took note that
In J Knwlsn's *Bcktt Rmbrng* Ed Albee usd
Beckett his way bt kept his own voice.

At The BL he re rd *The Unnmble*.
/As his Show came near in June Mac
hrd G Rosefield play cello and S Lepper
piano at The NPG. While he then rd
Sml *Pepys: An Unequal Self* by C Tomalin
he saw both *That Time* and *What Where*
by The Godot Co at The Theatre Bkshp.
He tk Pepys *Diaries* to Gldrs Grn whn
one more frnd was laid to rest thre.
In mid mnth at NPG The BBC Sngrs
led by Nick Kok sang 9 Motets in

the Frm of Sonic Prtrts by E Cowie.
On the Shw's eve at Rvrsde Mac sw
M Pwll & E Prssbrgr's *The Red Shoes*
as well as *Ballet Russe* by D Geller.
Mac's Show of Prnts fr The Bcktt Cntry
HOW IS IT? was at The Irish Centre
in Hamm frm 23rd June to 28th July.
It was based on Twenty One of the
Prints Mac had done in 7 years which
mrkd the wrd mu (sic) of Bcktt's txts.
The re verse side of his Invtn bore
an art wrk which said *ess is ore*.
The bk *my i to you* was shown
on a dais in front of a wind
des by John Carson. As Head of Fine
Art at St Martins he knew Mac's work
and oped the Show on his way to
Pittsburgh to tke up his fresh Post as
Hd of Carnegie Mlln Unv Schl of Art.
In Aug Mac took up his notes from
hs trwl thru The SOED for 'it' wrds
which he had put to one side, to
make a start on *The Book of It*.
He did not know then that it wld
tke him three mre years to do the
whole thing bt whn he looked bck he
had rd a lne frm *Lessness* which ran
'the sand no hold he will make it'.

251